JAMESTOWN EDUCATION

SIGNATURE READING

LEVEL L

Mc Graw Hill Glencoe

New York, New York   Columbus, Ohio   Chicago, Illinois   Peoria, Illinois   Woodland Hills, California

JAMESTOWN EDUCATION

Reviewers

Marsha Miller, Ed.D
Reading Specialist
Elgin High School
1200 Maroon Drive
Elgin, IL 60120

Kati Pearson
Orange County Public Schools
Literacy Coordinator
Carver Middle School
4500 West Columbia Street
Orlando, FL 32811

Lynda Pearson
Assistant Principal
Reading Specialist
Lied Middle School
5350 Tropical Parkway
Las Vegas, NV 89130

Suzanne Zweig
Reading Specialist/Consultant
Sullivan High School
6631 N. Bosworth
Chicago, IL 60626

Cover Image: Donald E. Carroll/Getty Images

ISBN: 0-07-861732-4 (Pupil's Edition)
ISBN: 0-07-861733-2 (Annotated Teacher's Edition)

Send all queries to:
Glencoe/McGraw-Hill
8787 Orion Place
Columbus, OH 43240-4027

ACC Library Services
Austin, Texas

2 3 4 5 6 7 8 9 113 09 08 07 06 05

Contents

How to Use This Book

Working Through the Lessons

The following descriptions will help you work your way through the lessons in this book.

Building Background will help you get ready to read. In this section you might begin a chart, discuss a question, or learn more about the topic of the selection.

Vocabulary Builder will help you start thinking about—and using—the selection vocabulary. You might draw a diagram and label it with vocabulary words, make a word map, match vocabulary words to their synonyms or antonyms, or use the words to predict what might happen in the selection.

Strategy Builder will introduce you to the strategy that you will use to read the selection. First you will read a definition of the strategy. Then you will see an example of how to use it. Often, you will be given ways to better organize or visualize what you will be reading.

Strategy Break will appear within the reading selection. It will show you how to apply the strategy you just learned to the first part of the selection.

Strategy Follow-up will ask you to apply the same strategy to the second part of the selection. Most of the time, you will work on your own to complete this section. Sometimes, however, you might work with a partner or a group of classmates.

Personal Checklist questions will ask you to rate how well you did in the lesson. When you finish totaling your score, you will enter it on the graphs on page 215.

Vocabulary Check will follow up on the work you did in the Vocabulary Builder. After you total your score, you will enter it on page 215.

Strategy Check will follow up on the strategy work that you did in the lesson. After you total your score, you will enter it on page 215.

Comprehension Check will check your understanding of the selection. After you total your score, you will enter it on page 215.

Extending will give ideas for activities that are related to the selection. Some activities will help you learn more about the topic of the selection. Others might ask you to respond to the selection by dramatizing, writing, or drawing something.

Resources such as books, recordings, videos, and Web sites will help you complete the Extending activities.

Graphing Your Progress

The information and graphs on pages 214–215 will help you track your progress as you work through this book. **Graph 1** will help you record your scores for the Personal Checklist and the Vocabulary, Strategy, and Comprehension Checks. **Graph 2** will help you track your overall progress across the book. You'll be able to see your areas of strength, as well as any areas that could use improvement. You and your teacher can discuss ways to work on those areas.

Priscilla and the Wimps

Building Background

At some point in life, everyone comes up against a bully. What experience have you had with a bully? How did you handle the situation? Recall a run-in that you or someone you know has had with a bully. Then fill in the chart below.

	The Bully	The Victim
Actions taken during the incident		
Feelings toward the other person during the incident		
Feelings toward the other person after the incident		

bionic

hammerlock

honcho

shakedowns

slithered

subtle

swaggers

threads

wimp

Vocabulary Builder

1. The words in the margin are from "Priscilla and the Wimps." Half of the words are **slang**—words used by a particular group of people for a short time. Slang is considered informal speech and usually uses common words in uncommon ways.

2. Before you begin reading this short story, see how many of the words you can match with their meanings.

   slang for *clothes* _____

   slang for "the acts of obtaining money from someone by a threat"

   _____

   slang for "person in charge" _____

   slang for "person regarded as weak" _____

   having extraordinary strength _____

   a wrestling hold _____

   glided or slid like a reptile _____

struts; walks in a boastful way _____

toned down; less obvious _____

3. As you read the story, watch for these words. Change your answers if necessary.

4. Then save your work. You will refer to it again in the Vocabulary Check.

Strategy Builder

Making Predictions While Reading a Short Story

- Some stories are told, or **narrated**, by a character who takes part in the story. That character uses words such as *I, me, my,* and *mine* to tell what he or she sees and hears throughout the story. Stories like these are said to be told in the **first-person point of view**.

- Because a first-person narrator cannot get inside the heads of the other characters, neither can readers. Both the narrator and readers must look at what the other characters say and do, and must use those clues to **predict**, or guess, what might happen next.

- The clues that the author gives you to help you predict are called context clues. **Context** is the information that comes before or after a word or a situation to help you figure it out. For example, read the following paragraphs. See if you can use the context clues to figure out what is happening and to predict what might happen next.

> Lisa arrived at the beach late, after 9 P.M., and the sky was already quite dark. Would she find her friends in time? There were so many people around that Lisa felt lost. But she had an idea of where to start looking. Her friends had come to the beach every July for three years, and they usually sat in the same area. Using her flashlight, Lisa quickly made her way past blankets and little American flags planted in the sand. Suddenly she saw a familiar picnic basket.
>
> "Lisa!" someone called. "Hurry up! We saved a space for you on the blanket!"
>
> As she ran to her friends, she heard a loud pop not far away. All around her were cries of "They're starting!" and everyone looked up over the lake.

- Can you predict what will happen over the lake? You can if you use context clues. By the end of these paragraphs, you probably figured out that the setting of this story is a beach on the Fourth of July, where a fireworks show is about to begin. Some of the clues are the time—after dark on a July night—and the flags that Lisa sees on the beach. Anyone who has attended a fireworks show also knows that a loud pop signals the firing of a fireworks canister. Now that you have added up the clues to figure out the time and place, you can use that information to predict that the next thing to happen will be an explosion of fireworks in the sky.

Priscilla and the Wimps

by Richard Peck

As you read this short story, look for context clues to help you predict what might happen next.

Listen, there was a time when you couldn't even go to the *rest room* around this school without a pass. And I'm not talking about those little pink tickets made out by some teacher. I'm talking about a pass that could cost anywhere up to a buck, sold by Monk Klutter.

Not that Mighty Monk ever touched money, not in public. The gang he ran, which ran the school for him, was his collection agency. They were Klutter's Kobras, a name spelled out in nailheads on six well-known black plastic windbreakers.

Monk's **threads** were more . . . **subtle**. A pile-lined suede battle jacket with lizard-skin flaps over tailored Levi's and a pair of ostrich-skin boots, brass-toed and suitable for kicking people around. One of his Kobras did nothing all day but walk a half step behind Monk, carrying a fitted bag with Monk's gym shoes, a roll of rest-room passes, a cashbox, and a switchblade that Monk gave himself manicures with at lunch over at the Kobras' table.

Speaking of lunch, there were a few cases of advanced malnutrition among the newer kids. The ones who were a little slow in handing over a cut of their lunch money and were therefore barred from the cafeteria. Monk ran a tight ship.

I admit it. I'm five foot five, and when the Kobras **slithered** by, with or without Monk, I shrank. And I admit

this, too: I paid up on a regular basis. And I might add: so would you.

This school was old Monk's Garden of Eden. Unfortunately for him, there was a serpent in it. The reason Monk didn't recognize trouble when it was staring him in the face is that the serpent in the Kobras' Eden was a girl.

Practically every guy in school could show you his scars. Fang marks from Kobras, you might say. And they were all highly visible in the shower room: lumps, lacerations, blue bruises, you name it. But girls usually got off with a warning.

Except there was this one girl named Priscilla Roseberry. Picture a girl named Priscilla Roseberry, and you'll be light years off. Priscilla was, hands down, the largest student in our particular institution of learning. I'm not talking fat. I'm talking big. Even beautiful, in a **bionic** way. Priscilla wasn't inclined toward organized crime. Otherwise, she could have put together a gang that would turn Klutter's Kobras into garter snakes.

Priscilla was basically a loner except she had one friend. A little guy named Melvin Detweiler. You talk about The Odd Couple. Melvin's one of the smallest guys above midget status ever seen. A really nice guy, but, you know—little. They even had lockers next to each other, in the same bank as mine. I don't know what they had going. I'm not saying this was a romance. After all, people deserve their privacy.

Priscilla was sort of above everything, if you'll pardon a pun. And very calm, as only the very big can be. If there was anybody who didn't notice Klutter's Kobras, it was Priscilla.

Until one winter day after school when we were all grabbing our coats out of our lockers. And hurrying, since Klutter's Kobras made sweeps of the halls for after-school **shakedowns**.

 Stop here for Strategy Break #1.

 **Strategy Break #1**

1. What do you predict will happen next? _____

_____

2. Why do you think so? _____

3. What clues from the story helped you make your prediction(s)? _____

_____

 Go on reading to see what happens.

Anyway, up to Melvin's locker **swaggers** one of the Kobras. Never mind his name. Gang members don't need names. They've got group identity. He reaches down and grabs little Melvin by the neck and slams his head against his locker door.

"Okay, let's see your pass," snarls the Kobra.

"A pass for what this time?" Melvin asks, probably still dazed.

"Let's call it a pass for very short people," says the Kobra, "a dwarf tax." He wheezes a little Kobra chuckle at his own wittiness. And already he's reaching for Melvin's wallet with the hand that isn't circling Melvin's wind-

pipe. All this time, of course, Melvin and the Kobra are standing in Priscilla's big shadow.

She's taking her time shoving her books into her locker and pulling on a very large-size coat. Then, quicker than the eye, she brings the side of her enormous hand down in a chop that breaks the Kobra's hold on Melvin's throat. You could hear a pin drop in that hallway. Nobody's ever laid a finger on a Kobra, let alone a hand the size of Priscilla's.

Then Priscilla, who hardly ever says anything to anybody except to Melvin, says to the Kobra, "Who's your leader, **wimp**?"

This practically blows the Kobra away. First he's chopped by a girl, and now she's acting like she doesn't know Monk Klutter, the Head **Honcho** of the World. He's so amazed, he tells her. "Monk Klutter."

"Never heard of him," Priscilla mentions. "Send him to see me." The Kobra just backs away from her like the whole situation is too big for him, which it is.

Pretty soon Monk himself slides up. He's going to handle this interesting case personally. "Who is it around here doesn't know Monk Klutter?"

He's standing inches from Priscilla. "Never heard of him," says Priscilla.

Monk's not happy with this answer, but by now he's spotted Melvin. Monk breaks his own rule by reaching for Melvin with his own hands. "Kid," he says, "you're going to have to educate your girl friend."

⬟ **Stop here for Strategy Break #2.**

Strategy Break #2

1. What do you predict will happen next? _____

_____

2. Why do you think so? _____

_____

3. What clues from the story helped you make your prediction(s)? _____

_____

➡ **Go on reading to see what happens.**

His hands never quite make it to Melvin. In a move of pure poetry Priscilla has Monk in a **hammerlock**.

Priscilla's behind him in another easy motion. And with a single mighty thrust forward, frog-marches Monk into her own locker. His ostrich-skin boots click once in the air. And suddenly he's gone, neatly wedged into a locker, a perfect fit. Priscilla bangs the door shut, twirls the lock, and strolls out of school. Melvin goes with her, of course, trotting along below her shoulder. The last stragglers leave quietly.

Well, this is where fate, an even bigger force than Priscilla, steps in. It snows all that night, a blizzard. The whole town ices up. And school closes for a week. ●

Strategy Follow-up

Now go back and look at the predictions that you wrote in this lesson. Do any of them match what actually happened in this story? Why or why not?

✓Personal Checklist

Read each question and put a check (✓) in the correct box.

1. How well were you able to use what you wrote in Building Background to help you understand the bullies in "Priscilla and the Wimps"?
   - ☐ 3 (extremely well)
   - ☐ 2 (fairly well)
   - ☐ 1 (not well)

2. In the Vocabulary Builder, how many words were you able to match with their meanings?
   - ☐ 3 (7–9 words)
   - ☐ 2 (4–6 words)
   - ☐ 1 (0–3 words)

3. How well were you able to use context clues to help you make predictions as you read?
   - ☐ 3 (extremely well)
   - ☐ 2 (fairly well)
   - ☐ 1 (not well)

4. How well were you able to identify the feelings of the characters in this story?
   - ☐ 3 (extremely well)
   - ☐ 2 (fairly well)
   - ☐ 1 (not well)

5. How well do you understand why Monk no longer has control of the school?
   - ☐ 3 (extremely well)
   - ☐ 2 (fairly well)
   - ☐ 1 (not well)

Vocabulary Check

Look back at the work you did in the Vocabulary Builder. Then answer each question by circling the correct letter.

1. If someone tells you that you have great threads, what is that person complimenting?
   a. your sewing ability
   b. your clothes
   c. your yarn collection

2. Which of these slang words is a title for somebody in charge?
   a. wimp
   b. swagger
   c. honcho

3. Imagine a person who walks around as if everyone should get out of his or her way. Which word describes how that person moves?
   a. swaggers
   b. slithers
   c. shakedowns

4. Which of these words is insulting to the person it describes?
   a. bionic
   b. honcho
   c. wimp

5. If you were applying a hammerlock to someone or something, in what activity would you be involved?
   a. wrestling
   b. carpentry
   c. burglary

Add the numbers that you just checked to get your total score. (For example, if you checked 3, 2, 3, 2, and 1, your total score would be 11.) Fill in your score here. Then turn to page 215 and transfer your score onto Graph 1.

▶ Personal
Vocabulary
Strategy
Comprehension
▶ TOTAL SCORE
T

Check your answers with your teacher. Give yourself 1 point for each correct answer, and fill in your Vocabulary score here. Then turn to page 215 and transfer your score onto Graph 1.

Personal
▶ Vocabulary
Strategy
Comprehension
TOTAL SCORE
✓ T

Strategy Check

Review what you wrote at each Strategy Break. Then answer these questions:

1. If you had predicted that Priscilla would somehow stop Monk's bullying, which clue would have best supported your prediction?
    a. The serpent in the Kobras' Eden was a girl.
    b. But girls usually got off with a warning.
    c. Picture a girl named Priscilla Roseberry, and you'll be light years off.

2. Which clue helped you predict that the narrator would *not* help stop Monk's bullying?
    a. And I'm not talking about those little pink tickets made out by some teacher.
    b. When the Kobras slithered by, with or without Monk, I shrank.
    c. They even had lockers next to each other, in the same bank as mine.

3. At Strategy Break #2, which prediction would *not* have fit the story?
    a. Priscilla will get a warning from Monk.
    b. Priscilla will stand up to Monk.
    c. Melvin will beat up Monk.

4. Which clue would have supported your prediction that Priscilla and Monk would fight?
    a. Priscilla wasn't inclined toward organized crime.
    b. But girls usually got off with a warning.
    c. She brings her hand down in a chop that breaks the Kobra's hold on Melvin's throat.

5. If you had predicted that Priscilla and Monk would *not* fight, which clue would have supported your prediction?
    a. Priscilla was sort of above everything. . . . And very calm, as only the very big can be.
    b. "Who's your leader, wimp?"
    c. Monk is going to handle this interesting case personally.

Comprehension Check

Review the story if necessary. Then answer these questions:

1. Why does Monk Klutter use a switchblade to give himself manicures at lunch?
    a. because he can't afford a manicure set
    b. because he has exceptionally hard nails
    c. because he wants everyone to see that he carries a switchblade

2. Why might the narrator call the school Monk's Garden of Eden?
    a. Adam and Eve had all they wanted in the Garden of Eden, and Monk gets all he wants in the school.
    b. The Garden of Eden was beautiful, and the school in the story is beautiful.
    c. The Garden of Eden had a serpent in it, and there were snakes in the area of this school.

3. Why is the narrator puzzled by the friendship between Priscilla and Melvin?
    a. Priscilla is usually too busy with her gang to develop friendships.
    b. Priscilla is a top student and Melvin is not very bright.
    c. Priscilla is exceptionally big and Melvin is exceptionally small.

4. Why does Priscilla take action against Monk?
    a. She doesn't like Monk's threads.
    b. She is protecting herself.
    c. She is protecting Melvin.

5. What happens to Monk at the end of the story?
    a. He gets lost in a blizzard.
    b. He is left locked in Priscilla's locker during the blizzard.
    c. He leaves town because he's embarrassed.

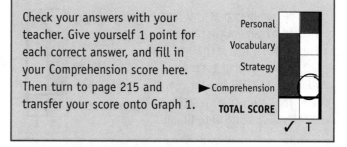

Check your answers with your teacher. Give yourself 1 point for each correct answer, and fill in your Strategy score here. Then turn to page 215 and transfer your score onto Graph 1.

Personal
Vocabulary
►Strategy
Comprehension
TOTAL SCORE
✓ T

Check your answers with your teacher. Give yourself 1 point for each correct answer, and fill in your Comprehension score here. Then turn to page 215 and transfer your score onto Graph 1.

Personal
Vocabulary
Strategy
►Comprehension
TOTAL SCORE
✓ T

Extending

Choose one or both of these activities:

LEARN HOW TO COPE WITH BULLIES

The fact that "Priscilla and the Wimps" is one of the most popular short stories written in the last 20 years suggests the seriousness of the problem of bullies. A good deal of research has been done on the subject, and much of what has been learned is available in books and on Web sites. Learn more about how to deal with bullies—in a manner more socially acceptable than the one described in this story—by exploring some of the resources listed on this page. (The first Web site discusses dealing with bullies.) Take notes on what you discover, organize your notes, and share your findings in a short speech.

DISCOVER RICHARD PECK

Richard Peck, the author of "Priscilla and the Wimps," is a prize-winning author. Read more of his works, and find out more about Peck himself. (Some of the resources listed on this page will help you get started.) Then write a brief biography that includes essential information about Peck's life and career, as well as a list of his works. If you have read any of the stories or novels on the list, include a few sentences about each story, along with your reactions to it. Then make copies of the biography and distribute it to all of your friends who might enjoy learning more about Richard Peck and his work.

Resources

Books

Gallo, Donald, ed. *Sixteen: Short Stories by Outstanding Writers for Young Adults.* Bt Bound, 1999.

Rue, Nancy N. *Everything You Need to Know About Peer Mediation.* The You Need to Know Library. Rosen, 1997.

Webster-Doyle, Terrence. *Why Is Everybody Always Picking on Me? A Guide to Understanding Bullies for Young People.* Weatherhill, 2000.

Web Sites

http://kidshealth.org/kid/feeling/emotion/bullies.html
This Web site offers advice for coping with bullies.

http://www.carolhurst.com/authors/rpeck.html
Read a short biography of Richard Peck and reviews of his books on this Web site.

Audio Recording

Gallo, Donald, ed. *Sixteen: Short Stories by Outstanding Writers for Young Adults.* Listening Library, 1987.

Building Background

Who doesn't like a good **mystery** or crime story? Detective novels, police dramas on TV, and all sorts of movie mysteries are always popular. Perhaps the reason is that humans are curious and enjoy solving puzzles. Perhaps the reason has something to do with our desire to test our wits against the writer's mix of clues and misdirection. Whatever the reason, almost all of us enjoy trying to solve the crime before the characters in the story do.

Where do we look for clues? Think of a particular type of crime, such as a murder or a burglary. On the concept map below, record your ideas for solving such a crime. Then, as you read "Sarah Tops," compare your ideas to the approaches that the characters use.

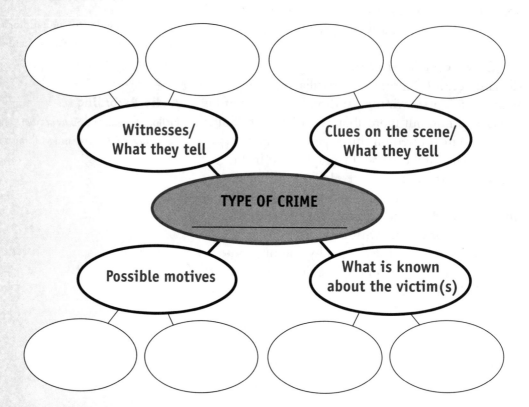

Witnesses/
What they tell

Clues on the scene/
What they tell

TYPE OF CRIME

Possible motives

What is known
about the victim(s)

Vocabulary Builder

1. The words in the margin are from the story "Sarah Tops." Write a meaning for each word on the clipboard. If a word has more than one meaning, predict how the word might be used in the story and write that meaning.

2. Then use the vocabulary words and the title to help you predict what might happen in this story. Write your prediction on the lines below. Use as many vocabulary words as possible in your prediction.

_____

_____

_____

_____

3. Save your work. You will refer to it again in the Vocabulary Check.

Strategy Builder

Mapping the Elements of a Short Story

- "Sarah Tops" is a short story. A **short story** is a piece of fiction that usually can be read in one sitting. Because it is much shorter than a novel, a short story often has fewer characters and takes place over a briefer period of time.

- One of the main elements of every short story is its **plot**, or sequence of events. In most stories, the plot revolves around a problem and what the main characters do to solve it.

- Another element is the **setting**—the time and place in which the story happens. In some stories the setting is a major element. For example, since "Sarah Tops" is a murder mystery, you can expect the scene of the murder to provide clues to solving the mystery.

- A good way to keep track of what happens in a short story is to record its elements on a **story map**. Study the story map below. It lists and defines the elements that you should look for as you read.

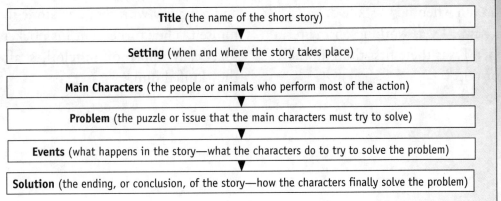

Title (the name of the short story)
▼
Setting (when and where the story takes place)
▼
Main Characters (the people or animals who perform most of the action)
▼
Problem (the puzzle or issue that the main characters must try to solve)
▼
Events (what happens in the story—what the characters do to try to solve the problem)
▼
Solution (the ending, or conclusion, of the story—how the characters finally solve the problem)

alive

gouged

hysterical

lead

magnificent

mentally

stashed

CLIPBOARD

alive
_____

gouged
_____

hysterical
_____

lead
_____

CLIPBOARD

magnificent
_____

mentally
_____

stashed
_____

Sarah Tops

by Isaac Asimov

As you begin reading this short story, apply the strategies that you just learned. Keep track of the characters, the setting, and other elements. You may want to underline them as you read.

I came out of the Museum of Natural History and was crossing the street on my way to the subway, when I saw the crowd about halfway down the block; and the police cars, too. I could hear the whine of an ambulance.

For a minute, I hesitated, but then I walked on. The crowds of the curious just get in the way of officials trying to save lives. Dad, who's a detective on the force, complains about that all the time.

I just kept my mind on the term paper I was going to have to write on air pollution, and **mentally** arranged the notes I had taken during the museum program on the subject.

Of course, I knew I would read about it in the afternoon papers. Besides, I would ask Dad about it after dinner. He sometimes talked about cases without telling too much of the real security details.

After I asked, Mom looked kind of funny and said, "The man was in the museum when he was killed."

I said, "I was working on my term paper. I was there first thing in the morning."

Mom looked very worried. "There might have been shooting in the museum."

"Well, there wasn't," said Dad, soothingly. "This man tried to lose himself there and he didn't succeed."

"*I* would have," I said. "I know the museum, every inch."

Dad doesn't like me bragging, so he frowned a little and said, "They didn't let him get away entirely—caught up with him outside, knifed him, and got away. We'll catch them, though. We know who they are."

He nodded his head. "They're what's left of the gang that broke into that jewelry store two weeks ago. We managed to get the jewels back, but we didn't grab all the men. And not all the jewels either. One diamond was left. A big one—worth $30,000."

"Maybe that's what the killers were after," I said.

"Very likely. The dead man was probably trying to cross the other two and get away with that one stone for himself. They turned out his pockets, practically ripped off his clothes, after they knifed him."

"Did they get the diamond?" I asked.

"How can we tell? The woman who reported the killing came on him when he was still just barely **alive**. She said he said three words to her, very slowly, 'Try—Sarah—Tops.' Then he died."

"Who is Sarah Tops?" asked Mom.

 **Stop here for the Strategy Break.**

Strategy Break

If you were to stop and begin a story map for "Sarah Tops," it might look like this so far:

Title: Sarah Tops

▼

Setting: modern times, in a city with a Museum of Natural History

▼

Main Characters: the narrator, his father, his mother

▼

Problem: A man has been killed outside the museum, and a large jewel that he probably was carrying is missing. The only clue in the case are the words, "Try Sarah Tops."

▼

Event 1: As the narrator leaves the museum, he sees a crowd and police cars nearby.

▼

Event 2: At dinner he asks his father (a police detective) what happened. His father explains that a man tried to hide in the museum but was found and stabbed just outside the building.

▼

Event 3: His father explains that the man was part of a gang of jewel thieves, and that his last words before he died were, "Try Sarah Tops."

▼

To be continued . . .

As you continue reading, keep paying attention to the events in this short story. You will use some of them to complete the story map in the Strategy Follow-up.

Go on reading to see what happens.

Dad shrugged. "I don't know. I don't even know if that's really what he said. The woman was pretty **hysterical**. If she's right and that's what he said then maybe the killers didn't get the diamond. Maybe the dead man left it with Sarah Tops, whoever she is. Maybe he knew he was dying and wanted to have it off his conscience."

"Is there a Sarah Tops in the phone book, Dad?" I asked.

Dad said, "Did you think we didn't look? No Sarah Tops, either one *P* or two *P*'s. Nothing in the city directory. Nothing in our files. Nothing in the FBI files."

Mom said, "Maybe it's not a person. Maybe it's a firm. Sarah Tops Cakes or something."

"Could be," said Dad. "There's no Sarah Tops firm, but there are other types of Tops companies and they'll be checked for anyone working there named Sarah."

I got an idea suddenly and bubbled over. "Listen, Dad, maybe it isn't a firm either. Maybe it's a *thing*. Maybe the woman didn't hear 'Sarah Tops' but 'Sarah's top'; you know, a *top* that you spin. If the dead guy has a daughter named Sarah, maybe he **gouged** a bit out of her top and **stashed** the diamond inside and—"

Dad grinned. "Very good, Larry," he said. "But he doesn't have a daughter named Sarah. Or any relative by that name as far as we know. We've searched where he lived and there's

nothing reported there that can be called a top."

"Well," I said, sort of let down and disappointed, "I suppose that's not such a good idea anyway, because why should he say we ought to *try* it? He either hid it in Sarah's top or he didn't. He would know which. Why should he say we should *try* it?"

And then it hit me. What if—

I said, "Dad, can you get into the museum this late?"

"On police business? Sure."

"Dad," I said, kind of breathless, "I think we better go look. *Now*. Before the people start coming in again."

"Why?"

"I've got a silly idea. I—I—"

Dad didn't push me. He likes me to have my own ideas. He thinks maybe I'll be a detective too, some day. He said, "All right. Let's follow up your **lead**."

We got there just when the last purple bit of twilight was turning to black. We were let in by a guard.

I'd never been in the museum when it was dark. It looked like a huge, underground cave, with the guard's flashlight seeming to make things even more mysterious.

We took the elevator up to the fourth floor, where the big shapes loomed in the bit of light that shone this way and that as the guard moved his flash. "Do you want me to put on the light in this room?" he asked.

"Yes, please," I said.

There they all were. Some in glass cases; but the big ones in the middle of the large room. Bones and teeth and spines of giants that ruled the earth, millions of years ago. I said, "I want to look close at that one. Is it all right if I climb over the railing?"

"Go ahead," said the guard. He helped me.

I leaned against the platform, looking at the grayish plaster material the skeleton was standing on.

"What's this?" I said. It didn't look much different in color from the plaster.

"Chewing gum," said the guard, frowning. "Those darn kids—"

I said, "The guy was trying to get away and he saw his chance to throw this—hide it from the gang—"

Dad took the gum from me, squeezed it, and then pulled it apart. Inside, something caught the light and *flashed*. Dad put it in an envelope and said to me, "How did you know?"

I said, "Well, look at it."

It was a **magnificent** skeleton. It had a large skull with bone stretching back over the neck vertebrae. It had two horns over the eyes, and a third one, just a bump, on the snout. The nameplate said: *Triceratops.* ●

Strategy Follow-up

Now complete the story map for "Sarah Tops." (Use a separate sheet of paper if you need more room to write.) Start with Event 4. Parts of the events have been filled in for you.

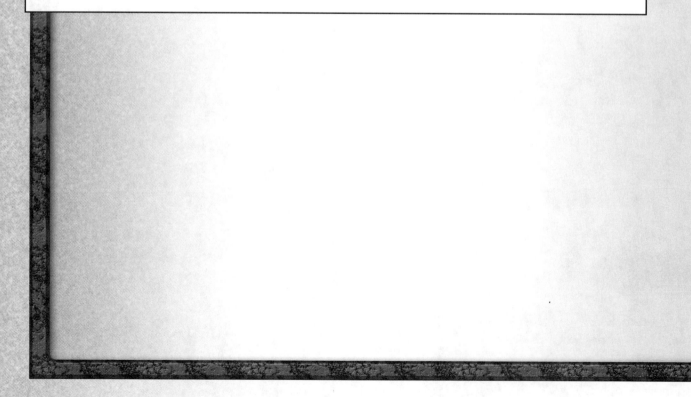

Problem: A man has been killed outside the museum, and a large jewel that he probably was carrying is missing. The only clue in the case are the words, "Try Sarah Tops."

▼

Event 4: Larry suggests checking the phone book for a Sarah Tops, but his father

▼

Event 5: Larry's mother suggests checking companies with the name Sarah Tops, and Larry suggests looking for a top belonging to a Sarah, but his father

▼

Event 6: Larry gets an idea and asks if

▼

Event 7: Larry and his father

▼

Event 8: Larry examines the platform under a dinosaur display and finds

▼

Solution: When Larry's father asks how he knew where to look, Larry

✓Personal Checklist

Read each question and put a check (✓) in the correct box.

1. In Building Background, how well were you able to use your concept map to help you understand how the characters might try to solve the crime?
   - ☐ 3 (extremely well)
   - ☐ 2 (fairly well)
   - ☐ 1 (not well)

2. In the Vocabulary Builder, how many vocabulary words were you able use in your prediction?
   - ☐ 3 (6–7 words)
   - ☐ 2 (4–5 words)
   - ☐ 1 (0–3 words)

3. How well were you able to complete the story map in the Strategy Follow-up?
   - ☐ 3 (extremely well)
   - ☐ 2 (fairly well)
   - ☐ 1 (not well)

4. How well do you understand the solution to the mystery?
   - ☐ 3 (extremely well)
   - ☐ 2 (fairly well)
   - ☐ 1 (not well)

5. How well do you understand why Larry had a better chance of understanding the thief's clue than other people did?
   - ☐ 3 (extremely well)
   - ☐ 2 (fairly well)
   - ☐ 1 (not well)

Vocabulary Check

Look back at the work you did in the Vocabulary Builder. Then answer each question by circling the correct letter.

1. What does *gouged* mean in the context of this story?
   a. cheated
   b. scratched
   c. scooped

2. Which of these words is the opposite of *calm*?
   a. alive
   b. hysterical
   c. stashed

3. Which word means the opposite of *magnificent*?
   a. hideous
   b. impressive
   c. extraordinary

4. After he leaves the museum, Larry mentally arranges the notes he had taken during the program on air pollution. What does this mean?
   a. He puts the notes in order as he says them aloud.
   b. In his mind, he puts the notes in order.
   c. He writes the notes down in order.

5. In the context of this story, what is a *lead*?
   a. a person in charge
   b. a piece of metal
   c. a hunch, or feeling

Add the numbers that you just checked to get your Personal Checklist score. Fill in your score here. Then turn to page 215 and transfer your score onto Graph 1.

Personal
Vocabulary
Strategy
Comprehension
TOTAL SCORE
✓ T

Check your answers with your teacher. Give yourself 1 point for each correct answer, and fill in your Vocabulary score here. Then turn to page 215 and transfer your score onto Graph 1.

Personal
Vocabulary
Strategy
Comprehension
TOTAL SCORE
✓ T

Strategy Check

Review the story map that you completed in the Strategy Follow-up. Then answer these questions:

1. How does Larry think a phone book might help solve the mystery?
   a. He thinks it might have a listing for someone named Sarah Tops.
   b. He thinks the missing jewel might be hidden in a phone book.
   c. He recalls seeing *Sarah Tops* listed under "Toy Manufacturers."

2. Why doesn't Larry's father look in the phone book for the names Larry and his mother suggest?
   a. He thinks their ideas are worthless.
   b. There is no telephone book in their house.
   c. The police have already looked.

3. What does Larry ask his father to do in Event 6?
   a. let him examine the clothing of the victim
   b. take him to the museum right away
   c. give him a copy of the witness's statement

4. What part of the museum is Larry interested in?
   a. the lobby
   b. the dinosaur exhibit
   c. the storage room

5. How does Larry use the clue "Try Sarah Tops" to lead him to the diamond?
   a. The words sound like the name of the dinosaur *triceratops.*
   b. Sarah Tops is the museum worker who assembled the display.
   c. The section of the museum where the dinosaurs are is labeled TST.

Comprehension Check

Review the story if necessary. Then answer these questions:

1. Why does Larry know that onlookers at a crime scene just get in the way?
   a. He has gotten into trouble before by interfering with police work.
   b. His father is on the force and has complained about this problem.
   c. Larry wants to be a police officer and has researched the job.

2. What does Larry brag about while he discusses the murder with his parents?
   a. that he knows the museum, every inch
   b. that he can solve crimes faster than the police
   c. that he could've caught the killers had he been closer to the scene

3. Who reported the clue of the victim's last words to the police?
   a. the guard at the door of the museum
   b. a woman who happened to find the man just before he died
   c. one of the thieves, who had already been caught

4. How can you tell that Larry's father thinks his son is smart?
   a. He doesn't like Larry bragging.
   b. He tells Larry that the police already checked the phone book.
   c. He goes along with Larry's suggestion to visit the museum.

5. Why do you think the man revealed the diamond's whereabouts before he died?
   a. He didn't want his killers to get the diamond.
   b. He had decided to turn his life around.
   c. He wanted to donate the diamond to the museum.

Check your answers with your teacher. Give yourself 1 point for each correct answer, and fill in your Strategy score here. Then turn to page 215 and transfer your score onto Graph 1.

Personal
Vocabulary
Strategy
Comprehension
TOTAL SCORE
✓ T

Check your answers with your teacher. Give yourself 1 point for each correct answer, and fill in your Comprehension score here. Then turn to page 215 and transfer your score onto Graph 1.

Personal
Vocabulary
Strategy
Comprehension
TOTAL SCORE
✓ T

Extending

Choose one or more of these activities:

READ MORE OF ISAAC ASIMOV'S WRITING

Isaac Asimov was one of the most prolific writers of our time. Best known for his science fiction, he also wrote hundreds of short stories and nonfiction in a number of fields. Using some of the resources listed on this page, investigate Asimov's work. Then read at least one more of his stories. (If you enjoyed "Sarah Tops," refer to the first Web site on this page for a list of other stories featuring Larry, the story's main character.) Compare your chosen story to "Sarah Tops." Do the two stories have any common characteristics? Which one did you enjoy more? Why? Write a short review of the second story. Begin with a summary to help readers understand what it is about, and then explain your reaction to it. End by explaining why you think the story is as good as, or better than, "Sarah Tops."

INVESTIGATE DINOSAURS

When and where did the triceratops live? How big was it? What did it eat? How do modern researchers know the answers to these questions? Using information from books, the Web, and local museums, create a poster about the triceratops. (The last Web site in the resource section will get you started online.) Answer all of the above questions and mention any other interesting facts that you think will interest your audience. Include a picture of the dinosaur, either photocopied or sketched from drawings or models that you find in your research. Also, be sure to include a list of the resources that you used.

WRITE A MYSTERY

Think about some mysteries that you have read or seen. (For examples of short but challenging mysteries, read some Encyclopedia Brown tales.) Then write your own mystery. Create a young detective with a connection to the police force, as in the Larry and Encyclopedia Brown stories. Be sure to make the problem clear and to provide some clues to give your reader a chance to figure out the solution as he or she reads. Before you begin writing, you may want to create a story map to help you outline the plot of your mystery.

Resources

Books

Asimov, Isaac. *The Disappearing Man, and Other Mysteries.* Walker, 1985.

———, Martin H. Greenberg, and Joseph D. Olander. *100 Malicious Little Mysteries.* Fromm International, 1993.

Sobol, Donald J. *Encyclopedia Brown and the Case of the Slippery Salamander.* Encyclopedia Brown. Skylark, 2000.

———. *Two-Minute Mysteries.* Scott Foresman, 1991.

Web Sites

http://www.asimovonline.com/oldsite/short_fiction_guide.html
This Web page offers a guide to Asimov's short fiction works. Click on the "Larry Mysteries" link in the Indexes section for a list of stories featuring Larry.

http://www.fieldmuseum.org/exhibits/exhibit_sites/dino/Triceratops1.htm
This Web site of the Field Museum contains information on triceratops.

affliction

aqualung

determination

earthbound

exploration

graduation

inflammation

underwater

Jacques Cousteau: Voice for a "Silent World"

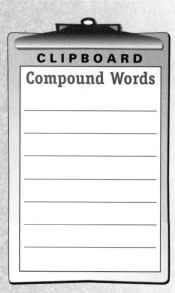

CLIPBOARD

Compound Words

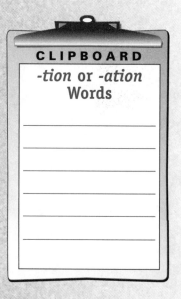

CLIPBOARD

***-tion* or *-ation* Words**

Building Background

In the article you are about to read, you will learn about a person who loved the earth's oceans. To understand his feelings, you should know something about the ocean yourself. Before you begin reading, find a partner and take a quick inventory of your knowledge of oceans. Make two lists. In the first, list all the different creatures you can think of that live in oceans around the world. In the second, list all the resources and benefits that oceans provide to humans.

After five minutes of brainstorming, share your list with other classmates. Which creatures and benefits did they think of that you can add to your lists?

Vocabulary Builder

1. Examine the vocabulary words in the margin. Four of them are **compounds**—words composed of two smaller words put together. Each of the other five words ends with the suffix *-tion* or *-ation,* which means "the act or process of _____ing" or "the condition or result of being _____ed."

2. Write each vocabulary word on the appropriate clipboard. Then, with your partner from Building Background, take turns defining each word. Write your definitions on another sheet of paper. Use a dictionary if you need help.

3. As you read this article, look for the boldfaced words. Do your definitions fit the way the words are used in the article?

4. Save your work. You will refer to it again in the Vocabulary Check.

Strategy Builder

Identifying Causes and Effects in Nonfiction

- When writing nonfiction, authors usually have a specific purpose in mind. For example, when authors write to give facts and information about a particular topic, their purpose is to **inform**. If they write to give their opinion about something, and try to convince others to share that opinion, their purpose is to **persuade**. If they write to describe how they feel about an experience—such as attending a sporting event or watching a sunrise—their purpose is to **express**. If they want to make readers smile, laugh, or be surprised, their purpose is to **entertain**. As you will see, the author's purpose for writing this article is to inform.

- Every piece of nonfiction follows a particular **organizational pattern**. The most common patterns are listed in the margin. The author of this article uses the pattern of **cause-effect** to describe the events that caused Jacques Cousteau to become interested in the "silent world" of the sea.

- To find cause-and-effect relationships while you read, keep asking yourself, "What happened?" and "Why did it happen?" Doing this will help you understand what has happened so far. As you read the following paragraphs, look for the chain of causes and effects.

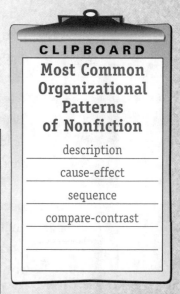

CLIPBOARD

Most Common Organizational Patterns of Nonfiction

description

cause-effect

sequence

compare-contrast

From the time Isaiah could hold a spoon, he loved to beat out rhythms. In kindergarten, whenever the children played with rhythm instruments, he was delighted. He asked for drums for his eighth birthday. By the time he entered fourth grade, he had talked his parents into letting him take drumming lessons. He practiced every chance he had and became a good drummer.

When Isaiah entered high school, he tried out for band and was immediately accepted. Soon he was given solos. In addition, he began to perform with a rock group and then to write music of his own. By the time he completed high school, he was sure he wanted to become a professional musician.

- If you wanted to track the causes and effects in the paragraphs above, you could put them on a **cause-and-effect chain**. It might look like this:

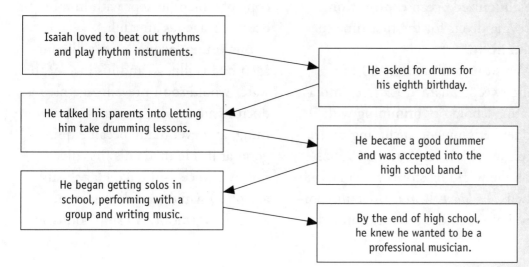

CAUSES

Isaiah loved to beat out rhythms and play rhythm instruments.

He talked his parents into letting him take drumming lessons.

He began getting solos in school, performing with a group and writing music.

EFFECTS

He asked for drums for his eighth birthday.

He became a good drummer and was accepted into the high school band.

By the end of high school, he knew he wanted to be a professional musician.

Jacques Cousteau: Voice for a "Silent World"

by Jim O'Leary and Stephen James O'Meara

As you read the first part of this article, apply the strategies that you just learned. To find the causes and effects, keep asking yourself, "What happened?" and "Why did it happen?"

Jacques-Yves Cousteau (1910–1997) spent his life exploring the Earth's oceans and communicating his love and concern for this vital resource to people of all ages around the world. An inscription on a Special Gold Medal presented to him by the National Geographic Society in 1961 reads: *To **earthbound** man he gave the key to the silent world.*

The "silent world" was the living ocean, a vast and uncharted territory that Cousteau tirelessly documented on paper and film. He first unlocked this mysterious and often feared realm in 1943, when he slipped beneath the ocean in a diving apparatus that he and engineer Émile Gagnan had designed. This invention, called the **aqualung** or "*self-c*ontained **underwater** *b*reathing *a*pparatus" (scuba), revolutionized ocean **exploration**, allowing divers for the first time to swim freely.

Cousteau converted a 400-ton mine-sweeper, named *Calypso*, into a floating laboratory brimming with modern equipment, including underwater television cameras. In 1953, he took the world by storm when he published *The Silent World*, a riveting portrayal of life under the sea captured both in words and in photographs like those never before seen. The book sold five million copies and was translated into 22 languages.

A Natural Passion

You can trace the roots of Cousteau's passion for the oceans to his childhood. Born on June 11, 1910, in Saint-André-de-Cubzac, France, Jacques-Yves Cousteau was a sickly boy. He suffered from *enteritis*, a painful **inflammation** of the intestines, and *anemia*, an **affliction** of the blood that left him weak. Confined by sickness, young Jacques read a great deal. His favorite stories were adventures of the sea—about pirates, smugglers, and pearl divers. He read Jules Verne's science-fiction novel, *20,000 Leagues Under the Sea*, a copy of which he kept with him on his ocean voyages as an adult.

But young Jacques wasn't discouraged by his illness, and his love of the water would soon prevail. Against his doctor's advice, Jacques took up swimming, and eventually became quite good at it. He made his first dive— not by choice—in Lake Harvey at the age of 10 while attending summer camp in Vermont. A camp counselor who didn't like Jacques very much forced him to clear fallen branches from the water under the lake's diving board. "I worked very hard," Cousteau recalled, "diving in that murk without goggles, without a mask, and that's where I learned to dive." Diving became his favorite camp activity—he would do it over and over again, testing how long he could stay under water.

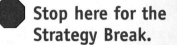 **Stop here for the Strategy Break.**

Strategy Break

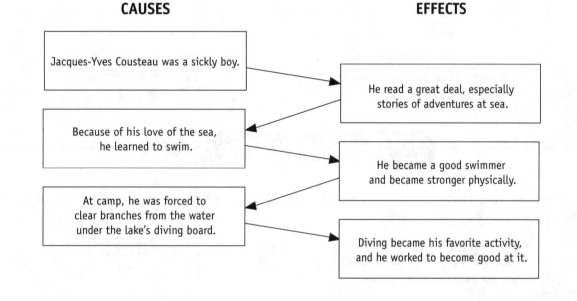

The first three paragraphs of this article are the introduction. The body of the article, which is the part organized by cause-and-effect, begins with "A Natural Passion." If you were to create a cause-and-effect chain for the body of the article so far, it might look like this:

CAUSES

Jacques-Yves Cousteau was a sickly boy.

Because of his love of the sea, he learned to swim.

At camp, he was forced to clear branches from the water under the lake's diving board.

EFFECTS

He read a great deal, especially stories of adventures at sea.

He became a good swimmer and became stronger physically.

Diving became his favorite activity, and he worked to become good at it.

As you continue reading, keep looking for causes and effects. At the end of this article, you will create a cause-and-effect chain of your own.

Go on reading.

As a teenager, Jacques also dabbled in constructing machines. He built a model crane and a battery-operated car. He used his allowance to buy a movie camera and experimented with it at home. He would take the camera apart and put it back together again. He remembered, "I was fascinated by the hardware. That's how I got started—the cameras, how to process film, and how to devise chemicals."

Lacking the excitement of diving and machinery, school seemed to bore Jacques. He insisted that 17 windows he broke at school were part of an experiment to prove that a strongly thrown stone would make smaller holes in glass. This incident prompted his parents to send him to a strict boarding school, where he eventually graduated with honors.

Upon **graduation**, Cousteau decided to enroll in the French naval academy, *l'École Navale,* where he was supposed to train as a navy pilot. A near-fatal car accident at the age of 26 weakened his arms and he was transferred to sea duty. Again, Cousteau's **determination** and love of the water prevailed, as he constantly swam to strengthen his arms. It was at this point in his life that he began to see the underwater world differently. As he explains in his book, *The Silent World,* "Sometimes we are lucky enough to know that our lives have been changed, to discard the old,

embrace the new, and run headlong down an immutable course. It happened to me . . . on that summer's day, when my eyes were opened to the sea."

Cousteau's Legacy

Before he passed away in Paris at the age of 87, on June 25, 1997, Cousteau had become the world's most famous underwater explorer. *The Undersea World of Jacques Cousteau,* a weekly television series of underwater documentaries which ran for eight years beginning in 1968, captured the attention of millions of viewers and is still run on some stations today. In all, Cousteau's television documentaries have won 40 Emmy Award nominations. ●

Strategy Follow-up

Now complete the cause-and-effect chain for the second part of this article. Some of the information has been provided for you.

CAUSES

| As a teen, Jacques was fascinated with machines—particularly |

| Lacking the excitement of diving and machinery, school |

| Upon graduation, |

| |

| |

EFFECTS

| |

| |

| |

| |

✓Personal Checklist

Read each question and put a check (✓) in the correct box.

1. How well do you understand why Jacques Cousteau is considered an important explorer?
   - ☐ 3 (extremely well)
   - ☐ 2 (fairly well)
   - ☐ 1 (not well)

2. How well were you able to work with your partner to create the two lists in Building Background?
   - ☐ 3 (extremely well)
   - ☐ 2 (fairly well)
   - ☐ 1 (not well)

3. How well were you able to complete the activity in the Vocabulary Builder?
   - ☐ 3 (extremely well)
   - ☐ 2 (fairly well)
   - ☐ 1 (not well)

4. In the Strategy Follow-up, how well were you able to complete the cause-and-effect chain for the second part of this article?
   - ☐ 3 (extremely well)
   - ☐ 2 (fairly well)
   - ☐ 1 (not well)

5. How well could you use this article to explain how Jacques Cousteau improved our knowledge of the earth's oceans?
   - ☐ 3 (extremely well)
   - ☐ 2 (fairly well)
   - ☐ 1 (not well)

Vocabulary Check

Look back at the work you did in the Vocabulary Builder. Then answer each question by circling the correct letter.

1. Which of the following vocabulary words is *not* a compound word?
   a earthbound
   b. underwater
   c. determination

2. If the word *aqua* means "water," what does *aqualung* mean?
   a. a device for breathing under water
   b. a lung that breathes water
   c. a device for breathing water

3. Which word describes a condition that causes swelling, redness, and pain?
   a. exploration
   b. inflammation
   c. affliction

4. Which vocabulary word means "limited to the land"?
   a. earthbound
   b. determination
   c. inflammation

5. What is an affliction?
   a. a condition that causes one to swell
   b. a change in one's tone of voice
   c. a condition of continued pain

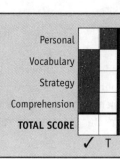

Add the numbers that you just checked to get your Personal Checklist score. Fill in your score here. Then turn to page 215 and transfer your score onto Graph 1.

Personal
Vocabulary
Strategy
Comprehension
TOTAL SCORE
✓ T

Check your answers with your teacher. Give yourself 1 point for each correct answer, and fill in your Vocabulary score here. Then turn to page 215 and transfer your score onto Graph 1.

Personal
Vocabulary
Strategy
Comprehension
TOTAL SCORE
✓ T

Strategy Check

Review the cause-and-effect chain that you completed in the Strategy Follow-up. Then answer the following questions:

1. What led Jacques to conduct an "experiment" in which he broke 17 windows?

   a. He was bored with school.

   b. He did it on a dare.

   c. He did it for an assignment.

2. What was the effect of the "experiment"?

   a. His parents took away his camera.

   b. His parents sent him to boarding school.

   c. His parents grounded him for a year.

3. What caused Jacques to transfer from training as a navy pilot to sea duty?

   a. He didn't get along well with the officers in charge of flight training.

   b. He discovered that he had a fear of heights.

   c. He was in a car accident that left his arms weak.

4. What did he do to improve his physical condition?

   a. He swam constantly to strengthen his arms.

   b. He took up running and eventually ran marathons.

   c. He became a weightlifter to strengthen his arms.

5. What was the long-term effect of his spending so much time in the water?

   a. His skin became wrinkled, and he aged very rapidly.

   b. He began to see the sea differently, and it became his lifelong passion.

   c. He lost interest in events on land for the rest of his life.

Comprehension Check

Review the article if necessary. Then answer these questions:

1. What is the "silent world" for which Cousteau spoke?

   a. the underwater world here on Earth

   b. the nearby planet of Mars

   c. the world of long ago, before people could write

2. What was Cousteau's invention that enabled divers to go underwater safely?

   a. the aqualung or "scuba"

   b. a 400-ton mine-sweeper

   c. a model crane

3. How did Cousteau communicate what he learned to the rest of the world?

   a. through words and photographs in a book

   b. through television documentaries

   c. through both ways listed above

4. What do you learn about Cousteau from his persistence in swimming despite his childhood illnesses and car accident?

   a. He liked to be disagreeable and do what he shouldn't do.

   b. He sometimes took the easy way out.

   c. Once he decided to do something, he didn't let anything stop him.

5. Which characteristic of Cousteau's ship, the *Calypso*, most clearly reflects his interests as a teenager?

   a. The *Calypso* was originally a 400-ton mine-sweeper.

   b. The *Calypso* was brimming with equipment, including underwater television cameras.

   c. The *Calypso* was named after the ship in Cousteau's favorite novel, *20,000 Leagues Under the Sea*.

Check your answers with your teacher. Give yourself 1 point for each correct answer, and fill in your Strategy score here. Then turn to page 215 and transfer your score onto Graph 1.

Check your answers with your teacher. Give yourself 1 point for each correct answer, and fill in your Comprehension score here. Then turn to page 215 and transfer your score onto Graph 1.

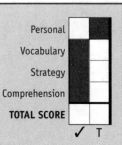

Extending

Choose one or more of these activities:

BUILD ON BUILDING BACKGROUND

Before reading this article, you made lists of sea creatures and benefits of the oceans. Which of the items on your lists would you like to know more about? In the library or on the Web, search for materials on that topic. At the library, in addition to books, be sure to investigate tapes of television documentaries made by Cousteau and others. As you skim the materials, keep these questions in mind:

- Why should people know more about this topic?
- How will the information help them?

Then write a report about your topic. Make the answers to the two questions clear.

EXPLORE THE TECHNOLOGY OF UNDERWATER EXPLORATION

How are underwater cameras different from regular cameras? How deep can divers go while exploring the ocean—either while swimming or traveling inside vessels? If the divers find samples that they want to bring back, what special methods do they use? Jacques Cousteau developed much of the equipment and many of the methods used to explore the undersea world. With a partner or small group, read about Cousteau's work, focusing on the technology and techniques he pioneered. Hold a panel discussion in which you describe some of his contributions.

READ A JULES VERNE CLASSIC

One of the experiences that drew Jacques Cousteau to the oceans was reading the Jules Verne novel *20,000 Leagues Under the Sea*. Read or listen to a shortened version of this classic, and summarize the story for your classmates. If several class members read or hear the tale, have a discussion about it. Compare your opinions of the novel.

Resources

Books

Cousteau, Jacques. *The Adventures of Life*. Abrams, 1975.

————. *The Ocean World of Jacques Cousteau*. Abradale Press, 1979.

————. *The Silent World*. Lyons Press, 1987.

Munson, Richard. *Cousteau: The Captain and His World*. Paragon House, 1991.

Verne, Jules. *20,000 Leagues Under the Sea*. Tor, 1995.

Web Sites

http://www.cousteau.org/en/
This is the Web site of the Cousteau Society.

http://www.seagrant.wisc.edu/madisonjason11/
This Web site on underwater exploration is sponsored by University of Wisconsin's Sea Grant Institute.

Audio Recording

Verne, Jules. *20,000 Leagues Under the Sea* (abridged). Naxos Audio Books, 1994.

Videos/DVDs

Amazon: River of the Future. Cousteau Society. Turner Home Video, 1991.

Cousteau: Pioneer of the Sea. Cousteau Society. Turner Home Video, 1990.

Vanishing Wonders of the Sea. Carousel Film and Video, 1998.

The Middle Ages

beautiful

exquisite

hostile

hovels

impoverished

lord

master

mighty

palaces

powerless

rich

unfriendly

Building Background

Knights in armor, princesses in cone-shaped hats, jousts, and quests. These are a few of the things that you might think of when you think of the Middle Ages. How typical are they of life at that time? The article you are about to read may provide a more accurate and complete picture of the Middle Ages than tales of King Arthur's court ever could.

Before you begin reading this article, choose a partner and fill in the first column of the chart below with at least four things that you know about life during the Middle Ages. Fill in the second column with at least four questions about the Middle Ages that you hope the article will answer. When you finish the article, you will fill in the last column.

Life During the Middle Ages

K (What I **K**now)	W (What I **W**ant to Know)	L (What I **L**earned)
1.	1.	1.
2.	2.	2.
3.	3.	3.
4.	4.	4.

Vocabulary Builder

1. Study the vocabulary words in the margin. Each word is half of a pair of **antonyms** (words with opposite meanings) or **synonyms** (words with similar meanings). Write the antonym pairs on the first clipboard. Write the synonym pairs on the second clipboard.

2. As you read this article, underline any other antonym or synonym pairs that you find.

3. Save your work. You will refer to it again in the Vocabulary Check.

CLIPBOARD 1

Antonym Pairs

1. _____

_____

2. _____

_____

3. _____

_____

CLIPBOARD 2

Synonym Pairs

1. _____

_____

2. _____

_____

3. _____

_____

Strategy Builder

Outlining Main Ideas and Supporting Details

- An **informational article** is a type of nonfiction that gives facts and details about a particular topic. As you know, the **topic** of an article is often mentioned or referred to in its **title**.

- You also know that every piece of nonfiction follows a particular organizational pattern. The pattern of this article is description. A **description** explains what something is, what it does, or how and why it works. For example, this article describes what the Middle Ages were, when they occurred, and what life was like during that time.

- Descriptions are usually organized into **main ideas** and **supporting details**. These ideas and details help explain or support the topic. In the article you are about to read, the main ideas are given in the boldfaced **headings**. The paragraphs below each heading contain details that support the main idea.

- There are several ways to keep track of main ideas and supporting details as you read an informational article. One way is to put them on a concept map, or web. Another way is to outline them. Some **outlines** use a system of Roman numerals (I, II, III, and so on), capital letters, Arabic numerals (1, 2, 3, and so on), and lowercase letters.

- Read the following paragraph from an article about the city of Calgary, Canada. Then read how one student outlined the main ideas and details.

Calgary

A Major City

To citizens of the United States, the Canadian city of Calgary is probably best known as the home of the Calgary Exhibition and Stampede. This annual affair—featuring rodeo events, livestock shows, and carnival rides and games—draws tourists from both Canada and the United States, as well as many other countries.

But the cattle industry that gave rise to the Stampede is no longer the major business in Calgary. In recent years, the oil industry has made Calgary one of the fastest-growing cities in Canada. Calgary is now the largest city in the province of Alberta and the second largest in population in all of Canada.

Calgary

I. A Major City
  A. Best known for the Calgary Exhibition and Stampede
    1. An annual event featuring rodeo and related events
    2. Draws tourists from Canada, the States, and elsewhere
  B. Calgary has two major industries
    1. Cattle industry was once the leading industry
    2. Recently, oil industry has made Calgary one of Canada's fastest-growing cities
      a. Calgary now the largest city in Alberta
      b. Is the second most populated city in Canada

The Middle Ages

As you read the first part of this article, apply some of the strategies that you just learned. Look for the main ideas and supporting details in this description, and think about how you might outline them.

A Complicated Time

The period we call the Middle Ages (the years from A.D. 1000 to 1500) was a time of great contrasts—between **mighty** lords and **powerless** peasants, saintly bishops and blood-thirsty soldiers, scholarly nuns and kings who could not read. Differences between people of title, rank, and status mattered far more than today. Most men and women had little chance of moving out of the social group into which they had been born.

The Middle Ages was a time of great achievements in art, architecture, music, poetry, and many highly skilled crafts. It was a time of great activity, when peasant farmers cleared land to grow food for their families and experimented with better ways of growing crops. It was a time of violence and lawlessness, but also a time when many men and women devoted their lives and their fortunes to the Christian faith.

However, the Middle Ages was also a time with many problems. From the windows of their fine houses, **rich** city merchants could see miserable beggars huddling at their gates. Magnificent castles, **exquisite palaces**, and lofty cathedrals were built within a stone's throw of flimsy countryside **hovels** and the **impoverished** conditions of inner-city slums. **Beautiful** silk and velvet robes, embroidered with gold, might be crawling with lice and fleas that carried disease. And, after the Black Death reached Europe in 1348, whole families could be wiped out by the plague within 24 hours.

Castles

Today, many impressive ruins of medieval castles remain throughout Europe, reminders of the wars fought in that period. Castles were built for defense. The earliest were simple wooden forts, hurriedly constructed to house a **lord** and his army in newly conquered lands. Later these first castles were rebuilt in stone, and became a safe place where the lord, his family, and everyone working for him could take shelter if they were attacked. By the end of the Middle Ages, castles had become little more than status symbols.

Building a castle could take years. Often, the person who commissioned it did not live to see it completed. It was also expensive. Even kings sometimes had to stop the work on their castles if they ran out of money.

Facts About Medieval Castles

- Castle servants often slept in the same room as their **master** and mistress to guard them.

- Sometimes prisoners in castles were left to starve. One type of French prison was called an *oubliette*—a place of forgetting.

- Castles were designed by engineers, but built by unskilled laborers. Edward I of England forced local peasants and prisoners to work on his castle-building sites.

- Blocks of stone were lifted into place with man-powered hoists. Medieval builders had no big machines to help them.

- Castle builders chose sites that would be easy to defend: steep cliffs, river banks, and rocky coasts. For extra security, the castle's keep—the central tower—was ringed with stone walls.

⬣ **Stop here for the
Strategy Break.**

Strategy Break

If you were to create an outline for this article so far, it might look like the one below. As you will notice, the information in the box, often called a *sidebar*, is not part of the article itself and is not covered in the outline.

The Middle Ages (A.D. 1000 to 1500)

I. A Complicated Time
  A. A time of great contrasts
    1. The mighty and the powerless
    2. The saintly and the bloodthirsty; the scholarly and the illiterate
    3. Title, rank, and status more important than today
  B. A time of great activity for peasant farmers
  C. A time of many problems
    1. Even the very rich could not avoid insects and disease
    2. Arrival of Black Death (1348) killed many
II. Castles
  A. Were built for defense during wars
    1. Earliest were wooden forts, built hurriedly in newly conquered lands
    2. By end of Middle Ages (and wars), castles were status symbols
  B. Took lots of time and money
    1. The person who commissioned it often didn't live to see it completed
    2. Building was so expensive that even kings ran out of money and had to stop the work

As you continue reading, keep paying attention to the main ideas and supporting details. At the end of this article, you will use some of them to complete an outline of your own.

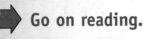 **Go on reading.**

Peasants

What would you notice about medieval peasants if you met them today? First, they would look dirty and would probably smell bad. It is difficult to keep clean and healthy if you live surrounded by farmyard mud. But they did try. Women washed clothes in streams, and in summer men and boys went swimming. (Women and girls could not take off their clothes in public.) Chewing twigs and rubbing salt into their gums was the only way they had to clean their teeth.

Second, you might think the peasants looked very old for their years. Hard work, hot sun, and winter winds made hands gnarled and skin rough and cracked. Accidents and diseases left unsightly scars or serious limps.

Third, the peasants would probably be **unfriendly** or even **hostile**. It was every villager's duty to be on the lookout for strangers and to raise the alarm if they saw anyone suspicious.

Homes

Today, many people think that medieval cottages look pretty and quaint. But what were they like to live in? In summer, they were probably cool and airy, thanks to the thick thatched roofs and unglazed windows, though the earth floor would have been dusty. In winter, most cottages would have been cold, damp, and very drafty. The wattle-and-daub walls were thin, and wind whistled through the wooden shutters covering the windows.

These houses needed constant repairs. Timber frames rotted where they rested on the damp ground, plaster walls cracked, and birds, rats, and mice nested in the roofs.

Families tried to warm their homes with fires, straw mattresses, and thick blankets. But the fire filled the house with smoke, the straw was prickly, and the blankets were rough.

In some parts of Europe, peasants and their animals lived together in the same building. Body heat from cows and horses gave extra warmth in winter, but in summer they would have been very smelly and would have attracted lots of flies.

Food

In medieval times, what you ate depended on who you were. Peasants ate coarse brown bread, pea soup, cabbages, onions, and garlic. If they were lucky, they might also have some ham or bacon, apples, pears, and homemade cheese.

Nobles liked rich meat cooked in sauces with strong tastes. Medieval cookbooks give recipes for hot and spicy dishes flavored with ginger and saffron. Sweet and sour foods were cooked with honey and unripe grapes, and puddings were made with eggs, almonds, and cream. This was an unhealthy diet—nobles did not eat much fresh fruit (they thought it was harmful), bread, or vegetables. In fact, they used *trenchers*, thick slices of bread used like disposable plates. They were used to soak up grease and spills, then given to the poor to eat.

Clothing

The rich loved fine clothes—the finer the better. People in cities and nobles at court followed the latest fashions. By the 15th century these could be extreme: tall "steeple" hats and low-cut dresses for young women; bottom-revealing tights and tunics, and ridiculously pointed shoes for young men.

Older nobles, merchants, lawyers, and their wives chose more sensible styles in expensive fabrics: silk, satin, velvet, and fine wool. Craftsmen wore practical woolen tunics and hose with a linen shirt. Their wives wore woolen dresses and linen kerchiefs. Peasants wore plain, simple clothes. In winter they wore several layers to try to keep warm.

The cost of a knight's clothes and armor would be like an expensive car today, and his warhorse was the equivalent of a small private jet.

Marriage

Marriage for love was rare. Among noble families marriages were arranged, often when children were still babies, to make political alliances, or to acquire land. Peasants were more likely to marry for love, but many peasant women married to find security and many peasant men to get a nanny, cleaner, and cook.

The average medieval marriage only lasted about 15 years. Many women died in childbirth, and many young and middle-aged men were killed in battles or farm accidents. And diseases killed rich and poor, young and old, men and women.

For noblewomen, marriage was a career, with many responsibilities. So young girls from rich or noble families were taught to read and write, to keep accounts, to manage servants, and to entertain important visitors with tact and charm.

Church law governed marriage. It taught that girls could marry when they were 12 years old and boys when they were 14.

Divorce was uncommon. The Church did not approve of it. But the rich could pay lawyers to persuade the Church to annul (cancel) a first marriage. An unhappy peasant simply left his wife. Deserted women and children were among the poorest people in medieval society.

Facts about Medieval Education

- In the early Middle Ages, monasteries were the main centers of learning. But after 1100, many schools and universities were built. They taught Latin, math, music, philosophy, medicine, and the law.

- Children from ordinary families did not go to school. Instead, they were trained by their parents at home. Boys were taught their fathers' occupation: farming, craftwork, or a trade. Girls learned housework, gardening, nursing, and how to take care of a baby.

The Plague

Men and women living in the Middle Ages faced far more pain and suffering than most people in developed countries today. Doctors, apothecaries (pharmacists), nuns, midwives, and wise women (witches) did their best with herbs, simple operations, and nursing, but they had few effective remedies. The Church taught that Christians should bear pain calmly. It might have been sent by God to purify the soul.

Medieval doctors were truly helpless faced with the bubonic plague, often called the Black Death. The first signs of the disease were painful black swellings under the arms. Then came a burning fever and a purple rash all over the body. Few people recovered. The disease reached Europe from Asia in the 1340s, killing millions of people. This disaster helped bring the Middle Ages to an end. So many people died, and normal routines were so thoroughly disturbed, that life could never go back to what it had been. ●

Strategy Follow-up

First, work with your partner to fill in the last column of the K-W-L chart on page 30. List at least four new things that you learned about the Middle Ages while reading this article.

Then, on a separate sheet of paper, work with your partner to complete an outline for the sections of this article called "Peasants," "Marriage," and "The Plague." When you are finished, compare your outline with those of other students. Do your outlines contain similar information? Why or why not? Revise your outline if necessary.

✓Personal Checklist

Read each question and put a check (✓) in the correct box.

1. How well do you understand the information presented in this article?
   - ☐ 3 (extremely well)
   - ☐ 2 (fairly well)
   - ☐ 1 (not well)

2. On the K-W-L chart, how easily were you and your partner able to list at least four new things that you learned while reading this article?
   - ☐ 3 (extremely well)
   - ☐ 2 (fairly well)
   - ☐ 1 (not well)

3. In the Vocabulary Builder, how well were you able to identify the synonym and antonym pairs?
   - ☐ 3 (extremely well)
   - ☐ 2 (fairly well)
   - ☐ 1 (not well)

4. How well were you able to help your partner complete the outline in the Strategy Follow-up?
   - ☐ 3 (extremely well)
   - ☐ 2 (fairly well)
   - ☐ 1 (not well)

5. After reading this article, how well do you think you could describe life during the Middle Ages?
   - ☐ 3 (extremely well)
   - ☐ 2 (fairly well)
   - ☐ 1 (not well)

Vocabulary Check

Look back at the work you did in the Vocabulary Builder. Then answer each question by circling the correct letter.

1. Which of these pairs of words from the article could you add to the clipboard of antonym pairs?
   a. silk/velvet
   b. easy/hard
   c. great/many

2. Which of these words from the story could you add to the clipboard of synonym pairs?
   a. magnificent/impressive
   b. wooden/stone
   c. mistress/master

3. Which of the following is a name for the nobleman in charge of a manor?
   a. lord
   b. master
   c. both of the above

4. Which of the following is a synonym for *hostile*?
   a. impoverished
   b. unfriendly
   c. both of the above

5. Which of the following is an antonym for *mighty*?
   a. exquisite
   b. powerless
   c. hostile

Add the numbers that you just checked to get your Personal Checklist score. Fill in your score here. Then turn to page 215 and transfer your score onto Graph 1.

Check your answers with your teacher. Give yourself 1 point for each correct answer, and fill in your Vocabulary score here. Then turn to page 215 and transfer your score onto Graph 1.

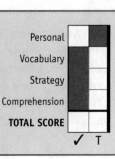

Strategy Check

Review the outline that you helped create in the Strategy Follow-up. Then answer these questions:

1. Which of these sentences would be a supporting detail under the main idea "Peasants"?

   a. Peasants looked very old for their years.

   b. People warmed their houses in different ways.

   c. The rich people loved fine clothes.

2. Which of these sentences would *not* be a supporting detail under the main idea "Marriage"?

   a. The average medieval marriage only lasted about 15 years.

   b. Among noble families, marriages were arranged for political or business reasons.

   c. Every villager looked out for strangers.

3. Which of these details would you include in the section called "The Plague"?

   a. The Church taught that pain might have been sent by God to purify the soul.

   b. Accidents and diseases left unsightly scars or serious limps.

   c. Chewing twigs and rubbing salt into their gums was how they cleaned their teeth.

4. Under which main idea would you include the detail that deserted women and children were among the poorest people in medieval society?

   a. "Peasants"

   b. "Marriage"

   c. "The Plague"

5. Under which main idea would you include the detail that people living in the Middle Ages faced more pain and suffering than most people in developed countries today?

   a. "Peasants"

   b. "Marriage"

   c. "The Plague"

Comprehension Check

Review the article if necessary. Then answer these questions:

1. Which of these things were peasants likely to eat?

   a. meat cooked in sauces with strong tastes

   b. brown bread, pea soup, cabbages, and onions

   c. sweet and sour foods cooked with honey and unripe grapes

2. Which of these types of dress was the most expensive?

   a. sensible dress styles in expensive fabrics

   b. practical woolen tunics and dresses

   c. a knight's suit of armor

3. Which of these statements is true?

   a. The only people who lived in castles were kings and their families.

   b. People of the Middle Ages chewed twigs to clean their teeth.

   c. Almost all peasants married for love.

4. Which of the following was *not* a teaching of the Church?

   a. Every villager should raise the alarm if he or she saw a stranger.

   a. Girls could marry at 12 years of age and boys at 14.

   c. People should bear pain calmly.

5. Which sentence best summarizes this article?

   a. The homes, food, clothing, and customs of the Middle Ages were not very different from the homes, food, clothing, and customs of today.

   b. The Middle Ages was not as wonderful as legend portrays the era, but it was less stressful and more enjoyable than today.

   c. The Middle Ages was a much more uncomfortable and difficult time for most people than modern times.

Check your answers with your teacher. Give yourself 1 point for each correct answer, and fill in your Strategy score here. Then turn to page 215 and transfer your score onto Graph 1.

Check your answers with your teacher. Give yourself 1 point for each correct answer, and fill in your Comprehension score here. Then turn to page 215 and transfer your score onto Graph 1.

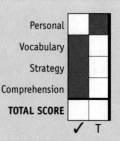

Extending

Choose one or both of these activities:

EXAMINE ART OF THE MIDDLE AGES

Visit a museum (or Web site) that has paintings, statues, and objects such as jewelry, silver, and tapestries that were created during the Middle Ages. Find a work that you consider exceptionally beautiful and examine it carefully. Write a detailed description of the work that will help others imagine it, and explain why you find the piece particularly noteworthy.

BUILD A CASTLE

Using the resources on this page or ones you find yourself, learn about castles and how they were built. Then build a model castle, or produce a small book of drawings that show the various parts, buildings, and rooms of a castle. Add labels that identify the parts of the castle and explain their uses. Put your castle or book on display, and provide a notebook next to it in which viewers can write comments and questions. These responses may help you determine how clear your model or drawings and your explanations are.

Resources

Books

Gravett, Christopher. *Castle.* Eyewitness. Knopf, 1994.

Macaulay, David. *Castle.* Houghton Mifflin, 1982.

Petty, Kate, and Caroline Pitcher. *Build Your Own Castle.* Franklin Watts, 1985.

Web Sites

http://www.medieval-castles.net/
This Web site offers information on castles in the Middle Ages.

http://www.metmuseum.org/collections/department.asp?dep=17
You can view examples of artwork created during the Middle Ages on this Web page of the Metropolitan Museum of Art.

CD-ROM

Destination: Castle. Imagination Express. Edmark, 1995.

Video/DVD

Castle. Tours of the World's Most Magnificent Structures. Based on the book by David Macaulay. PBS Home Video, 1998.

A Habit for the Voyage

Building Background

The story you are about to read takes place on a ship. Unlike the huge cruise ships of today, this ship carries only a few passengers—perhaps only a few dozen—and it also carries cargo, or freight. Here are some facts about ships and some ship-related terms that are used in the story:

Each level of a ship is called a deck, rather than a floor. When passengers board the ship, they walk up a gangplank—a removable ramp—from the dock to the main deck. The main deck is open to the water on all sides and is circled by a railing. Small lifeboats hang on the outside of the ship, below the railing. There may be four or five decks above, and another four or five decks below, the main deck. Also above the main deck is the bridge, an enclosed area from where the ship is controlled. Besides the captain and officers, who operate the ship, the crew includes deckhands who maintain the ship and stewards who care for the passengers.

Rooms for the passengers, called staterooms or cabins, are usually on decks other than the main deck. Large staterooms may have freestanding beds, but smaller ones have bunks—narrow beds built like a shelf against the wall. Cabins along the outer wall may have small round windows, called portholes. On most ships, staterooms are equipped with call buttons that passengers can push to call for a steward. Hallways connecting the rooms are called passageways. All the passengers eat meals together in the dining room.

dingy

dispose of

ptomaine

tarantula

Vocabulary Builder

1. Before you begin reading "A Habit for the Voyage" match each vocabulary word in Column 1 with its definition in Column 2.

COLUMN 1	COLUMN 2
dingy	poison produced in food
dispose of	dirty and drab
ptomaine	tropical spider, once considered poisonous
tarantula	get rid of; kill or destroy

2. Predict how each vocabulary word might help tell the story. Then, as you read each boldfaced word in the story, see if your prediction was accurate.

3. Save your work. You will refer to it again in the Vocabulary Check.

Strategy Builder

Drawing Conclusions While You Read

- A **conclusion** is a decision that you reach after thinking about certain facts or information. When you read a story, you often draw conclusions based on information that the author gives you about the characters, setting, or events.

- In order to draw conclusions, you must pay attention to details. To better understand the characters, for example, you must examine their words, thoughts, feelings, and actions. To discover the importance of certain events, you must look for possible connections between them.

- Read the following passage. See what conclusions you can draw about the setting, the characters, or the events.

> Donna leaned over the table to whisper to Felice. "Eat more slowly," she urged. "They won't throw us out of here while we're still eating, and the movie isn't scheduled to end for another 10 minutes."
>
> "But what if the boys walk past while I'm still eating?" Felice whispered back. "I'm still hungry, and I don't want to waste the food—especially since I already paid for it!"
>
> "Okay, okay, but if—Uh-oh, you'd better eat fast! I see people coming out of the theater already. We'd better get across the street if we're going to 'accidentally' bump into Richie and James there!"
>
> As the girls dashed out the door, the ceiling lights were already being turned off.

- What conclusions can you draw about the paragraphs that you just read? Here are some conclusions that one reader drew:

First, I can draw some conclusions about the setting. I think the two girls are in a restaurant. It's probably a fast-food place, since they paid for their food before they ate it. The restaurant is just across the street from a theater. It must be closing time for the restaurant, since the girls are worried about being thrown out, and someone starts turning out the lights as soon as the girls start to leave. Conclusions I can draw about the girls are that they are anxious to meet up with some boys at the theater, but they want to make the boys think that the meeting is accidental.

A Habit for the Voyage

by Robert Edmond Alter

As you read this short story, apply the strategies that you just learned. Look for clues that the author provides to help you draw conclusions about the characters, setting, and events.

The moment Kreuger stepped aboard the ship, he sensed that something was wrong. He had never really understood these warnings, but he had had them before, and usually he had been right.

He paused on the gangplank and looked around. He could see the deckhands loading the last of the cargo aboard. The steward was standing about twenty feet ahead, with Kreuger's shabby suitcase in his hand. He looked back at Kreuger impatiently.

Kreuger took one final look around, saw nothing out of the ordinary, and stepped across the deck to follow the steward.

It came again—a sudden sense of danger—so sharply that he actually flinched. Then, as a black object went flying past his sight, he threw himself to one side. The object, whatever it was, smacked to the deck right at his feet with a thudding crash.

Kreuger took one glance at it—a metal bucket filled to the top with nails and screws. He stepped quickly to his right and thrust his hand under his raincoat to get at the pistol in his right-hand pocket. Then he stared upward at the shadowy deck above him and to the railing on the deck above that.

Kreuger couldn't see anything. Nothing moved up there.

The steward was coming back toward him, a look of shock on his face. "What happened?" he called.

Kreuger quickly withdrew his empty hand from under his coat. He realized that the incident had drawn attention.

"Some fool nearly killed me with that bucket—that's what!"

The steward looked at the bucket, still half full. "Those deckhands," he remarked, "are careless fellows."

Kreuger was getting back his breath. The steward was right, he thought to himself. It had been an accident, of course. "Please show me to my cabin," he said softly.

The steward nodded and led him down a poorly lit corridor to his stateroom. It was on the starboard side, in the second-class section, and it wasn't very large. It contained a porthole, a sink, a closet, and a bunk. That was all.

Kreuger was careful to give the steward a modest tip. Then he seated himself on the bunk with a sigh, as though prepared to relax and enjoy his trip. Kreuger always tried to maintain a mild, bland air in front of people who served him. It was one of his rules: never do anything that makes you stand out. Stewards, waiters, and desk clerks had an annoying way of being able to remember certain *mannerisms*—habits or traits—about you, when questioned later.

The steward thanked Kreuger and left the room. For a moment, Kreuger stayed where he was. Then he got up and went over to lock the door. He opened his suitcase, took out a roll of adhesive tape, and cut four eight-inch strips. Then, getting down on his knees, he placed his pistol underneath the sink and taped it there. Just a precaution—in case someone went through his things when he was out of the room.

Kreuger never relied on a firearm for his work. It was messy and much too obvious. No, he was a man who arranged innocent-looking *accidents*. The pistol was a weapon he used only in self-defense—in case there was a hitch and he was forced to fight his way out. This had happened more than once during his career. For Kreuger was what is known in the trade as a secret agent. He was one of the best. Among other things, he knew seven languages and felt completely comfortable speaking any one of them. That was important in his business.

Kreuger sat back in his bunk and thought for a while about the man, the man aboard this ship—the man he was going to do away with.

Unconsciously, Kreuger brought his right hand up to his ear and began to tug gently at the lobe. When he caught himself doing this, he hurriedly snatched his hand away. That was a *bad habit* with him—one that he had to watch. Bad habits were dangerous in his business. Exceedingly dangerous. They gave away your identity. They gave an enemy agent a chance to spot you. It was like walking around in public wearing a sign that said: *I am Kreuger. I am Kreuger, the Secret Agent.*

He remembered only too well what had happened to his old friend, Delchev. Delchev had developed a bad habit—of occasionally pulling at his tie. Over the years, the word had gotten around. The habit had been noted and recorded. It went into all the enemy files and folders on Delchev. Delchev was identified by his habit. And no matter what alias or disguise he used, sooner or later it gave him away. In the end, it had cost him his life.

Kreuger had known of another agent who liked to break toothpicks in half. He was dead now too.

And there was one fellow who used so many different disguises, he was simply referred to by those in the business as Mr. D. Kreuger believed that he could have tracked down Mr. D. within six months, had someone made it worth his while, because there was a note in the file on Mr. D.—of a bad habit, one that identified him. Mr. D. always revealed himself by scratching a paper matchbook with his thumbnail.

Well, at least tugging at your ear wasn't that bad. Not as bad as scratching a matchbook with your thumbnail. But it was bad enough and Kreuger knew it. He must be more careful about his habits in the future. He had to weed out anything that could give him away.

The distant clang of a ship's bell reached him. Dinnertime.

All right. Time to go to work, to proceed. Time to view the future victim.

⬡ **Stop here for the Strategy Break.**

Strategy Break

What conclusions can you draw about this story so far? Using information from the story and what you learned in Building Background, try to answer the following questions. The hints below each question will help you draw your conclusions.

1. Is it possible that the falling bucket was not an accident? Why or why not?
Hint: Consider Kreuger's job and background. _____

_____

_____

2. Does the incident of the falling bucket frighten Kreuger much?
Hint: Think of his thoughts and actions after being shown to his room. _____

_____

_____

3. Kreuger carries a shabby suitcase. Does that mean he is poor?
Hint: Recall what he thinks about while the steward is in the room with him. _____

_____

_____

As you continue reading, keep looking for clues that the author gives about the characters and their actions. At the end of this selection, you will be asked to draw more conclusions.

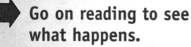 **Go on reading to see what happens.**

In the dining room, Kreuger looked around, found the table he wanted, and sat down. The room seemed to him dull and **dingy.** This suggested that the food would be poorly prepared. But Kreuger knew in advance that he would say nothing. Never call attention to yourself by being a complainer.

He picked up a napkin and started to tuck it into his collar. Then he caught himself in time and put it on his lap instead.

Watch it! Watch that sort of thing. You put your napkin in your collar on your last assignment. Never repeat the same mannerism twice in a row!

Kreuger smiled at the man across the table and said, "If you don't mind, pass the menu, please."

The man Kreuger addressed was a harmless-looking, slender little fellow of about forty, with thinning hair and glasses. His name was Amos Bicker—and he was the man slated for a fatal accident—one arranged by Kreuger.

While he pretended to examine the menu, Kreuger secretly studied his intended victim. He certainly didn't look like the sort who needed killing. However, Kreuger's instructions were quite clear. So be it then. Now for the means to accomplish the . . .

Kreuger caught his hand halfway to his ear. *Blast it!* He continued the gesture but scratched the back of his neck. He put the menu down and ordered oysters for an appetizer. Then, turning to the woman on his left, he began speaking to her in Spanish, which she understood. All the time, however, he was thinking about the man across the table—Bicker—and wondering how to **dispose of** him.

Kreuger always preferred obvious accidents. Therefore, when aboard a ship, man overboard. This could be accomplished in a variety of ways. The simplest was to make friends with the victim, then arrange an evening stroll along the deck. A sudden, sharp push would achieve the goal. Man overboard.

The waiter brought Kreuger his oysters. As Kreuger reached for his fork, he gave a start. Something was brushing against his leg under the table. He leaned back in his chair and raised the cloth. A scruffy-looking cat—the ship's cat, probably—was standing there.

"Here, kitty, kitty," Kreuger said. He loved animals. Had he led a quieter, more peaceful life, he would have had a home, and the home would have been filled with pets. He'd have been married too.

A ship's officer appeared in the doorway. "Who is Señor Werfel?" he called into the room.

"Here!" Kreuger replied. That was one thing he never slipped up on. He could pick up and drop an alias with the snap of his fingers. And on this voyage, he had signed on as Señor Werfel.

"The captain wishes to see you for a moment, señor."

The word *why* flashed into Kreuger's brain. Then he found the obvious answer and stood up, smiling. The incident with the bucket, no doubt. This was annoying because it called further attention to him. However there was really nothing that he could do.

Moments later Kreuger met the captain on the bridge of the ship. There, the captain repeatedly apologized for the unfortunate accident. Kreuger laughed it off. "It was really nothing, Captain," he said. "I wish that you would put it out of your mind." He shook the captain's hand and returned at once to the dining room.

But something had happened during his absence.

Passengers were crowded around a space near his table. Kreuger could see that the cook and the waiter were attending to something on the floor. It was the ship's cat, and it was stretched out and lying there silently.

"*Oh*, Mr. Werfel," said the lady who had been seated next to Kreuger, "I did a *terrible* thing. No, come to think of it, it was fortunate that I did. Certainly fortunate for *you*!"

"What?" Kreuger said sharply, his eyes fixed on the cat. "What did you do?"

"That *poor* little dear jumped up on your seat after you left. He wanted your oysters. Of course I held him off, but you were so long in returning. . . ."

"You gave him the oysters I ordered," said Kreuger.

"Yes! I finally did. And before any of us knew it, the poor thing began to shake terribly—and then it was gone."

"I better take care of this," said the ship's doctor, who had arrived on the scene.

Kreuger waited until the passengers had thinned out, then he took the waiter aside. "What was wrong with those oysters?" he demanded.

The waiter seemed utterly astonished. "I don't know. Perhaps **ptomaine.** They were canned, of course."

"Let's see the can," said Kreuger.

There was a faint, unpleasant scent to the can, one able to be detected if held close to the nose.

Kreuger put down the can and looked at the waiter.

"Anyone else order oysters?"

"No, señor. Only yourself."

Kreuger forced a smile. "Well, accidents will happen," he said. But he certainly wished there were some way he could have analyzed the contents of that can. He returned to his room more angry than shaken.

Well, that had been close. Very close. *Too* close. But no matter how you looked at it, he had been very lucky. Of course it *could* have been ptomaine . . . food poisoning sometimes happened . . . but when you combined it with the business about the bucket—

He went to the sink and reached under for his gun.

It wasn't there! The tape was there, neatly, but not the pistol.

Now wait, he warned himself, tugging at his ear. A sailor *could* have kicked over the bucket by accident. Ptomaine poisoning *does* occur in carelessly canned meats. And things *are* sometimes stolen from compartments . . .

But the combination still spelled suspicion. Yet even if his suspicions were right, what could he do? He couldn't prove that the bucket and the food poisoning weren't accidents. He couldn't reveal that he'd brought a loaded pistol aboard.

I must tread very carefully, he thought. Very, very carefully, until this business is over. Tugging furiously at his ear, he read for a while. Then he undressed, turned out the light, and got into his bunk.

At first he thought it must be the wool blanket that was scratching him. Then he remembered that there was a sheet between his body and the blanket. Then he was certain that it wasn't the blanket—because it seemed to be moving.

He felt something fuzzy on his bare chest, something crawling sluggishly under the blanket. Kreuger started to raise the edge of the blanket, and the thing—whatever it was—scrambled onto his stomach. He froze, sucking in his breath, too scared to move a muscle.

It stopped, too, as if waiting for the man to make the first move. He could feel it there, on his bare skin, squatting, poised and waiting. He could feel the tiny feet advancing toward his rib cage.

He'd had it. Coordinating his movements, he threw the blanket and sheet aside with his left hand, as he swung his right arm across his stomach. Then he rolled off the bunk to the floor.

He was up instantly and frantically fumbling for the light switch.

The thing scurried across the sheet—a thick-legged, deadly **tarantula.** Kreuger snatched up a shoe and with two sharp blows disposed of the spider.

He threw the shoe aside and went to the sink. There he washed the beads of perspiration from his face. He opened his door and shouted, "Steward!"

A few minutes later the steward, with a sleepy smile, looked in. "Yes, Señor Werfel?"

Silently, Kreuger pointed to the crushed spider on his bed. The steward looked at it, made a face, and grunted. But he didn't seem particularly surprised.

"It happens. It is from the cargo, señor. They come aboard in the bananas. Some of them sometimes find their way through the ship."

It was the kind of answer Kreuger had expected, a reasonable explanation that left no room for argument. But this was getting to be too much. The tarantula was the last straw.

"See if you can find me the captain," said Kreuger, flatly.

The steward shrugged. He was not eager to bother the captain at this time of night.

"Never mind!" said Kreuger rudely, as he shoved by the steward. "I'll find him myself!" Kreuger paused and took a deep breath. He was starting to forget all his rules.

The captain was no help at all. He merely repeated all of his sad, tiresome excuses: clumsy deckhands, careless canning, the bothersome little hazards of taking on bananas as cargo.

"Now look here, Captain," said Kreuger, angrily pulling at his ear, "I'm a reasonable man, and I'll go along with everyday accidents as long as they stay within the limits of probability. But all of these accidents have happened to *me*. All within one day!"

"What is it that you're trying to say, Mr. Werfel? Surely you're not implying that someone aboard this ship is trying to kill you, are you? You're not suggesting that? You don't have enemies, do you?"

Kreuger balked at that. It was a subject he wanted to stay away from.

"I said no such thing, Captain! All I'm saying is that these things keep happening aboard your ship. And I expect you to offer some protection."

"Certainly, Mr. Werfel. Let me see. Yes . . . I can give you your choice of any of my officers' cabins, if you like, my own included. I can assign a competent officer to stay by your side and—"

"No, no, no!" Kreuger said, hastily. "That isn't at all necessary, Captain. I don't intend to act like a prisoner aboard this ship!"

Turning angrily on his heels, Kreuger began to make his way back to his stateroom. He needed to relax, to think. The whole game was going very badly, turning sour on him. He was calling attention to himself and . . .

He paused on the passageway that overlooked the dark deck below. Someone was down there on the deck, someone familiar, leaning over the low rail, staring out to the sea.

The man on the deck was Amos Bicker. He was looking out at the black, rambling sea, his elbows up on the rail, his thin back to Kreuger.

Kreuger quietly came down another step. His eyes quickly checked out everything with professional interest.

Bicker was leaning over the low railing. Below him was nothing—nothing except the open sea.

Kreuger could finish his business here and now. Then he could concentrate on his own survival, guard himself against those recurring accidents—if accidents, indeed, were what they were.

Kreuger came down the last step. He planted both feet on the deck. He looked around once more. Kreuger and the victim were the only ones there—and the unsuspecting victim thought that he was alone!

It wouldn't take much—just a short, sudden run and a shove—to thrust Bicker over the rail and into the sea. Kreuger smiled a tight grin.

All the lifeboats had returned and the captain had received their reports. Shaking his head sadly, he entered his office and sat down at the seat behind the desk.

"Well," he said, "this is certainly a sorry business. Unfortunate that you had to be involved in it, Mr. Bicker."

Amos Bicker was sitting bent over in his chair facing the desk. His nerves were obviously in a bad state. His hands trembled, his voice trembled too.

"You didn't recover the—uh—"

"Not a sign of the body," the captain said. "He must have gone down like a stone. But please, Mr. Bicker, please do not let it prey on your mind."

Mr. Bicker shivered, and the captain thought that he might be going into shock.

"He must have been mad—crazy," Bicker said, finally. "I didn't know the man, had never seen him, except in the dining room this evening. I was just standing there at the rail minding my own business, watching the sea without a thought in my head. And then I heard a—a movement, a sort of quiet rushing motion, and I looked around and there he was. Coming right at me! And the look on his face!"

"Yes, yes, Mr. Bicker," the captain said sympathetically. "We quite understand. There's no doubt in anyone's mind that there was something—well, odd in Mr. Werfel's behavior. I have reason to believe that he actually thought that someone aboard the ship was trying to kill him. Strange fellow. Lucky for you that you stepped aside at the last minute—or he might have taken you over the side with him."

Mr. Bicker stared at the carpet and nodded. One of his thumbnails was idly scratching the edge of a paper matchbook. ●

Strategy Follow-up

Use information from the story to help you answer these questions on a separate sheet of paper:

1. What does the last sentence of the story help you conclude about Mr. Bicker's identity?

2. What does knowing Mr. Bicker's identity help you conclude about Kreuger's death?

3. Consider Kreuger's experiences from the moment he boarded the ship. What does the ending of the story help you conclude about those experiences?

✓Personal Checklist

Read each question and put a check (✓) in the correct box.

1. How well do you understand the importance of the final sentence in this story?
   - ☐ 3 (extremely well)
   - ☐ 2 (fairly well)
   - ☐ 1 (not well)

2. How well were you able to use what you learned in Building Background to help you understand Kreuger's movement around the ship?
   - ☐ 3 (extremely well)
   - ☐ 2 (fairly well)
   - ☐ 1 (not well)

3. In the Vocabulary Builder, how well were you able to match the vocabulary words with their definitions?
   - ☐ 3 (extremely well)
   - ☐ 2 (fairly well)
   - ☐ 1 (not well)

4. How well were you able to draw conclusions as you read this story?
   - ☐ 3 (extremely well)
   - ☐ 2 (fairly well)
   - ☐ 1 (not well)

5. How well do you understand how and why Kreuger fell overboard?
   - ☐ 3 (extremely well)
   - ☐ 2 (fairly well)
   - ☐ 1 (not well)

Vocabulary Check

Look back at the work you did in the Vocabulary Builder. Then answer each question by circling the correct letter.

1. How would the average person feel about having a meal in a dingy restaurant?
   a. The average person would be eager to eat in a dingy restaurant.
   b. The average person wouldn't be happy eating in a dingy restaurant.
   c. The average person wouldn't care if the restaurant was dingy.

2. If you had all of the following, which one would you want to dispose of?
   a. A mosquito on your arm
   b. A valuable watch
   c. A good friend

3. Which of the following has been blamed for food poisoning?
   a. tarantulas
   b. ptomaine
   c. disposals

4. Which of the following is a false definition?
   a. dispose of—get rid of
   b. tarantula—a deceitful person
   c. ptomaine—a chemical compound produced in food

5. What kind of creature is a tarantula?
   a. an oyster
   b. a person
   c. a spider

Add the numbers that you just checked to get your Personal Checklist score. Fill in your score here. Then turn to page 215 and transfer your score onto Graph 1.

Check your answers with your teacher. Give yourself 1 point for each correct answer, and fill in your Vocabulary score here. Then turn to page 215 and transfer your score onto Graph 1.

Strategy Check

Review the conclusions that you drew in this lesson. Also review the story if necessary. Then answer these questions:

1. As he walks up the gangplank and senses danger, why does Kreuger pay attention to this feeling?
   a. He doesn't understand the feeling.
   b. He has had the feeling before and has usually been right.
   c. The feeling reminds him of a nightmare he had not long ago.

2. Kreuger can speak seven languages fluently. What does this help you conclude about him?
   a. He takes his job as an agent seriously.
   b. He went to school for a very long time.
   c. He likes talking to lots of different people.

3. Why does Mr. Bicker's habit of scratching the edge of a matchbook reveal his identity?
   a. When the captain sees him do it, he recognizes Bicker as an old friend.
   b. Earlier in the story, Kreuger recalls an agent who has that habit.
   c. The steward complains that a passenger has that habit.

4. Mysterious "accidents" began happening to Kreuger even as he boards the ship. What does that help you conclude?
   a. Kreuger has a truly terrible string of bad luck.
   b. Everybody on the ship is against him.
   c. He was a target from the beginning of the voyage.

5. Taking all the clues about Kreuger and Bicker into consideration, which conclusion would you say is most accurate?
   a. A better player beat Kreuger at his own game.
   b. Kreuger was killed through bad luck.
   c. Bicker was lucky to survive.

Comprehension Check

Review the story if necessary. Then answer these questions:

1. When a heavy metal bucket narrowly misses Kreuger, for what does he reach?
   a. the gun he has under his coat
   b. the railing along the deck
   c. the medicine for his heart

2. What is Kreuger's major concern?
   a. He feels bad about killing a harmless-looking man.
   b. He's afraid he'll forget which alias he is using.
   c. He's afraid that his mannerisms will give him away.

3. Who or what does Kreuger honestly like?
   a. the steward
   b. animals
   c. Mr. Bicker

4. How does the ship's cat die?
   a. The bucket that misses Kreuger hits the cat instead.
   b. The cat eats the poisoned oysters intended for Kreuger.
   c. When Kreuger goes overboard, he knocks the cat overboard too.

5. How does the steward explain the presence of a tarantula on the ship?
   a. The crew keeps tarantulas aboard to control the insects.
   b. One of the passengers is a scientist who is studying tarantulas.
   c. Tarantulas probably came aboard with the cargo of bananas.

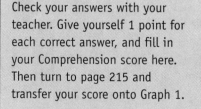

Check your answers with your teacher. Give yourself 1 point for each correct answer, and fill in your Strategy score here. Then turn to page 215 and transfer your score onto Graph 1.

Personal
Vocabulary
Strategy
Comprehension
TOTAL SCORE
✓ T

Check your answers with your teacher. Give yourself 1 point for each correct answer, and fill in your Comprehension score here. Then turn to page 215 and transfer your score onto Graph 1.

Personal
Vocabulary
Strategy
Comprehension
TOTAL SCORE
✓ T

Extending

Choose one or more of these activities:

MAKE A STORYBOARD

When directors are working on a movie, they often make storyboards to help them picture what happens in the story. On a storyboard, important scenes are depicted and arranged in sequence on a large bulletin board. Decide what the important scenes in this story are. Draw sketches of the scenes, including details about the people in each scene, as well as the setting. Arrange the sketches in sequence on a large board. See if others can tell what is happening in each scene.

WRITE A MINI-PLAY

Alone or with a few other students, transform this short story into a play. Write lines for a narrator who will explain what Krueger is thinking and feeling. The narrator's lines can come straight from the story. Also write lines for the other characters. Put them in play form, as in the example:

Captain (*apologetically*): Nothing like the accident with the bucket has ever happened on this ship before, and I'm sincerely sorry. I assure you, Señor Werfel, that we will find and punish the clumsy deckhand responsible for the accident.

Whenever possible, take the characters' lines directly from the story. Then, ask some friends to help you perform your play. Practice it a few times, and then present it to the rest of the class.

DEFEND TARANTULAS

According to the experts, the bite of the tarantula, while painful, is not necessarily poisonous enough to kill a person. How did these spiders get such a frightening reputation? Investigate tarantulas, and then give a short speech presenting tarantulas in a more balanced way than the story does. The Web site listed on this page might help you.

Resources

Book

Alter, Robert Edmond. *Who Goes Next? True Stories of Exciting Escapes.* Putnam, 1966.

Web Site

http://www.atshq.org/articles/found.html
This page on the Web site of the American Tarantula Society contains information about tarantulas native to the United States.

Learning New Words

VOCABULARY

From Lesson 4
- beautiful
  exquisite
- hostile
  unfriendly
- lord
  master

Synonyms

A synonym is a word that means the same thing—or close to the same thing—as another word. For example, the author of "The Middle Ages" uses the words *lord* and *master* to describe the nobleman in charge of a manor.

Draw a line from each word in Column 1 to its synonym in Column 2.

COLUMN 1	COLUMN 2
happiness	center
battle	regal
middle	monarch
king	combat
royal	contentment

From Lesson 4
- hovels
  palaces
- impoverished
  rich
- mighty
  powerless

Antonyms

An antonym is a word that means the opposite of another word. For example, in "The Middle Ages" you read that exquisite palaces were built within a stone's throw of flimsy hovels. Although *palaces* and *hovels* are both places to live, very wealthy people live in palaces, and very poor people live in hovels.

Draw a line from each word in Column 1 to its antonym in Column 2.

COLUMN 1	COLUMN 2
wealth	priests
nuns	motionless
major	tenderness
violence	poverty
moving	minor

Compound Words

A compound word is made up of two words put together. When you read about Jacques Cousteau in Lesson 3, you learned that before he passed away he had become the world's most famous underwater explorer. *Underwater* is made up of the words *under* and *water* and refers to anything that is below the surface of the water or made for use under the water.

Fill in each blank with a compound word by combining a word from Row 1 with a word from Row 2.

Row 1:	ever	river	frost	lay
Row 2:	bite	away	lasting	boat

1. skin damage done by severe cold = _____

2. floating vessel with a flat bottom = _____

3. never ending = _____

4. plan of making partial payments = _____

Suffixes

A suffix is a word part that is added to the end of a root word. When you add a suffix, you often change the root word's meaning and function. For example, the suffix *-ful* means "full of," so the root word *respect* changes from a noun or verb to an adjective meaning "full of respect."

-tion and -ation

The suffixes *-tion* and *-ation* both mean the same thing: "the act or process of _____ing" or "the condition or result of being _____ed." In Lesson 3 you learned that Jacques Cousteau's aqualung revolutionized ocean exploration. *Exploration* is the act or process of exploring.

Write the word for each definition below.

1. result of being invented   _____

2. act or process of realizing   _____

3. act or process of introducing   _____

4. result of being organized   _____

VOCABULARY

From Lesson 1
- hammerlock
- shakedown

From Lesson 3
- aqualung
- earthbound
- underwater

From Lesson 3
- affliction
- determination
- exploration
- graduation
- inflammation

allay

anesthetics

apprehension

chloroform

extricate

incredible

ominous

perilous

phobia

premonition

spirits of camphor

The Night the Bed Fell

Building Background

Sleep is something we all do, but we all have individual ways of doing it. For example, some people fall asleep almost instantly and enjoy a sound sleep no matter where they are. Other people can sleep well at home but not on a strange bed. Some people lie in one position all night, but others move repeatedly. Some people walk in their sleep, and some even eat in their sleep.

There are different ways of waking up too. Some people wake up on time without an alarm clock, while others need more than one alarm to get them moving. What are your sleep-related habits? Write them on the concept map below. Then, as you read "The Night the Bed Fell," compare your habits to those of the speaker and his relatives.

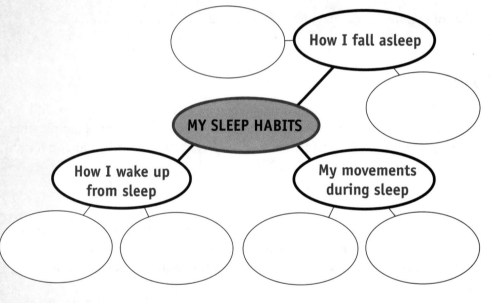

CLIPBOARD

Medicines or Drugs

CLIPBOARD

Adjectives

Vocabulary Builder

1. Before you begin reading "The Night the Bed Fell," read the vocabulary words in the margin. Write any of the words that you already know on the appropriate clipboards. (Hint: One of the words belongs in two groups.)

2. Later, as you read the story, find any vocabulary words that you don't know. Read them in context, and decide what they mean. If using context doesn't help, look up the words in a dictionary. Then write each one on the appropriate clipboard.

3. Save your work. You will refer to it again in the Vocabulary Check.

Strategy Builder

Identifying Causes and Effects in Fiction

- In many fictional stories, events are connected by time order. One event happens, and then another, and then another. In other stories, however, events are connected by **cause and effect**. One event will cause another event to happen, which will cause another event, and so on. Like the falling dominoes on this page, a single event can cause a chain reaction of more effects and causes. When an author's purpose is to **entertain**, as it is in this story, some of those causes and effects can be quite comical.

- To find cause-and-effect relationships while you read, keep asking yourself, "What happened?" and "Why did it happen?" Doing this will help you understand what has happened so far. It also will help you predict what might happen next.

- Read the following paragraph, and look for the chain of causes and effects.

Jackson was ravenously hungry after his football game, so he made himself a sandwich with everything on it. Just as Jackson was sitting down to eat, his dog Angel walked up and gave Jackson her paw. Jackson shook Angel's hand and gave her a corner of his sandwich. Angel gobbled it down and howled as if she were singing Jackson a song. Jackson applauded and gave Angel another piece of his sandwich. Angel ate that piece and rolled over twice. Jackson gave Angel another piece of his sandwich. Suddenly Jackson realized that he had given Angel almost all of his sandwich! He gave Angel the rest of his sandwich and got up and made himself another one.

CLIPBOARD
Verbs

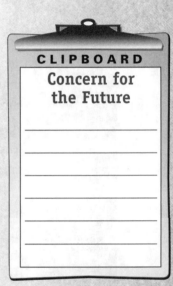

CLIPBOARD
Concern for the Future

- If you wanted to highlight the causes and effects in this paragraph, you could use a **cause-and-effect chain** like this one:

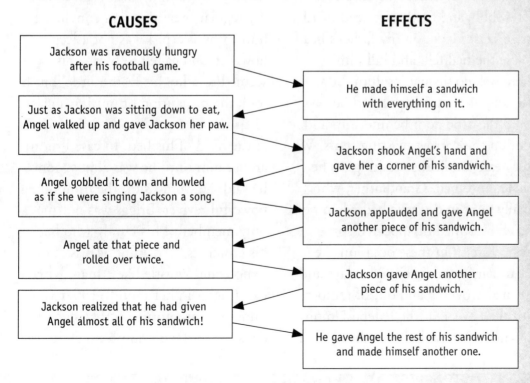

CAUSES

| Jackson was ravenously hungry after his football game. |
| Just as Jackson was sitting down to eat, Angel walked up and gave Jackson her paw. |
| Angel gobbled it down and howled as if she were singing Jackson a song. |
| Angel ate that piece and rolled over twice. |
| Jackson realized that he had given Angel almost all of his sandwich! |

EFFECTS

| He made himself a sandwich with everything on it. |
| Jackson shook Angel's hand and gave her a corner of his sandwich. |
| Jackson applauded and gave Angel another piece of his sandwich. |
| Jackson gave Angel another piece of his sandwich. |
| He gave Angel the rest of his sandwich and made himself another one. |

The Night the Bed Fell

by James Thurber

As you read the first part of this story, apply the strategies that you just learned. To find the causes and effects, keep asking yourself, "What happened?" and "Why did it happen?"

I suppose that the high-water mark of my youth in Columbus, Ohio, was the night the bed fell on my father. It makes a better recitation (unless, as some friends of mine have said, one has heard it five or six times) than it does a piece of writing, for it is almost necessary to throw furniture around, shake doors, and bark like a dog, to lend the proper atmosphere and verisimilitude to what is admittedly a somewhat incredible tale. Still, it did take place.

It happened, then, that my father had decided to sleep in the attic one night, to be away where he could think. My mother opposed the notion strongly because, she said, the old wooden bed up there was unsafe: it was wobbly and the heavy headboard would crash down on my father's head in case the bed fell, and kill him. There was no dissuading him, how-ever, and at a quarter past ten he closed the attic door behind him and went up the narrow twisting stairs. We later heard **ominous** creakings as he crawled into bed. Grandfather, who usually slept in the attic bed when he was with us, had disappeared some days before. (On these occasions he was usually gone six or eight days and returned growling and out of temper, with the news that the federal Union was run by a passel of blockheads and that the Army of the Potomac didn't have a chance.)

We had visiting us at this time a nervous first cousin of mine named Briggs Beall, who believed that he was likely to cease breathing when he was asleep. It was his feeling that if he were not awakened every hour during the night, he might die of suffocation. He had been accustomed to setting an alarm clock to ring at intervals until morning, but I persuaded him to abandon this. He slept in my room and I told him that I was such a light sleeper that if anybody quit breathing in the same room with me, I would wake instantly. He tested me the first night—which I had suspected he would—by holding his breath after my regular breathing had convinced him I was asleep. I was not asleep, however, and called to him. This seemed to **allay** his fears a little, but he took the precaution of putting a glass of **spirits of camphor** on a little table at the head of his bed. In case I didn't arouse him until he was almost gone, he said, he would sniff the camphor, a powerful reviver. Briggs was not the only member of his family who had his crotchets. Old Aunt Melissa Beall (who could whistle like a man, with two fingers in her mouth) suffered under the **premonition** that she was destined to die on South High Street, because she had been born on South High Street and married on South High Street. Then there was Aunt Sarah Shoaf, who never went to bed at night without the fear that a burglar was going to get in and blow **chloroform** under her door through a tube. To avert this calamity—for she was in greater dread of **anesthetics** than of losing her household goods—she always piled her money, silverware, and other valuables in a neat stack just outside her bedroom, with a note reading: "This is all I have. Please take it and do not use your chloroform, as this is all I have." Aunt Gracie Shoaf also had a burglar **phobia,** but she met it with more fortitude. She was confident that burglars had been getting into her house every night for forty years. The fact that she never missed anything was to her no proof to the contrary. She always claimed that she scared them off before they could take anything, by throwing shoes down the hallway. When she went to bed she piled, where she could get at them handily, all the shoes there were about her house. Five minutes after she had turned off the light, she would sit up in bed and say "Hark!" Her husband, who had learned to ignore the whole situation as long ago as 1903, would either be sound asleep or pretend to be sound asleep. In either case he would not respond to her tugging and pulling, so that presently she would arise, tiptoe to the door, open it slightly and heave a shoe down the hall in one direction, and its mate down the hall in the other direction. Some nights she threw them all, some nights only a couple of pair.

⬢ **Stop here for the Strategy Break.**

Strategy Break

So far, the narrator has described the strange habits of two aunts and a first cousin. If you were to create a cause-and-effect chain for the narrator's dealings with his cousin Briggs Beall, it might look like this:

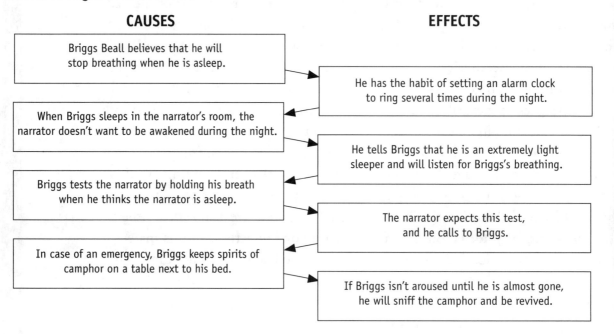

CAUSES

Briggs Beall believes that he will stop breathing when he is asleep.

When Briggs sleeps in the narrator's room, the narrator doesn't want to be awakened during the night.

Briggs tests the narrator by holding his breath when he thinks the narrator is asleep.

In case of an emergency, Briggs keeps spirits of camphor on a table next to his bed.

EFFECTS

He has the habit of setting an alarm clock to ring several times during the night.

He tells Briggs that he is an extremely light sleeper and will listen for Briggs's breathing.

The narrator expects this test, and he calls to Briggs.

If Briggs isn't aroused until he is almost gone, he will sniff the camphor and be revived.

As you continue reading, keep looking for causes and effects. At the end of this story you will create a cause-and-effect chain of your own.

 Go on reading to see what happens.

But I am straying from the remarkable incidents that took place during the night that the bed fell on Father. By midnight we were all in bed. The layout of the rooms and the disposition of their occupants is important to an understanding of what later occurred. In the front room upstairs (just under Father's attic bedroom) were my mother and my brother Herman, who sometimes sang in his sleep, usually "Marching Through Georgia" or "Onward Christian Soldiers." Briggs Beall and myself were in a room adjoining this one. My brother Roy was in a room across the hall from ours. Our bull terrier, Rex, slept in the hall.

My bed was an army cot, one of those affairs which are made wide enough to sleep on comfortably only by putting up, flat with the middle section, the two sides which ordinarily hang down like the sideboards of a drop-leaf table. When these sides are up, it is **perilous** to roll too far toward the edge, for then the cot is likely to tip completely over, bringing the whole bed down on top of one, with a tremendous banging crash. This, in fact, is precisely what happened, about two o'clock in the morning. (It was my mother who, in recalling the scene later, first referred to it as "the night the bed fell on your father.")

Always a deep sleeper, slow to arouse (I had lied to Briggs), I was at first unconscious of what had happened when the iron cot rolled me onto the floor and toppled over on me. It left me still warmly bundled up and unhurt, for the bed rested above me like a canopy. Hence I did not wake up, only reached the edge of consciousness and went back. The racket, however, instantly awakened my mother, in the next room, who came to the immediate conclusion that her worst dread was realized: the big wooden bed upstairs had fallen on Father. She therefore screamed, "Let's go to your poor father!" It was this shout, rather than the noise of my cot falling, that awakened Herman, in the same room with her. He thought that Mother had become, for no apparent reason, hysterical. "You're all right, Mamma!" he shouted, trying to calm her. They exchanged shout for shout for perhaps ten seconds: "Let's go to your poor father!" and "You're all right!" That woke up Briggs. By this time I was conscious of what was going on, in a vague way, but did not yet realize that I was under my bed instead of on it. Briggs, awakening in the midst of loud shouts of fear and **apprehension,** came to the quick conclusion that he was suffocating and that we were all trying to "bring him out." With a low moan, he grasped the glass of camphor at the head of his bed and instead of sniffing it poured it over himself. The room

reeked of camphor. "Ugf, ahfg," choked Briggs, like a drowning man, for he had almost succeeded in stopping his breath under the deluge of pungent spirits. He leaped out of bed and groped toward the open window, but he came up against one that was closed. With his hand, he beat out the glass, and I could hear it crash and tinkle on the alleyway below. It was at this juncture that I, in trying to get up, had the uncanny sensation of feeling my bed above me! Foggy with sleep, I now suspected, in my turn, that the whole uproar was being made in a frantic endeavor to **extricate** me from what must be an unheard-of and perilous situation. "Get me out of this!" I bawled. "Get me out!" I think I had the nightmarish belief that I was entombed in a mine. "Gugh," gasped Briggs, floundering in his camphor.

By this time my mother, still shouting, pursued by Herman, still shouting, was trying to open the door to the attic, in order to go up and get my father's body out of the wreckage. The door was stuck, however, and wouldn't yield. Her frantic pulls on it only added to the general banging and confusion. Roy and the dog were now up, the one shouting questions, the other barking.

Father, farthest away and soundest sleeper of all, had by this time been awakened by the battering on the attic door. He decided that the house was on fire. "I'm coming, I'm coming!" he wailed in a slow, sleepy voice—it took him many minutes to regain full consciousness. My mother, still believing he was caught under the bed, detected in his "I'm coming!" the mournful, resigned note of one who is preparing to meet his Maker. "He's dying!" she shouted.

"I'm all right!" Briggs yelled to reassure her. "I'm all right!" He still believed that it was his own closeness to death that was worrying Mother. I found at last the light switch in my room, unlocked the door, and Briggs and I joined the others at the attic door. The dog, who never did like Briggs, jumped for him—assuming that he was the culprit in whatever was going on—and Roy had to throw Rex and hold him. We could hear Father crawling out of bed upstairs. Roy pulled the attic door open, with a mighty jerk and Father came down the stairs, sleepy and irritable but safe and sound. My mother began to weep when she saw him. Rex began to howl. "What in the name of God is going on here?" asked father.

The situation was finally put together like a gigantic jigsaw puzzle. Father caught a cold from prowling around in his bare feet but there were no other bad results. "I'm glad," said Mother, who always looked on the bright side of things, "that your grandfather wasn't here." ●

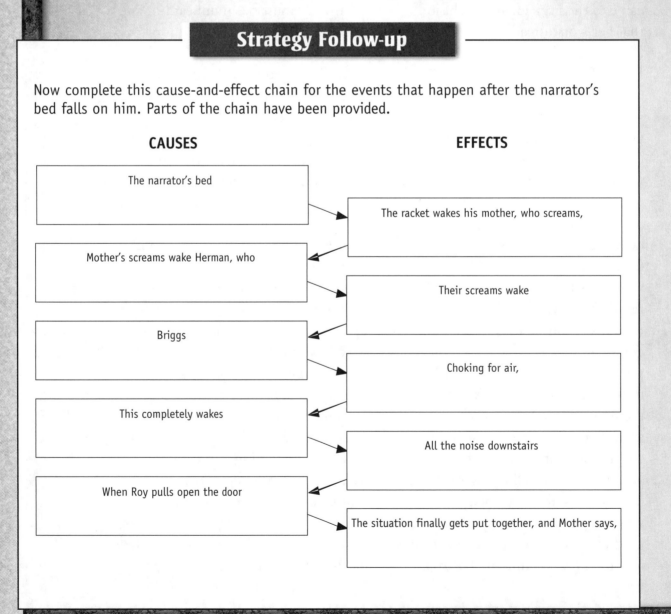

Strategy Follow-up

Now complete this cause-and-effect chain for the events that happen after the narrator's bed falls on him. Parts of the chain have been provided.

CAUSES

- The narrator's bed
- Mother's screams wake Herman, who
- Briggs
- This completely wakes
- When Roy pulls open the door

EFFECTS

- The racket wakes his mother, who screams,
- Their screams wake
- Choking for air,
- All the noise downstairs
- The situation finally gets put together, and Mother says,

✓Personal Checklist

Read each question and put a check (✓) in the correct box.

1. How well were you able to use what you wrote in Building Background to compare your sleep habits to those of the speaker and his relatives?
   - ☐ 3 (extremely well)
   - ☐ 2 (fairly well)
   - ☐ 1 (not well)

2. By the time you finished reading this story, how many vocabulary words were you able to put on the appropriate clipboards?
   - ☐ 3 (8–11 words)
   - ☐ 2 (4–7 words)
   - ☐ 1 (0–3 words)

3. How well were you able to help your partner or group create a cause-and-effect chain in the Strategy Follow-up?
   - ☐ 3 (extremely well)
   - ☐ 2 (fairly well)
   - ☐ 1 (not well)

4. How well could you explain why Mother's reference to "the night the bed fell on your father" is not an accurate description of the night?
   - ☐ 3 (extremely well)
   - ☐ 2 (fairly well)
   - ☐ 1 (not well)

5. How well could you explain why everyone but Father becomes hysterical when the bed falls?
   - ☐ 3 (extremely well)
   - ☐ 2 (fairly well)
   - ☐ 1 (not well)

Vocabulary Check

Look back at the work you did in the Vocabulary Builder. Then answer each question by circling the correct letter.

1. Which of the following sets contains three terms relating to medicines or drugs?
   - a. anesthetics, chloroform, spirits of camphor
   - b. phobia, premonition, ominous
   - c. extricate, chloroform, allay

2. Imagine that in taking off your sweater you get tangled in it. Which action would you choose to take?
   - a. extricate yourself
   - b. allay yourself
   - c. chloroform yourself

3. Which word is both an adjective and a word that describes concern for the future?
   - a. incredible
   - b. phobia
   - c. ominous

4. Which of the following is *not* an adjective?
   - a. ominous
   - b. premonition
   - c. perilous

5. Briggs awoke in the midst of loud shouts of fear and apprehension. What does *apprehension* mean in this context?
   - a. the ability to understand
   - b. the act of capturing or arresting
   - c. fearful or uneasy anticipation of the future

Add the numbers that you just checked to get your Personal Checklist score. Fill in your score here. Then turn to page 215 and transfer your score onto Graph 1.

Personal
Vocabulary
Strategy
Comprehension
TOTAL SCORE
✓ T

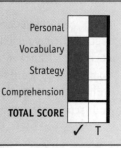

Check your answers with your teacher. Give yourself 1 point for each correct answer, and fill in your Vocabulary score here. Then turn to page 215 and transfer your score onto Graph 1.

Personal
Vocabulary
Strategy
Comprehension
TOTAL SCORE
✓ T

Strategy Check

Review the cause-and-effect chain that you helped create in the Strategy Follow-up. Then answer the following questions:

1. What causes the tremendous crash in the middle of the night?
   a. The bed that the narrator's father is in falls.
   b. The bed that the narrator is in tips over.
   c. The narrator's bother Herman falls out of bed.

2. What is the immediate effect of the crash?
   a. Mother wakes up and thinks that Father has been hurt.
   b. The narrator wakes up and screams for help.
   c. Herman yells for someone to help him get back into bed.

3. What causes Briggs to wake up?
   a. He hears the shouts of the narrator's mother and brother.
   b. The narrator pours the spirits of camphor on him.
   c. He hears the narrator's father's bed fall in the attic.

4. How does the glass of spirits of camphor make the situation worse?
   a. When Briggs pours it on himself, he is almost overcome by the fumes.
   b. When the narrator accidentally drinks it, he begins choking.
   c. When Herman spills it on the floor, everyone starts slipping and falling.

5. When the noise awakes the narrator's father, what does he think is happening?
   a. He thinks there's a burglar in the house.
   b. He thinks the house is on fire.
   c. He thinks there has been an earthquake.

Comprehension Check

Review the story if necessary. Then answer these questions:

1. Who usually sleeps in the attic bed?
   a. the narrator's grandfather
   b. the narrator's father
   c. the narrator's brother

2. Why does Aunt Gracie Shoaf pile up shoes near her bed before going to sleep each night?
   a. She needs to throw them at the burglars that she thinks are in the house.
   b. She is a sleepwalker and needs to keep shoes handy for her nightly walks.
   c. She considers shoes her most valuable items and wants to protect them.

3. For what purpose do you think the author has the narrator describe the odd habits of his aunts?
   a. He wants to inform readers.
   b. He wants to persuade readers.
   c. He wants to entertain readers.

4. Why do you think Mother refers to the incident as "the night the bed fell on your father"?
   a. She doesn't know that it was really the narrator's bed that fell.
   b. She injured her head that night and has amnesia.
   c. She's referring to the night that she thought the bed fell on Father.

5. Why is Mother's comment, "I'm glad that your grandfather wasn't here," silly?
   a. Grandfather really would have enjoyed watching the events.
   b. If Grandfather had been there, the events would not have happened.
   c. Grandfather was there all along.

Check your answers with your teacher. Give yourself 1 point for each correct answer, and fill in your Strategy score here. Then turn to page 215 and transfer your score onto Graph 1.

Personal
Vocabulary
Strategy
Comprehension
TOTAL SCORE
✓ T

Check your answers with your teacher. Give yourself 1 point for each correct answer, and fill in your Comprehension score here. Then turn to page 215 and transfer your score onto Graph 1.

Personal
Vocabulary
Strategy
Comprehension
TOTAL SCORE
✓ T

Extending

Choose one or both of these activities:

RESEARCH SLEEP DISORDERS

Although in this story the writer invites readers to laugh at Briggs Beall's fear of dying in his sleep, there is a sleep disorder that causes some people to stop breathing during sleep. With one or two classmates, research sleep apnea, insomnia, sleep walking, and other problems related to getting a good night's rest. Present your findings in a panel discussion. Explain each problem, describe what research has been conducted on it, and present researchers' recommendations for avoiding or reducing the problem.

SHARE THE HUMOR OF JAMES THURBER

"The Night the Bed Fell" is one of James Thurber's most popular short stories, but it is by no means his only one. Read several of Thurber's fables or such tales as "Many Moons," "The Great Quillow," or "The Secret Life of Walter Mitty." Choose one of these pieces, and present it to your class in an oral reading. Prepare by reading the story aloud in front of a mirror and deciding on the attitude you wish to project. After you present the reading, you may choose to lead a discussion about what makes the story humorous.

Resources

Books

Simpson, Carolyn. *Coping with Sleep Disorders.* Coping. Rosen, 1996.

Thurber, James. *Fables for Our Times, and Famous Poems Illustrated.* Harper, 1940.

———. *Many Moons.* Illus., Louis Slobodkin. Harcourt, 1981.

Web Sites

http://www.bigeye.com/thurber.htm
Several of Thurber's parables are available on this Web site. There are also links to information about the author.

http://www.sleepapnea.org/
This is the home page of the American Sleep Apnea Association.

http://www.sleepfoundation.org/disorder.cfm
This Web page of the National Sleep Foundation provides links to information on sleep disorders.

Audio Recording

Thurber, James. *Fables for Our Time, Further Fables for Our Time.* Books on Tape, 1983.

Levi's: The Pants That Won the West

Building Background

There is an old saying that states, "Necessity is the mother of invention." Do you agree? Why or why not? Look around the room right now. What inventions do you see? If you're in a classroom, you might see anything from paper clips and writing utensils to calculators and computers. Although inventions vary in their size and importance in our lives, they all have one thing in common: Each one was a solution to a problem that someone once had. The same thing can be said of Levi's— another invention you might see often as you look around the room. In "Levi's: The Pants That Won the West" you will read about how Levi's were invented and what problems they solved as they evolved into the pants that we wear today.

As you read the following selection, think about the saying about necessity. Decide whether Levi Strauss and the California gold miners would agree or disagree with it.

Vocabulary Builder

1. **Specialized vocabulary** words are words that are all related to a particular topic. The words in the margin are all related to the topic of Levi's.

2. Use the specialized vocabulary words to create a diagram of a pair of Levi's. First, draw the back of a pair of Levi's in the box below. (If you're wearing a pair of jeans right now, you can use them as a reference.) Then label your drawing with the vocabulary words.

3. Save your work. You will refer to it again in the Vocabulary Check.

denim

label

leg

pockets

rivets

seams

waist

Levi's

Strategy Builder

Identifying Problems and Solutions in Nonfiction

• As you know, every piece of nonfiction follows an organizational pattern. The most common patterns are description, cause-effect, sequence, and compare-contrast. Another organizational pattern, however, is **problem-solution**. When a piece of writing follows this pattern, the problem is first described, and then the solution or solutions are presented. The problem is finally solved when the solution that works—called **the end result**—is found.

• The selection you are about to read actually describes three separate problems and their solutions. First you will read about the problem that led to the invention of Levi's. The information in the Strategy Break will show you how to record that problem and solutions on a **problem-solution frame**. When you finish this selection, you will record one of the other problems on a problem-solution frame of your own.

Levi's: The Pants That Won the West

by Hilda Withrow

As you read the first part of this selection, apply the strategies that you just learned. Look for the miners' problem and what Levi Strauss does to solve it.

As anyone knows who watches TV, the West was won by just about everybody from Wild Bill Hickok to the U.S. Cavalry. But no one man captured the West so completely or so uniquely as a pint-sized, bearded Bavarian immigrant named Levi Strauss. And he did it not with a gun but with a pair of pants!

More incredible, Mr. Strauss's remarkable pants are not only still winning the West but the world in general. Today, more than a century since the first pair was made, his blue **denim** Levi's are setting trends in leisure wear around the globe. But fashion was the least of anyone's concern back in the gold-rush days of San Francisco.

The discovery of gold in California in 1848 set off such a stampede of young men rushing west to "strike it rich" that the population of San Francisco jumped from about eight hundred to twenty-five thousand within two years. Most of them lived in tents, covered wagons, or makeshift houses crudely constructed of canvas.

This was the view of San Francisco that greeted twenty-year-old Levi Strauss, Bavarian-born New Yorker, when he landed in 1850 after having made the seventeen-thousand-mile journey around the Horn by clipper ship. Unlike most of the others, Strauss didn't arrive empty-handed; he carried with him a small stock of dry goods, including some precious canvas, which he intended to sell for a grubstake in the Mother Lode country. But like the others, he had visions of making his fortune in gold nuggets and little dreamed he was toting his own "gold mine" in his bundle of fabrics.

According to local legend, Strauss sold most of his wares—at 50 per cent higher than Eastern prices—within minutes after his ship docked. When he walked ashore he had little left except a roll of heavy brown tent canvas. By chance he met a prospector, just in from the mining country, who asked him what he had brought from the East. Strauss pointed to his roll of canvas.

"Should have brought pants," snorted the disappointed miner.

"Pants? Why *pants*?" asked the surprised youngster.

"Because pants don't wear a hoot up in the diggings," the prospector grumbled. "Can't get a pair to last no time at all."

Since Strauss intended to pan for gold himself, he decided he might as well be outfitted for the rough work.

He took the miner and his roll of canvas to a tailor. "Make my friend and me each a pair of pants out of this," he said.

The miner was so pleased he became a walking advertisement as he strutted around San Francisco, boasting, "See these pants of Levi's—strongest doggone pair of pants a man ever had."

The name stuck. Other miners came looking for "the fellow with those Levi's," and even though more than 300 million pairs have been made since that time, the sturdy work pants have rarely been called by any other name. Today, "Levi's" is included in many reputable dictionaries.

Strauss soon abandoned the idea of digging for gold. He sent his grub-stake money to his two merchandising brothers in New York, along with an order for a larger stock of goods.

Before long, he had a modest store in newly founded Sacramento, the jumping-off place to the gold fields, where he supplied overland traders with dry goods. But as word-of-mouth advertising swamped him with orders for Levi's, Strauss began sending urgent letters to his brothers in the East to "buy all the canvas and duck you can find," and he scurried around in pursuit of every available tailor and seamstress in the area.

By 1853 he had convinced his brothers that they should combine their capital into one wholesale, jobbing, and manufacturing operation under the name of Levi Strauss and Company, with buying offices in New York and central headquarters in San Francisco.

 Stop here for the Strategy Break.

Strategy Break

If you were to create a problem-solution frame for the miners' problem and what Levi did to solve it, your frame might look like this:

What is the problem?
The miners needed pants that stood up to their rough work.

Why is it a problem?
Their pants didn't last long up in the diggings, and the miners had to keep replacing them.

Solutions	Results
1. Levi took his canvas to a tailor and had pants made for himself and his miner friend.	1. The miner was so pleased that he became a walking advertisement for his "pants of Levi's."
2. Other miners started looking for "the fellow with those Levi's," and they started wearing his pants.	2. **END RESULT:** Levi Strauss succeeded in providing sturdy work pants for the miners—and, eventually, for more than 300 million other people.

As you continue reading, watch for other problems and their solutions. At the end of this selection, you will create a problem-solution frame of your own.

Go on reading.

Somewhere along the line, Strauss switched from making Levi's of canvas and duck and began using a tough cotton fabric originally loomed in Nimes, France, and first known as *serge de Nimes.* This fabric, now called denim, came in three colors: light blue, brown, and gray. Because two pieces rarely dyed exactly the same shade, Strauss ordered a deeper indigo blue, which has remained the color for standard Levi's ever since.

No other change was made for about a decade. Meanwhile, Strauss's blue britches were becoming regulation garb for men who toiled at outdoor work, and they were gaining a widespread reputation for being as sturdy and tough as the rugged pioneers who wore them. Then they met up with a man who was tougher.

Local yarn-spinners claim it was along in the 1860s when a pair of Levi's tangled with a grizzled prospector, Alkali Ike, and came out the worst for the encounter.

Alkali Ike prospected for ore in Nevada, and he had an incurable habit of carrying jagged ore samples in the back **pockets** of his Levi's, repeatedly ripping out the **seams**. Alkali also had a set habit of making the rounds of the saloons every time he came to Virginia City and getting in a boisterous mood before he stomped into the tailoring shop of Jacob W. Davis and demanded to have his pockets mended. Jake Davis finally got fed up. He took Alkali's pants to a blacksmith and had the pockets riveted at the corners with black-iron square nails.

On his next trip to Strauss's factory to purchase materials, Jake told his friend Levi about the joke he had played on Alkali Ike. But Strauss thought the idea more ingenious than funny. He urged Davis to apply for a patent on the idea, suggested a copper rivet to avoid rust and discoloration of the fabric, and promptly made the tailor foreman of his clothing plant.

The protective patent was granted in 1873. Those copper **rivets**, leather **label**, and printed oilcloth ticket were the distinguishing features of Levi's until 1936. That was the year a bobcat inspired the first change to be made in the construction of Levi's in over sixty years.

It happened when two company executives went hunting and one of them bagged a bobcat.

Observation of the animal's concealed claws started them thinking about some letters the company had received complaining that the rivets on the back pockets of Levi's scratched furniture, upholstery, and fine leather saddles. When a way was

finally found to conceal the back-pocket rivets, it was the last major change to be made on the famous blue jeans that had become the accepted work uniform of miners, railroaders, lumberjacks, farmers, construction crews, oil drillers, cowboys, and all men who engaged in rugged outdoor labor.

Of course, what really established fame and a permanent market for Levi's was their symbolic identification with the American cowboy of the old "Wild West." Traditionally, especially in Western fiction tales, the cowboy totes a Colt in his holster, wears a Stetson on his head, and strolls around in a pair of low-hipped, tight-legged *faded* Levi's. Also traditionally, the cowboy will not part with his saddle once it is broken to fit his anatomy; neither will he part with his broken-in Levi's. It's also supposed to be tradition that cowboys used to jump into a rain barrel and let their Levi's shrink-to-fit as they dried on their bodies. Present-day teen-agers get the same skin-tight effect by wearing their blue denim Levi's in the shower. Average shrinkage: about an inch around the **waist** and two inches in length. Levi's also still fade to a washed-out blue, apparently to the satisfaction of customers who don't want to be dubbed "dudes" in new pants.

In the 1930s the company came out with "Lady Levi's," and found an instant market among women, who quickly discovered how practical the sturdy blue denims were.

The indigo-blue denim used in Levi's is exclusive with the company and reputed to be the strongest loomed in the world. For extra durability and functional fit, there are forty-seven separate sewing operations and seventeen different kinds of thread used in each pair.

For decades the Strauss trademark, etched on the leather label, has been two horses straining to pull apart a pair of Levi's; their guarantee: "A New Pair If They Rip." Every so often some wag hitches up two horses and pulls a pair of Levi's apart. "Whenever that happens," one executive said, "we always send the person another pair."

However, company files bulge with letters like this one from Mrs. M. H. English of Otto, Wyoming, who wrote: "Going between here and Basin we found a man who had run his car off the highway and was stuck. We had no chains or rope . . . but we found an old pair of Levi's in the back of our car. We tied one **leg** to our car and one to the front of his. We really had to pull, but the pants held and out he came."

That was an easy tow job compared to the time, back in 1899, when a pair of Levi's substituted for a broken coupling on an old wood-burning locomotive pulling seven cars piled high with logs. But the most remarkable testimony of Levi's longevity came from a woman who found a pair in an abandoned mine in the desert. She took them home, washed them, and then discovered from the markings on the back that they were eighty years old.

So far Merle Harjo is the only man who has credited Levi's with saving his life. It happened when Harjo was working on a fifty-two-story building in Fort Worth and a crane hook caught under the back pocket of his Levi's and swung him over the street. "I thought I was a goner," he wrote the company, ". . . but the Levi's didn't rip."

When the Strauss patent on the copper-rivet feature expired in 1908, there was an immediate rush of other manufacturers to turn out copper-studded clothing, creating unprecedented competition for the Levi Strauss Company. But the original blue jeans were so deeply rooted in the tradition of the old West they managed to stand firm against the new brands flooding the market.

Levi Strauss never saw the many imitations of his copper-reinforced pants. He died in 1902 at the age of seventy. Having remained a bachelor all his life, he left the business to his only surviving relative, a sister, Mrs. David Stern.

The firm has since expanded from two plants in San Francisco to seventy factories and distribution centers in North America and thirty-seven elsewhere in the world. Products are now sold by more than thirty-five thousand retailers, including distribution in seventy countries, and the company's line has expanded from blue jeans into a variety of casual clothes. Today, the Levi Strauss catalogue lists thousands of items in every fabric from the original denim to the latest synthetics, ranging from ladies' bright-hued beach wear to men's white Bermuda shorts.

What happened to the old-time Levi's in the face of these newcomers?

They're still the company's best sellers, with over one billion pairs sold since their early days.

Originally made for gold miners, Levi's literally stepped into a gold mine when they became a campus uniform for teen-agers. Since World War II young people have been a major market, and the demand for the indigo-blue old-timers is on the increase. Naturally, the popularity of Western movies and TV shows, both here and abroad, has also enhanced their appeal.

If imitation is truly a tribute to genius, then Levi Strauss must be hailed as such, for he originated the most imitated, copied, counterfeited, plagiarized, and pirated article of clothing in the world today. ●

Strategy Follow-up

Now complete the following problem-solution frame with information about Alkali Ike's problem. Some of the information has been provided for you.

What is the problem?

Alkali Ike kept

Why is it a problem?

Solutions	Results
1. Tailor Jacob W. Davis	**1.** The pockets
2. Davis told Strauss	**2.** Strauss suggested
3. The patent	**3. END RESULT:**

✓Personal Checklist

Read each question and put a check (✓) in the correct box.

1. How well were you able to decide if Levi Straus and the gold miners would agree or disagree with the idea that necessity is the mother of invention?
   - ☐ 3 (extremely well)
   - ☐ 2 (fairly well)
   - ☐ 1 (not well)

2. In the Vocabulary Builder, how well were you able to draw a diagram of a pair of Levi's and label it with the specialized vocabulary words?
   - ☐ 3 (extremely well)
   - ☐ 2 (fairly well)
   - ☐ 1 (not well)

3. How well were you able to complete the problem-solution frame in the Strategy Follow-up?
   - ☐ 3 (extremely well)
   - ☐ 2 (fairly well)
   - ☐ 1 (not well)

4. How well do you understand why Strauss's first pants became so popular?
   - ☐ 3 (extremely well)
   - ☐ 2 (fairly well)
   - ☐ 1 (not well)

5. How well could you explain why Levi's are so popular today?
   - ☐ 3 (extremely well)
   - ☐ 2 (fairly well)
   - ☐ 1 (not well)

Vocabulary Check

Look back at the work you did in the Vocabulary Builder. Then answer each question by circling the correct letter.

1. Which meaning of the word *rivets* is used in this selection?
   a. attracts and holds someone's attention
   b. looks firmly at someone or something
   c. metal bolts used to join things together

2. What is depicted on the leather label of a pair of Levi's?
   a. two miners panning for gold in a stream
   b. two horses straining to pull apart a pair of Levi's
   c. a man hanging by the back pocket of his Levi's

3. Levi's original denim came in what three colors?
   a. indigo blue, light blue, and brown
   b. light blue, brown, and gray
   c. gray, brown, and indigo blue

4. What did Alkali Ike keep ripping out with jagged ore samples?
   a. the rivets in his pockets
   b. the seams of his pockets
   c. the label on his pocket

5. If you were to wear a pair of Levi's in the shower, what part of them would shrink about an inch?
   a. the waist
   b. the leg
   c. the pockets

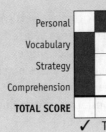

Add the numbers that you just checked to get your Personal Checklist score. Fill in your score here. Then turn to page 215 and transfer your score onto Graph 1.

Personal
Vocabulary
Strategy
Comprehension
TOTAL SCORE
✓ T

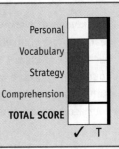

Check your answers with your teacher. Give yourself 1 point for each correct answer, and fill in your Vocabulary score here. Then turn to page 215 and transfer your score onto Graph 1.

Personal
Vocabulary
Strategy
Comprehension
TOTAL SCORE
✓ T

Strategy Check

Review the problem-solution frame that you completed in the Strategy Follow-up. Also review the selection if necessary. Then answer these questions:

1. How did Jacob Davis solve Alkali Ike's problem?
   a. He had Alkali's pockets riveted with iron nails.
   b. He advised the miner to start wearing Levi's.
   c. He suggested that Alkali go see a blacksmith.

2. When Davis told Strauss what he had done, how did Davis expect Strauss to react?
   a. by asking to meet Alkali Ike
   b. by becoming angry at Davis
   c. by laughing at his joke

3. What did Strauss do instead?
   a. He urged Davis to patent copper rivets.
   b. He made Davis the foreman of his plant.
   c. He did both of the above.

4. A major design change in Levi's was covering the rivets on the back pockets. What problem did that solve?
   a. The back rivets used to scratch furniture.
   b. The back rivets didn't look attractive.
   c. The back rivets were uncomfortable.

5. What observation inspired two Levi's executives to cover the rivets on the back pockets?
   a. the way workmen engaged in rugged outdoor labor
   b. the way a bobcat's claws are concealed
   c. the way a cowboy won't part with his broken-in Levi's

Comprehension Check

Review the selection if necessary. Then answer these questions:

1. Why did Levi Strauss go to California?
   a. to open a dry goods business
   b. to search for gold
   c. to make pants for miners

2. When did Strauss go to California?
   a. 1845—just before the United States took over California
   b. 1850—just after gold had been discovered there
   c. 1870—just after the railroads across the continent were completed

3. Which of these statements is false?
   a. Today, Strauss's are considered stylish rather than merely work clothes.
   b. Today, very few people are impressed by the strength of Strauss's.
   c. Today, Strauss's products are distributed in seventy countries.

4. Recall how Strauss reacted to Jacob Davis's rivet joke. What does that reaction suggest about Strauss's success as a business person?
   a. He recognized problems and practical solutions that he could sell to people.
   b. He used people's names to sell his products.
   c. Both of the above answers are correct.

5. Which sentence best states the main idea, or theme, of this selection?
   a. Everyone should wear Levi's.
   b. Levi Strauss was never a good gold miner.
   c. Levi Strauss has had a lasting effect on American culture.

Check your answers with your teacher. Give yourself 1 point for each correct answer, and fill in your Strategy score here. Then turn to page 215 and transfer your score onto Graph 1.

Personal
Vocabulary
Strategy
Comprehension
TOTAL SCORE
✓ T

Check your answers with your teacher. Give yourself 1 point for each correct answer, and fill in your Comprehension score here. Then turn to page 215 and transfer your score onto Graph 1.

Personal
Vocabulary
Strategy
Comprehension
TOTAL SCORE
✓ T

Extending

Choose one or both of these activities:

PROPOSE A THEORY

Other clothing styles that have been popular in the United States in the last 150 years include the bustle, the top hat, the Nehru jacket, and the leisure suit. Why have Levi's persisted, while other types of clothing have disappeared? Develop your own answer to this question—either a reasonable one or a humorous one—and write a short essay explaining your theory and providing evidence to support it.

EXAMINE A CURRENT STYLE

Choose a particular type or style of clothing that is popular today. Investigate its beginnings. Who wears this clothing? Did one person develop the style? Was developing this type of clothing a conscious effort, or did it evolve gradually? Did one person (such as a movie, sports, or music figure) make the style popular, or did a large group accept it over a period of time? What makes this clothing or style popular today? Do your peers think the popularity of this clothing will last, as the popularity of Levi's has lasted? With a partner or a small group, investigate these questions by using print materials, TV commercials, and polls that you find or conduct. Report your findings with illustrations and any relevant charts and graphics.

Resources

Books

Finlayson, Iain. *Denim: An American Legend.* Fireside, 1990.

Henry, Sondra, and Emily Taitz. *Everyone Wears His Name: A Biography of Levi Strauss.* People in Focus. Dillion Press, 1990.

Little, David. *Vintage Denim.* Gibbs Smith, 1996.

Web Site

http://www.levistrauss.com/about/history/timeline.asp This Web page presents a time line of Levi Strauss and Company, from its beginning in the 1800s to today.

Video/DVD

Blue Jeans. Landmark Media, 1995.

This Farm for Sale

Building Background

When people say, "The grass is always greener on the other side of the fence," what do you think they mean? Why do you think this expression is so widely used? What does it say about people's satisfaction with their lives? Think of an example that illustrates this expression, either from your own life or someone else's. Explain the situation on a separate piece of paper. Then explain why the expression proved to be true or untrue in that situation.

As you read this story, look at both sides of the "fence," or issue. Notice what the characters learn as they deal with the sale of the farm.

balks

bottoms

lean

mast

plunder

stage

virgin

Vocabulary Builder

1. You know that a single word can have more than one meaning. To figure out which meaning an author is using, you have to use context. **Context** is the information surrounding a word or situation that helps you understand it.

2. Read each multiple-meaning word in Column 1 below. For most of the words, the meanings used in this story will be unfamiliar if you've never been on a farm. Before you begin reading, see if you can match the words in Column 1 with their meanings in Column 2. Don't worry if you can't match them all.

3. As you read the story, find the boldfaced words that you were unable to match and use context to figure out their meanings. If you still haven't matched all the words by the end of the story, look them up in a dictionary.

4. Save your work. You will refer to it again in the Vocabulary Check.

COLUMN 1	COLUMN 2
balks	containing little or no fat
bottoms	low lands along a river
lean	household goods
mast	unplowed strips of land
plunder	in an untouched, natural state
stage	height of a river at a set point
virgin	nuts from trees, piled on the ground and used especially as food for pigs

Strategy Builder

Drawing Conclusions About Characters

- As you know, a **conclusion** is a decision that you reach after thinking about certain facts or information. When you read a story, you often draw conclusions based on information that the author gives you about the characters, the setting, or particular events.

- You can draw conclusions about the **characters** in a story by paying attention to their words, thoughts, feelings, and actions. These clues can help you understand the characters better. They also can help you understand why the characters do what they do.

- Read the following paragraph about a character named Louis. Then look at the **character map** below the paragraph. It shows the conclusions that one student drew about Louis, and why.

One night Louis was working on a homework assignment when a thunderstorm woke up his little brothers. Both of them ran into Louis's room. "Louis, can we sleep with you tonight?" Matt begged.

"Hey, I don't need you to protect me," Louis protested, smiling. "I know we're safe inside this building. But if you want to keep me company for a while, that's okay." The two little boys crawled into his bed and watched him read. After a while, they were both asleep. They didn't wake up even when Louis carried them back to their beds.

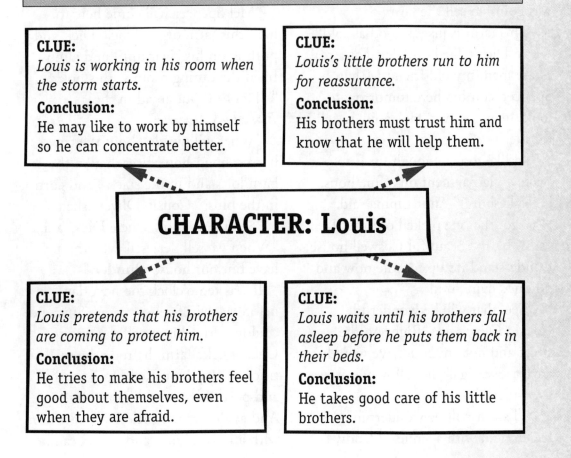

CLUE:
Louis is working in his room when the storm starts.
Conclusion:
He may like to work by himself so he can concentrate better.

CLUE:
Louis's little brothers run to him for reassurance.
Conclusion:
His brothers must trust him and know that he will help them.

CHARACTER: Louis

CLUE:
Louis pretends that his brothers are coming to protect him.
Conclusion:
He tries to make his brothers feel good about themselves, even when they are afraid.

CLUE:
Louis waits until his brothers fall asleep before he puts them back in their beds.
Conclusion:
He takes good care of his little brothers.

This Farm for Sale

by Jesse Stuart

As you read this story, apply the strategies that you just learned. Look for clues that the author provides to help you draw conclusions about the members of the family.

"This time we're goin' to sell this farm," Uncle Dick said to Aunt Emma. "I've just learned how to sell a farm. Funny, I never thought of it myself."

My cousins—Olive, Helen, Oliver, and Little Dick—all stopped eating and looked at one another and then looked at Uncle Dick and Aunt Emma. When Aunt Emma smiled, they smiled, too. Everybody seemed happy because Uncle Dick, who had just come from Blakesburg, had found a way to sell the farm. Everybody was happy but me. I was sorry Uncle Dick was going to sell the farm.

"This farm is just as good as sold!" Uncle Dick talked on. "I've got a real estate man, my old friend Melvin Spencer, coming here tomorrow to look the place over. He's goin' to sell it for me."

"I'd like to get enough for it to make a big payment on a fine house in Blakesburg," Aunt Emma said. "I've got the one picked out that I want. It's the beautiful Coswell house. I understand it's up for sale now and no one's livin' in it!"

"Gee, that will be wonderful," Cousin Olive said. "Right on the street and not any mud. We wouldn't have to wear galoshes all winter if we lived there!"

"I'll say it will be wonderful," Helen said, with a smile. "Daddy, I hope Mr. Spencer can sell this place."

I wanted to tell Aunt Emma the reason why no one was living in the Coswell house. Every time Big River rose to flood **stage**, the water got on the first floor in the house; and this was the reason why the Coswells had built a house on higher ground outside Blakesburg and had moved to it. And this was the reason why they couldn't keep a renter any longer than it took Big River to rise to flood stage. But this wasn't my business, so I didn't say anything.

"Mel Spencer will come here to look this farm over," Uncle Dick said, puffing on his cigar until he'd almost filled the dining room with smoke. "Then he'll put an ad in the *Blakesburg Gazette*."

"What will we do about the cows, horses, hogs, honeybees, hay in the barn lofts and in the stacks, and corn in the bins?" Cousin Oliver asked.

"Sell them, too," Uncle Dick said. "When we sell, let's sell everything we have but our house **plunder**."

It was ten o'clock the next day before Melvin Spencer came. Since he couldn't drive his car all the way to Uncle Dick's farm, he rode the mail truck to Red Hot. Red Hot is a store and post office on the Tiber River. And at Red Hot, Uncle Dick met him with an extra horse and empty saddle.

So Melvin Spencer came riding up with Uncle Dick. And I'll never forget the first words he said when he climbed down from the saddle.

"Richard, it's a great experience to be in the saddle again," he said, breathing deeply of the fresh air. "All this reminds me of another day and time."

Oliver, Little Dick, and I followed Melvin Spencer and Uncle Dick as they started walking toward the Tiber **bottoms**.

"How many acres in this farm, Richard?" Melvin Spencer asked.

"The deed calls for three hundred, more or less," Uncle Dick said.

"How many acres of bottom land?" he asked Uncle Dick.

"I'd say about sixty-five," Uncle Dick replied.

We walked down the jolt-wagon road, where my cousins and I had often ridden Nell and Jerry to and from the field.

"What kind of land is this?" Melvin Spencer asked. He had to look up to see the bright heads of cane.

"It's limestone land," Uncle Dick bragged. "Never had to use fertilizer. My people have farmed these bottoms over a hundred years."

Then Uncle Dick showed Melvin Spencer the corn we had laid by. It was August, and our growing corn was maturing. Melvin Spencer looked at the big cornfield. He was very silent. We walked on to the five acres of tobacco, where the broad leaves crossed the **balks** and a man couldn't walk through. Then we went down to the river.

"My farm comes to this river," Uncle Dick said. "I've often thought what a difference it would be if we had a bridge across this river. Then I could reach the Tiber road and go east to Blakesburg and west to Darter City. But we don't have a bridge; and until we go down the river seven miles to Red Hot where we can cross to the Tiber road, we'll always be in the mud. I've heard all my life that the county would build a bridge. My father heard it, too, in his lifetime."

"You *are* shut in here," Melvin Spencer agreed, as he looked beyond the Tiber River at the road.

"Now, we'll go to the house and get some dinner," Uncle Dick said. "Then I'll take you up on the hill this afternoon and show you my timber and the rest of the farm."

⬣ **Stop here for the Strategy Break.**

Strategy Break

If you were to create a character map for the narrators' cousins based on what you have learned about them so far, it might look like this:

CLUE:
When their father says he will sell the farm, they look at one another and then at their parents. When their mother smiles, they smile too.

Conclusion:
They follow their parents' lead when deciding how they should feel.

CLUE:
Olive and Helen say they'll be happy not to wear galoshes all winter.

Conclusion:
They want to be more stylish and comfortable.

CHARACTERS:
Olive, Helen, Oliver, and Little Dick

CLUE:
Oliver asks what will happen to the animals, the hay, and the corn.

Conclusion:
He is a practical boy and is perhaps more concerned about the farm than his own feelings.

CLUE:
Oliver and Little Dick, along with Shan, silently trail after their father and Melvin Spencer as they walk around the farm.

Conclusion:
They are curious about what's happening but polite enough not to interrupt or ask questions.

As you continue reading, keep looking for clues that the author gives about all the characters, but particularly Uncle Dick. At the end of this selection, you will create a character map of your own.

➡ **Go on reading to see what happens.**

When we reached the big house, Melvin Spencer stopped for a minute and looked at the house and yard.

"You know, when I sell a piece of property, I want to look it over," he told Uncle Dick. "I want to know all about it. How old is this house?"

"The date was cut on the chimney," Uncle Dick said.

Melvin Spencer looked over the big squat log house with the plank door, big stone steps, small windows, the moss-covered roof. Then we went inside, and he started looking again. That is, he did until Uncle Dick introduced him to Aunt Emma and Aunt Emma introduced him to a table that made him stand and look some more.

"I've never seen anything like this since I was a boy," Melvin Spencer said, showing more interest in the loaded table than he had in the farm.

"All of this came from our farm here," Uncle Dick said.

I never saw a man eat like Melvin Spencer. He ate like I did when I first came to Uncle Dick's and Aunt Emma's each spring when school was over. He tried to eat something of everything on the table, but he couldn't get around to it all.

"If I could sell this farm like you can prepare a meal, I'd get a whopping big price for it," he said with a chuckle as he looked at Aunt Emma.

"I hope you can," Aunt Emma said. "We're too far back here. Our children have to wade the winter mud to get to school. And we don't have electricity. We don't have the things that city people have. And I think every country woman wants them."

Melvin Spencer didn't listen to all that Aunt Emma said. He was much too busy eating.

"The old place is as good as sold, Mother," Uncle Dick said with a wink. "You're a-goin' to be out of the mud. We'll let some other woman slave around here and wear galoshes all winter. We'll be on the bright, clean streets wearin' well-shined shoes—every blessed one of us. We'll have an electric washer, a radio where we won't have to have the batteries charged, a bathroom, and an electric stove. No more of this stove-wood choppin' for the boys and me."

When Uncle Dick said this, Olive and Helen looked at Aunt Emma and smiled. I looked at Oliver and Little Dick, and they were grinning. But Melvin Spencer never looked up from his plate.

When we got up from the table, Melvin Spencer thanked Aunt Emma, Cousin Olive, and Helen for the "best dinner" he'd had since he was a young man. Then he asked Aunt Emma for a picture of the house.

Aunt Emma sent Helen to get it. "If you can, just sell this place for us," Aunt Emma said to Melvin Spencer.

"I'll do my best," he promised her. "But as you ought to know, it will be a hard place to sell, located way back here and without a road."

"Are you a-goin' to put a picture of this old house in the paper?" Uncle Dick asked, as Helen came running with the picture.

"I might," Melvin Spencer said. "I never say much in an ad, since I have to make my words count. A picture means a sale sometimes. Of course, this expense will come from the sale of the property."

He said good-by to Aunt Emma, Olive, and Helen. Little Dick, Oliver, and I followed him and Uncle Dick out of the house and up the hill where the yellow poplars and the pines grow.

"Why hasn't this timber been cut long ago?" Melvin Spencer asked, looking up at the trees.

"Not any way to haul it out," Uncle Dick told him.

"That's right," Melvin Spencer said. "I'd forgot about the road. If a body doesn't have a road to his farm, Richard, he's not got much of a place."

While we walked under the beech grove, we came upon a drove of slender bacon hogs eating beechnuts.

"Old skinny bacon hogs," Uncle Dick said, as they scurried past us. "They feed on the **mast** of the beeches and oaks, on saw-briar, green-briar, and pine-tree roots, and on mulberries, persimmons, and pawpaws."

When we climbed to the top of a hill, the land slanted in all directions.

"Show me from here what you own," Melvin Spencer said.

"It's very easy, Mel," Uncle Dick said. "The stream on the right and the one on the left are the left and right forks of Wolfe Creek. They are boundary lines. I own all the land between them. I own all the bottom land from where the forks join, down to that big bend in the Tiber. And I own down where the Tiber flows against those white limestone cliffs."

"You are fenced in by natural boundaries," Melvin Spencer said. "They're almost impossible to cross. This place will be hard to sell, Richard."

Then we went back down the hill, and Melvin and Uncle Dick climbed into the saddles and were off down the little narrow road toward Red Hot. Their horses went away at a gallop, because Melvin Spencer had to catch the mail truck, and he was already behind schedule.

On Saturday, Uncle Dick rode to Red Hot to get the paper. Since he didn't read very well, he asked me to read what Melvin Spencer had said about his house. When I opened the paper and turned to the picture of the house, everybody gathered around.

"Look, here's two columns all the way down the page," I said. "The other four places advertised here have only a paragraph about them."

"Read it," Uncle Dick said. "I'd like to know what Mel said about this place. Something good, I hope."

So I read this aloud:

Yesterday, I had a unique experience when I visited the farm of Mr. and Mrs. Richard Stone, which they have asked me to sell. I cannot write an ad about this farm. I must tell you about it.

I went up a winding road on horseback. Hazelnut bushes, with clusters of green hazelnuts bending their slender stems, swished across my face. Pawpaws, heavy with green clusters of fruit, grew along this road. Persimmons with bending boughs covered one slope below the road. Here are wild fruits and nuts of Nature's cultivation for the one who possesses land like this. Not any work but just to go out and gather the fruit. How many of you city dwellers would love this?

"What about him a-mentionin' the persimmons, pawpaws, and hazelnuts!" Uncle Dick broke in. "I'd never have thought of them. They're common things!"

This peaceful Tiber River, flowing dreamily down the valley, is a boundary to his farm. Here one can see to the bottoms of the deep holes, the water is so clear and blue. One can catch fish from the river for his next meal. Elder bushes, where they gather the berries to make the finest jelly in the world, grow along this riverbank as thick as ragweeds. The Stones have farmed this land for four generations, have lived in the same house, have gathered elderberries for their jelly along the Tiber riverbanks, and fished in its sky-blue waters that long—and yet they will sell this land.

"Just a minute, Shan," Uncle Dick said as he got up from his chair. "Stop just a minute."

Uncle Dick pulled a handkerchief from his pocket and wiped the sweat from his forehead. His face seemed a bit flushed. He walked a little circle around the living room and then sat back down in his chair. But the sweat broke out on his face again when I started reading.

*The proof of what a farm produces is at the farm table. I wish that whoever reads what I have written here could have seen the table prepared by Mrs. Stone and her two daughters. Hot fluffy biscuits with light-brown tops, brown-crusted cornbread, buttermilk, sweet milk (cooled in a freestone well), wild-grape jelly, wild-crab-apple jelly, mast-fed **lean** bacon that melted in my mouth, fresh apple pie, wild-blackberry cobbler, honey-colored sorghum from the limestone bottoms of the Tiber, and wild honey from the beehives.*

"Oh, no one ever said that about a meal I cooked before," Aunt Emma broke in.

"Just a minute, Shan," Uncle Dick said, as he got up from his chair with his handkerchief in his hand again.

This time Uncle Dick went a bit faster as he circled the living room. He wiped sweat from his face as he walked. He had a worried look on his face. I read on:

Their house, eight rooms and two halls, would be a show place if close to some of our modern cities. The house itself would be worth the price I will later quote you on this farm. Giant yellow poplar logs with twenty- to thirty-inch facings, hewed smooth with broad-axes by the mighty hands of Stone pioneers, make the sturdy walls in this termite-proof house. Two planks make the broad doors in this house that is one-hundred-and-six years old. This beautiful home of pioneer architecture is without modern conveniences, but since a power line will be constructed up the Tiber River early next spring, a few modern conveniences will be possible.

"I didn't know that!" Aunt Emma was excited. "I guess it's just talk, like about the bridge across the Tiber."

*After lunch I climbed a high hill to look at the rest of this farm. I walked through a valley of **virgin** trees, where there were yellow poplars and one sixty feet to the first limb. Beech trees with tops big enough to shade twenty-five head of cattle. Beechnuts streaming down like golden coins, to be gathered by the bacon hogs running wild. A farm with wild game and fowl, and a river bountiful with fish. And yet, this farm is for sale!*

Uncle Dick walked over beside his chair. He looked as if he were going to fall over.

Go see for yourself roads not exploited by the county or state, where the horse's shoe makes music on the clay, where apple orchards with fruit are bending down, and barns and bins are full. Go see a way of life, a richness and fulfillment that make America great, that put solid foundation stones under America! This beautiful farm, fifty head of livestock, honeybees, crops old and new, and a home for only $22,000!

"Oh!" Aunt Emma screamed. I thought she was going to faint. "Oh, he's killed it with that price. It's unheard of, Richard! You couldn't get $6000 for it."

Uncle Dick still paced the floor.

"What's the matter, Pa?" Oliver finally asked.

"I didn't know I had so much," Uncle Dick said. "I'm a rich man and didn't know it. I'm not selling this farm!"

"Don't worry, Richard," Aunt Emma said. "You won't sell it at that price!"

I never saw such disappointed looks as there were on my cousins' faces.

"But what will you do with Mr. Spencer?" Aunt Emma asked. "You've put the farm in his hands to sell."

"Pay him for his day and what he put in the paper," Uncle Dick told her. "I know we're not goin' to sell now, for it takes two to sign the deed. I'll be willing to pay Mel Spencer a little extra because he showed me what we have."

Then I laid the paper down and walked quietly from the room. Evening was coming on. I walked toward the meadows. I wanted to share the beauty of this farm with Melvin Spencer. I was never so happy. ●

Strategy Follow-up

Copy the character map for Uncle Dick onto a sheet of paper. Then complete the map by filling in the conclusions that you draw based on the clues given.

CLUE:
Uncle Dick brags about the farm while showing it to Melvin Spencer.
Conclusion:

CLUE:
He is amazed at Melvin's mention of characteristics of the farm that seem like "common things."
Conclusion:

CHARACTER: Uncle Dick

CLUE:
He asks Shan to stop reading several times, and he walks around and wipes sweat from his face.
Conclusion:

CLUE:
After hearing all of Melvin's column, Uncle Dick announces "I'm a rich man and didn't know it. I'm not selling the farm."
Conclusion:

✓Personal Checklist

Read each question and put a check (✓) in the correct box.

1. How well do you understand what the characters learned about "the grass being greener" as they dealt with the sale of the farm?
   ☐ 3 (extremely well)
   ☐ 2 (fairly well)
   ☐ 1 (not well)

2. By the time you finished reading this story, how many farm terms were you able to match with their meanings in the Vocabulary Builder?
   ☐ 3 (6–7 words)
   ☐ 2 (3–5 words)
   ☐ 1 (0–2 words)

3. How well were you able to complete the character map in the Strategy Follow-up?
   ☐ 3 (extremely well)
   ☐ 2 (fairly well)
   ☐ 1 (not well)

4. How well do you understand why Uncle Dick changes his mind about selling the farm?
   ☐ 3 (extremely well)
   ☐ 2 (fairly well)
   ☐ 1 (not well)

5. How well do understand why Shan is so happy at the end of the story?
   ☐ 3 (extremely well)
   ☐ 2 (fairly well)
   ☐ 1 (not well)

Vocabulary Check

Look back at the work you did in the Vocabulary Builder. Then answer each question by circling the correct letter.

1. In the context of this story, which vocabulary word means "household goods"?
   a. mast
   b. plunder
   c. stage

2. The hogs in this story are mast-fed. What does that mean?
   a. They feed on the nuts that fall from the surrounding trees.
   b. They feed on wooden poles that grow out of the ground.
   c. They feed on the part of a ship that supports a sail.

3. Which word or phrase is a synonym of *untouched*?
   a. lean
   b. virgin
   c. bottom

4. How is the word *stage* used in this story?
   a. one step in a process of development
   b. level to which water rises
   c. raised platform on which plays are acted

5. Which of these could *not* be described by the word *lean* as it is used in this story?
   a. a cut of meat
   b. a slender person
   c. rely on

Add the numbers that you just checked to get your Personal Checklist score. Fill in your score here. Then turn to page 215 and transfer your score onto Graph 1.

Personal
Vocabulary
Strategy
Comprehension
TOTAL SCORE
✓ T

Check your answers with your teacher. Give yourself 1 point for each correct answer, and fill in your Vocabulary score here. Then turn to page 215 and transfer your score onto Graph 1.

Personal
Vocabulary
Strategy
Comprehension
TOTAL SCORE
✓ T

Strategy Check

Review the character map that you completed, and the selection. Then answer these questions:

1. Why is Uncle Dick surprised that Melvin Spencer mentions the wild fruits and nuts on the farm?

   a. He thinks that readers won't know what wild fruits and nuts are.

   b. He has seen these things so often that he doesn't appreciate them.

   c. The fruits and nuts are just common ones.

2. When Uncle Dick says that he won't sell the farm, the children don't say a word. What is not a reasonable conclusion you can draw from this?

   a. The children don't say anything because they don't know how to talk.

   b. They always lose arguments with their father.

   c. They know they must accept his decision.

3. Why would you think that Spencer disagrees with Uncle Dick's decision to sell the farm?

   a. He has to ride a horse to get from the closest road to the house.

   b. He writes a glowing description of the farm and sets the price very high.

   c. He says that the farm will be hard to sell.

4. Why does Uncle Dick declare "I'm a rich man and didn't know it"?

   a. He thinks that Melvin wants the farm and figures he can raise the price even higher.

   b. He finds gold in the bottom soil of his farm.

   c. He sees the farm in a new way and appreciates what he has taken for granted.

5. Which conclusion about Uncle Dick would you say is most accurate?

   a. He tends to make up his mind quickly, but he's willing to change his thinking.

   b. He lets others talk him into doing things.

   c. Uncle Dick is never satisfied with anything.

Comprehension Check

Review the story if necessary. Then answer these questions:

1. Aunt Emma wants to move into the "beautiful Coswell house" in town. Why does Shan say that house is empty?

   a. Whenever the Big River goes over its banks, the house gets flooded.

   b. The house has a reputation for being haunted.

   c. The owners have set too high a price.

2. Why does Melvin Spencer come to look over the farm?

   a. He has heard about Aunt Emma's cooking and wants a free meal.

   b. He is considering buying the farm himself and wants to check it out.

   c. He likes to know what it is he's selling.

3. How long has the Stone family been living on this farm?

   a. about 20 years

   b. about 50 years

   c. more than 100 years

4. Why have the trees on the farm never been cut down and sold?

   a. The Stone family like to keep the trees there to protect their pigs.

   b. There is no road to the farm by which to remove the cut timber.

   c. The trees are not worth very much.

5. Why does Aunt Emma want to leave the farm?

   a. She wants to open a restaurant in town.

   b. She's allergic to many of the things that grow on the farm.

   c. She wants electricity and other things available only in town.

Check your answers with your teacher. Give yourself 1 point for each correct answer, and fill in your Strategy score here. Then turn to page 215 and transfer your score onto Graph 1.

Personal
Vocabulary
Strategy
Comprehension
TOTAL SCORE
✓ T

Check your answers with your teacher. Give yourself 1 point for each correct answer, and fill in your Comprehension score here. Then turn to page 215 and transfer your score onto Graph 1.

Personal
Vocabulary
Strategy
Comprehension
TOTAL SCORE
✓ T

Extending

Choose one or more of these activities:

RESEARCH MODERN FARMS

Are any farms in America today like the farm in this story? How many are still without electricity? How many are still owned and operated by a family that draws most of its food from the crops and animals grown there? Can a farmer still make a profit without having access to roads? How much does it cost to operate a successful farm today? With a small group, research today's farms. All group members should do some preliminary research to get an overall idea of the condition of modern farms. Then the group should divide the possible subtopics and do more detailed research. Together, decide how to present your findings: in a panel discussion, in a booklet with a page or more from each subcommittee, in video or poster form, or in another way.

HAVE A DEBATE

Uncle Dick's family is very traditional, with the father being responsible for major decisions and the entire family working together on chores. Decide whether you agree or disagree with this statement: Today's families would be happier and more successful if they were more like Uncle Dick's family. Meet with others who agree with you, and develop arguments for your side of the issue. Then hold a debate with students taking the opposite view.

READ OTHER WORKS BY JESSE STUART

Jesse Stuart was born and raised on a Kentucky farm much like the one in this story. He grew up to become a teacher and an author of novels, short stories, books for children, essays, and poetry. In most of his writing, he records the Appalachian way of life. Choose one of Jesse Stuart's books or shorter works, such as those listed on this page, and report on it to the class. You can give your report orally or in writing. If you'd like, read aloud or mention some of your favorite passages, and explain why they appeal to you.

Resources

Books

Stuart, Jesse. *Men of the Mountains.* University of Kentucky Press, 1979.

———. *Mongrel Mettle: The Autobiography of a Dog.* Dutton, 1944.

———. *My World.* University Press of Kentucky, 1992.

———. *A Ride with Huey, the Engineer.* Jesse Stuart Foundation, 1988.

———. *Tales from the Plum Grove Hills.* Jesse Stuart Foundation, 1998.

———. *The Thread That Runs So True.* University Press of Kentucky, 1974.

———. ed. *A Jesse Stuart Reader: Stories and Poems.* McGraw-Hill, 1963.

Web Sites

http://www.acci.org/aici/info/history.html
On this Web page, read an account of how the U.S. government brought electricity to rural areas in the 1930s.

http://www.morehead-st.edu/projects/village/jshome.html
This Web site presents a short biography of Jesse Stuart. It also contains a poem and a short story by the author.

http://www.usda.gov/
This is the Web site of the U.S. Department of Agriculture.

Neighbors

churchgoing

farewell

greenhouse

newcomers

overturned

rosebud

uproot

Building Background

Think about the title of this article. What does the word *neighbors* mean to you? What might you expect to learn from a nonfiction selection about neighbors? Before you begin reading this selection, take a few moments to answer these questions:

1. What makes a good neighbor? _____

   _____

2. Of the neighbors you have had, which ones are your favorites? Why? _____

   _____

3. If you have had some bad neighbors, what made them undesirable? _____

   _____

4. How do you think the people who live near you rate you and your family as neighbors, and why? _____

   _____

5. Do you predict that this article will be about good or bad neighbors? _____

   Why? _____

   _____

CLIPBOARD

churchgoing
_____

_____

farewell
_____

_____

greenhouse
_____

_____

CLIPBOARD

newcomers
_____

_____

overturned
_____

_____

rosebud
_____

_____

uproot
_____

_____

Vocabulary Builder

1. The words in the margin are all compound words. As you know, a **compound word** is made up of two words put together. Separating the words that make up a compound can help you figure out its meaning. For example, look at the words that make up *sundial*. Of course you know what the *sun* is, and you've seen a *dial* on a watch. A sundial has more in common with a watch than just its shape. Many years ago, a sundial was used to tell time. People figured out the time by measuring the shadow cast on the dial by the sun.

2. On the clipboards, draw a line between the words that make up each compound. Then use the words to figure out and write a meaning for each compound. If a compound has more than one meaning, find how it is used in the selection and write that meaning.

3. Save your work. You will refer to it again in the Vocabulary Check.

Strategy Builder

Summarizing Nonfiction

- As you know, every piece of nonfiction follows a particular organizational pattern. The main pattern of "Neighbors" is **description**. However, the author also uses sequence as he describes what happens to two neighboring families as a result of events during World War II.

- Sometimes when you read nonfiction, you're given a great deal of information at once. To keep the information straight—and to remember it better—you might stop from time to time and summarize what you've read. When you **summarize** a section of text, you list or retell the most important ideas in your own words.

- Read the following description of peasants from the selection "The Middle Ages." Then read how one student summarized the paragraphs.

Peasants

What would you notice about medieval peasants if you met them today? First, they would look dirty and would probably smell bad. It is difficult to keep clean and healthy if you live surrounded by farmyard mud. But they did try. Women washed clothes in streams, and in summer men and boys went swimming. (Women and girls could not take off their clothes in public.) Chewing twigs and rubbing salt into their gums was the only way they had to clean their teeth.

Second, you might think the peasants looked very old for their years. Hard work, hot sun, and winter winds made hands gnarled and skin rough and cracked. Accidents and diseases left unsightly scars or serious limps.

If we met medieval peasants today, here is what we'd notice about them:

1. They'd be dirty. They'd probably smell bad, too, because of all the farmyard mud they were surrounded by. But they did try to stay clean. Females washed clothes in streams, and in summer males went swimming. They also cleaned their teeth by chewing twigs and rubbing salt into their gums.

2. They'd look very old for their years. Hard work, the sun, and the wind gnarled their hands and made their skin rough. Accidents and diseases caused scars or limps.

Neighbors

by John Sherrill

As you read the first part of this selection, think about how you might summarize it. Jot down your ideas on a separate sheet of paper. When you get to the Strategy Break, you can compare your summary with the sample provided.

Once there was a man who loved roses. His name was Jiro Ninomiya. Mr. Ninomiya came to this country from Japan at the turn of the century and bought a few acres of land just northeast of San Francisco. There under a palm tree Mr. Ninomiya built a house for himself and his family. Behind his home he grew roses that each morning he trucked into San Francisco to be sold.

It happened that immediately across Route 17 from the Ninomiyas lived a second immigrant, a man named Frederick Aebi (pronounced A-bee), who had come to this country from Switzerland about the same time as Jiro Ninomiya. Like the Ninomiyas, the Aebis struggled to make a living growing quality roses on a strip of land behind their home.

The Ninomiyas and the Aebis were just the kind of **newcomers** who have given America its strength—hard-working, family-centered, churchgoing people (the Ninomiyas were Methodists; the Aebis, Lutherans). And they were raising their sons, Tamaki Ninomiya and Francis Aebi, with the same standards.

For three decades the rose-growing neighbors lived across from one another. By now Tamaki and Francis had taken over the rose farms. Both men worked too hard to do much

socializing, and neither family were great talkers, but each enjoyed the other's culture. The Aebis, for example, often admired a Japanese doll which the Ninomiyas kept in their living room: a dancer wearing an elaborate costume of black-and-white silk, encased in glass. The taciturn youngsters of the third generation were allowed to look at the doll, never to touch it.

In time both families became modestly successful; their roses were known in the markets of San Francisco for their long vase-life.

Then on December 7, 1941, Japan attacked the U.S. Naval Base at Pearl Harbor. And in California, reports of violence in nearby Richmond reached the truck farms out on Route 17: a Japanese car had been **overturned**, a Japanese **greenhouse** stoned. Rumors spread that soon Japanese people, especially those on the West Coast, were going to be rounded up and sent away to internment camps.

Francis Aebi, his wife, Carrie, and their two children walked across Route 17 and knocked on the door of Tamaki's house, under its palm tree. While skinny nine-year-old Lina Aebi stood looking at the dancing doll, her father spoke. "Tamaki," Francis said, "we've lived across from each other for a long time."

"Three generations," Tamaki said, glancing at his own five children.

"We are your neighbors," Francis Aebi said, and with that meaningful statement Francis went on to make clear that if need arose, he would look after the Ninomiya nursery. It was simply something that each family had learned in church: *Love thy neighbor as thyself.* "You would do the same for us," Francis said.

The possibility that Tamaki would be interned was not far-fetched.

Tamaki's wife, Hayane, was an American citizen. Their children were Americans too, but Tamaki was an alien; he had been born in Japan and never naturalized.

Meanwhile the fear and animosity grew. There were stories of stonings and boycotts not only of Japanese but also of those who befriended them.

⬟ **Stop here for the Strategy Break.**

Strategy Break

Did you jot down your summary as you read? If you did, see if it looks anything like this:

Two immigrants, Mr. Ninomiya from Japan and Mr. Aebi from Switzerland, lived across Route 17 from each other near San Francisco. For 30 years the Ninomiyas and the Aebis grew and sold roses. Eventually the older men turned their businesses over to their sons, who kept up the relationship and enjoyed each other's culture. The Aebis especially loved the Japanese doll that the Ninomiyas kept in their living room.

On December 7, 1941, Japan attacked Pearl Harbor, and things in California began to change. When rumors spread that Japanese people living on the West coast would be sent away to internment camps, Francis told Tamaki that he and his family would take care of the Ninomiyas' nursery if necessary. Tamaki's internment was not an impossibility, since he was not an American citizen.

Things grew worse. There were stories of stonings and boycotts of not only Japanese people but their friends as well.

➡ **Go on reading.**

On February 19, 1942, ten weeks after Pearl Harbor, President Roosevelt signed Executive Order 9066, providing for the designation of "military areas . . . from which any or all persons may be excluded." Speculation was that it might be

used to get Japanese people off the West Coast.

When the news of the Executive Order was broadcast, Tamaki and Hayane immediately paid a visit to the Aebis to discuss the quirks of the watering system in the Ninomiyas' greenhouse. They came carrying a gift-wrapped package:

the exquisite dancing doll in its glass case.

Little Lina jumped up and down in delight, but Francis had trouble finding words. "I couldn't possibly accept this, Tamaki," he finally said. "But we'll keep the doll safe until . . . things are back to normal."

Every day when the Aebis awoke, they checked to see if the Ninomiyas were still there. Then at noon one day in late February 1942 a black car pulled up to the Ninomiyas' home. Four men dressed in business suits went inside. Tamaki came in from the sorting shed. The Aebis watched from their front window as he was escorted to the car and driven off.

That same day, Hayane, the five children and old Jiro Ninomiya, Tamaki's father, went to live with friends in Livingston, which was farther from the coast; they reasoned it would not be considered a "sensitive area," and citizens of Japanese ancestry would be left alone. They loaded the pickup with clothes, a few pots and pans and some favorite toys, and drove away from the home that Jiro had built with his own hands. Hayane's last sight of their rose farm was of Francis, his work-worn wife, Carrie, and their two children, Lina and her older brother, standing under the palm tree waving **farewell**.

The move inland didn't help. On May 3, 1942, a new Civilian Exclusion Order was issued by the Western Defense Command. *All* persons of Japanese ancestry, citizens included, were to be evacuated from the area. Assistance would be granted for the disposition of property, such as real estate and automobiles. Evacuees were required to carry with them bedding, clothing and table articles, including a bowl for each member of the family. In August the Ninomiyas boarded a crowded train, having been told only that they were going east.

"East" turned out to be Granada, Colorado. The train stopped in the middle of a barren **landscape** from which the family was transported by truck to a relocation center of tarpaper-roofed barracks surrounded by barbed wire and armed guards.

While Hayane was trying to settle into the living space allotted each family in the barracks, her father-in-law came running in. He led the family outside and pointed excitedly to a sandy bit of ground. Each family had been given a plot of land, 10 feet by 50 feet, for a garden. "We'll grow flowers!" Jiro said. "Annuals," he added. "It takes years to grow roses. They won't keep us here that long."

Back in California Francis Aebi didn't mind the longer hours running two nurseries. But one thing he did mind. To qualify for a farmer's ration of fuel he had to **uproot** the roses and plant vegetables. In the Ninomiya greenhouses he planted cucumbers; in his own, tomatoes. In both, he left room for a few roses. "For tomorrow," he explained to his children.

Months passed. The whole Aebi family labored beside Francis. The children worked in the greenhouses before school, and on Saturdays they also had to work instead of going to Luther League at church. Even with their help, Francis's work stretched to 16, 17 hours a day.

A full year went by. Then two years. Then three. Occasionally a letter arrived from the internment camp. The best news was that after two and a half years Tamaki had been allowed to join his family again. Tamaki's only son, David, cried when this stranger picked him up.

Francis and Carrie and the children continued their exhausting labors, but at least Lina's brother was now 16, old enough to drive. That helped. Japanese property was still being vandalized, and Francis kept lights burning all night in the Ninomiya home across the way. Another child was born to the Ninomiyas in the camp. Hayane knit wool socks and sweaters for the Aebis.

At long, long last the war in Europe ended. Word came through the public address system in the relocation center cafeteria that the detainees were to be sent home. Once again they boarded a train.

In his letters Francis had reported that all was well at the Ninomiya nursery, but Tamaki wondered: Could that really be true? What would they actually find when they reached their rose farm?

Finally the train came to a stop in Richmond. There on the platform, waving his wide-brimmed hat in welcome, was a man so drawn and thin that his cheekbones showed. The oldest Ninomiya girl whispered reverently to little David, now five, "That's Mr. Aebi, our *neighbor!*"

Francis and Tamaki shook hands a bit awkwardly, as if they wanted to hug, but couldn't quite. There were so many Ninomiyas that Francis had brought along a friend to help transport them. The Ninomiyas piled their pots and pans into the vehicles and stared anxiously out the windows as Francis and his friend drove them through Richmond, then into the country and onto Route 17.

Finally they were turning into the crunchy drive, stopping beneath the palm tree in the front yard. Tamaki and Hayane got out, followed by Jiro and the children. They stared.

There was their nursery, intact, scrubbed and shining in the sunlight . . . looking neat, prosperous and healthy. And so was the balance in the bank passbook that Francis turned over to Tamaki.

Carrie Aebi came running across the road, followed by the Aebi children, who were not too old at 12 and 16 to dance their greeting. Together the families stepped into the Ninomiyas' home, which was as clean and welcoming as the nursery.

There on the dining room table was the dancing doll in its glass case. And next to it was one perfect red **rosebud**, just waiting to unfold—the gift of one neighbor to another. ●

Strategy Follow-up

Work with a small group of students to complete this activity. First, skim the second part of "Neighbors," and divide it into two or three sections. (Try to divide the sections at logical stopping points.) Assign each section to a pair or group of students. Then work with your partner or group to write a summary for your particular section of text. Be sure to use your own words, and include only the most important information. When everyone is finished, put the summaries in order and review them together. Revise any information as necessary.

✓Personal Checklist

Read each question and put a check (✓) in the correct box.

1. In Building Background, how well were you able to describe what makes a good neighbor?
   ☐ 3 (extremely well)
   ☐ 2 (fairly well)
   ☐ 1 (not well)

2. How well were you able to separate and define the compound words in the Vocabulary Builder?
   ☐ 3 (extremely well)
   ☐ 2 (fairly well)
   ☐ 1 (not well)

3. In the Strategy Follow-up, how well were you able to help write a summary for your section of text?
   ☐ 3 (extremely well)
   ☐ 2 (fairly well)
   ☐ 1 (not well)

4. Now that you've read this article, how well would you be able to explain why Japanese residents in the United States were placed in internment camps?
   ☐ 3 (extremely well)
   ☐ 2 (fairly well)
   ☐ 1 (not well)

5. How well do you understand why the Aebis helped their neighbors, the Ninomiyas?
   ☐ 3 (extremely well)
   ☐ 2 (fairly well)
   ☐ 1 (not well)

Vocabulary Check

Look back at the work you did in the Vocabulary Builder. Then answer each question by circling the correct letter.

1. Which of the following can be uprooted?
   a. people
   b. plants
   c. both of the above

2. Which word describes a person who attends worship services on a regular basis?
   a. churchgoing
   b. newcomers
   c. greenhouse

3. If greenhouses have a glass ceiling and glass windows, why are they called greenhouses?
   a. because they are used for growing greenery and keeping it healthy
   b. because they are painted green inside to make the flowers grow
   c. because the people who work in them wear green clothing

4. Why are Jiro Ninomiya and Frederick Aebi called newcomers in this selection?
   a. because they were new neighbors to each other on Route 17
   b. because they both arrived in the United States from other countries
   c. because they were very young men when they became neighbors

5. In the context of this selection, what does *overturned* mean?
   a. upset
   b. turned upside down
   c. made powerless

Add the numbers that you just checked to get your Personal Checklist score. Fill in your score here. Then turn to page 215 and transfer your score onto Graph 1.

	Personal
	Vocabulary
	Strategy
	Comprehension
TOTAL SCORE	✓ T

Check your answers with your teacher. Give yourself 1 point for each correct answer, and fill in your Vocabulary score here. Then turn to page 215 and transfer your score onto Graph 1.

	Personal
	Vocabulary
	Strategy
	Comprehension
TOTAL SCORE	✓ T

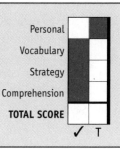

Strategy Check

Review the summary that you worked on in the Strategy Follow-up. Then answer these questions:

1. Why did the Aebis keep checking to see if the Ninomiyas were home?
   a. because they were afraid that Mr. Ninomiya would be sent away
   b. because the Ninomiyas were spies
   c. because the children wanted the Japanese doll

2. Which sentence best summarizes what some people thought of Executive Order 9066?
   a. They thought it might be used to help protect Japanese people on the West coast.
   b. They thought it might be used to force Japanese people to move to Japan.
   c. They thought it might be used to get Japanese people off the West coast.

3. Which sentence best summarizes why Tamaki's family went to live in Livingston?
   a. They thought that living with Tamaki was way too risky.
   b. They started a business in Livingston.
   c. They thought they'd be left alone, since the area was not "sensitive."

4. What summarizes the Civilian Exclusion Order issued by the Western Defense Command?
   a. All persons born in Japan but living in the States were to be interned.
   b. All persons of Japanese ancestry, including those born in the States, were to be interned.
   c. All persons of Japanese ancestry, excluding those born in the States, were to be interned.

5. Which sentence best summarizes this story?
   a. The Aebis acted like good neighbors.
   b. The Aebis and the Ninomiyas lived across Route 17 from each other for many years.
   c. Both families grew roses for many years.

Check your answers with your teacher. Give yourself 1 point for each correct answer, and fill in your Strategy score here. Then turn to page 215 and transfer your score onto Graph 1.

Personal
Vocabulary
Strategy
Comprehension
TOTAL SCORE
✓ T

Comprehension Check

Review the selection if necessary. Then answer these questions:

1. What possession of the Ninomiyas did the Aebi children like best?
   a. the Ninomiya children's favorite toys
   b. their greenhouse
   c. a Japanese dancer doll in a silk costume

2. Which of the following statements is false?
   a. The Aebis were more concerned about themselves than anyone else.
   b. The Aebis took risks for their neighbors.
   c. What the Aebis did for the Ninomiyas was unusual.

3. What conclusion can you draw from the sentences *There was their nursery . . . looking neat, prosperous, and healthy. And so was the balance in the bank passbook that Francis turned over to Tamaki?*
   a. Francis kept the accounts of the nurseries separate and returned to Tamaki all the profits that came from the Ninomiya nursery.
   b. Anything that Francis wrote in Tamaki's bank passbook was easy to read.
   c. Although the Aebis had worked hard to keep the Ninomiya nursery looking good, it hadn't made any money during the war years.

4. Why does the author use the word *reverently* in the sentence *The oldest Ninomiya girl whispered reverently, "That's Mr. Aebi, our neighbor!"?*
   a. to teach readers a new word
   b. to stress how much she respected Mr. Aebi
   c. to show that Mr. Aebi was a minister

5. If anyone had attacked the Ninomiya nursery, what would the Aebis have done?
   a. They would have tried to stop the violence.
   b. They would have watched from their home.
   c. They would have left the area.

Check your answers with your teacher. Give yourself 1 point for each correct answer, and fill in your Comprehension score here. Then turn to page 215 and transfer your score onto Graph 1.

Personal
Vocabulary
Strategy
Comprehension
TOTAL SCORE
✓ T

Extending

Choose one or both of these activities:

CREATE AN EXHIBIT

Using sources listed on this page or ones you find yourself, research the actions taken by the U.S. government against its Japanese residents during World War II. Put together a time line for the years that the internment camps existed, and mount it on one or more poster boards. Obtain short accounts of life at the camps, reproduce the accounts on separate sheets of paper, and attach them to the time line at appropriate points. Create a map showing the location of the camps, including the one at Granada, Colorado, at which the Ninomiyas were held. Also indicate where the events described in the posted accounts took place. If possible, obtain permission to display your exhibit in a school or public library.

INTERVIEW MEMBERS OF THE WORLD WAR II GENERATION

Most people in the United States at the time of the events described in this article were not aware of what was happening to Japanese citizens. They were more concerned with the progress of the war and their relatives on the battlefront. Interview several people who were teenaged or older by the end of World War II. With their permission, tape the interviews and play them for the class. Or write an article reporting on their memories of the war years here in the States.

Resources

Books

Adams, Ansel, photog., and John Hersey, writ. *Manzanar.* Ed. John Armor and Peter Wright. Times Books, 1988.

Alonso, Karen. *Korematsu v. United States: Japanese-American Internment Camps.* Landmark Supreme Court Cases. Enslow, 1998.

Axford, Roger W. *Too Long Been Silent: Japanese Americans Speak Out.* Media Publishing, 1986.

Brimner, Larry Dane. *Voices from the Camps: Internment of Japanese Americans During World War II.* Franklin Watts, 1994.

Denenberg, Larry. *The Journal of Ben Uchida: Citizen 13559, Mirror Lake Internment Camp.* My Name Is America. Scholastic, 1999.

Stanley, Jerry. *I Am an American: A True Story of the Japanese Internment.* Crown, 1996.

Uchido, Yoshiko. *The Bracelet.* Bt Bound, 2000.

Web Sites

http://www.children-of-the-camps.org/
This is the Web site for the documentary film *Children of the Camps.* Click on the "History" link for background information, including a time line of the World War II years.

http://www.momomedia.com/CLPEF/camps.html
This Web page offers photographs and short descriptions of the internment camps and detention centers where people of Japanese descent were held during World War II.

Viva New Jersey

anemic

bolted

cantina

exotic

panoramic

pitched

qué pasó

CLIPBOARD 1
Spanish Words

CLIPBOARD 2
Verbs

bolted:

pitched:

CLIPBOARD 3
Adjectives

Building Background

Every piece of writing has at least one **theme**, or message. Different writers may have different ideas about the same theme, and they may use different forms of writing to present their ideas. For example, the selection you just read, "Neighbors," is a nonfiction account that illustrates how neighbors can become good friends. "Viva New Jersey" is a fictional story about a girl who is new to her neighborhood and wants to make friends. As you read, compare the two writers' ideas about friendship. Before you read, however, consider your own ideas about friendship. What have you felt and done when you've wanted to make new friends? In the box below, write at least six words or phrases that describe your feelings or experiences.

Feelings Related to Making Friends

Vocabulary Builder

1. The words in the margin are from "Viva New Jersey." Before you read the story, discover how much you know about these words by sorting them into different categories. First, identify which terms come from Spanish, and write them on the first clipboard.

2. Next, identify two words that have multiple meanings. Write those words on the second clipboard, along with at least two definitions for each word.

3. Last, write the words that are adjectives on the third clipboard.

4. On your clipboards for Spanish words and adjectives, put a check (✔) next to each word whose meaning you know. As you read, watch for all the boldfaced words. Compare your definitions for the words with their meanings given in the story.

5. Save your work. You will refer to it again in the Vocabulary Check.

Strategy Builder

Making Predictions While You Read

- As you may remember from reading "Priscilla and the Wimps," you can understand a story better when you try to **predict**, or guess, what will happen next. When you predict, you pay attention to clues that the author gives, and you try to make connections between them. Then you use what you know to make your predictions.

- Some of the clues that an author might give you are **story elements**. For example, if you know that a story's **setting** is a desert island, you can suppose that whatever happens will involve water, sand, tropical weather conditions, and/or the plants and animals found in such a place.

- What the **characters** do for a living might help you make predictions too. Also, consider the conflict, or **problem**, that the main character faces. If you were in that character's place, what might you do? Use that knowledge to help you make your prediction.

- Still another clue that an author might provide is the **title** of a story. Look, for example, at the title of this story. In movies involving kings, you may have heard the cheer "Long live the king!" The Spanish word *viva* means "long live," so the title of this story means "Long Live New Jersey!" What might this title have to do with the main character and her problem?

Viva New Jersey

by Gloria Gonzalez

As you begin reading, keep the story elements and the title in mind, and look for context clues to help you predict what might happen next.

As far as dogs go, it wasn't much of a prize—a hairy mongrel with clumps of bubble gum wadded on its belly. Pieces of multicolored hard candies were matted in its fur. The leash around its neck was fashioned from a cloth belt, the kind usually seen attached to old bathrobes. The dog's paws were clogged with mud from yesterday's rain, and you could see where the animal had gnawed at the irritated skin around the swollen pads.

The dog was tied to an **anemic** tree high above the cliffs overlooking the Hudson River and the majestic New York City skyline.

Lucinda traveled the route each day on her way to the high school, along the New Jersey side of the river. The short walk saddened her, despite its **panoramic** vista of bridges and sky-scrapers, for the river reminded her of the perilous journey six months earli-er, when she and her family had escaped from Cuba in a makeshift boat with seven others.

They had spent two freezing nights adrift in the ocean, uncertain of their destination, till a U.S. Coast Guard cutter towed them to the shores of Key West.

From there they wound their way north, staying temporarily with friends in Miami and finally settling in West New York, New Jersey, the most densely populated town in the United States. Barely a square mile, high above the Palisades, the town boasted a population of 85,000. Most of the community was housed in mammoth apartment buildings that seemed to reach into the clouds. The few private homes had cement lawns and paved driveways where there should have been backyards.

Lucinda longed for the spacious front porch where she'd sat at night with her friends while her grandmoth-er bustled about the house, humming her Spanish songs. Lucinda would ride her bike to school and sometimes not see a soul for miles, just wild flowers amid a forest of greenery.

Now it was cement and cars and trucks and motorcycles and clanging fire engines that seemed to be in con-stant motion, shattering the air with their menacing roar.

Lucinda longed painfully for her grandmother. The old woman had refused to leave her house in Cuba, despite the family's pleas, so she had remained behind, promising to see them again one day.

The teenager, tall and slight of build with long dark hair that reached down her spine, was uncomfortable among her new classmates, most of whom she towered over. Even though the majori-ty of them spoke Spanish and came from Cuba, Argentina, and Costa Rica, they were not like any of her friends back home. These "American" girls wore heavy makeup to school, dressed in jeans and high heels, and talked about rock singers and TV stars that she knew nothing of. They all seemed to be busy, rushing through the school corridors, huddling in laughing groups, mingling freely with boys, and chatting openly with teachers as if they were personal friends.

It was all too confusing.

Things weren't much better at home. Her parents had found jobs almost immediately and were often away from the tiny, cramped apartment. Her brother quickly made friends and was picked for the school baseball team, traveling to nearby towns to compete.

All Lucinda had were her memories—and now this dog, whom she untied from the tree. The animal was frightened and growled at her when she approached, but she spoke softly and offered a soothing hand, which he tried to attack. Lucinda persisted, and the dog, perhaps grateful to be freed from the mud puddles, allowed her to lead him away.

She didn't know what she was going to do with him now that she had him. Pets were not allowed in her building, and her family could be evicted. She couldn't worry about that now. Her main concern was to get him out of the cold.

Even though it was April and supposedly spring, the weather had yet to top fifty degrees. At night she slept under two blankets, wearing warm socks over her cold feet. Another night outdoors, and the dog could freeze to death.

Lucinda reached her building and comforted the dog, "I'm not going to hurt you." She took off her jacket and wrapped it quickly around the animal, hoping to disguise it as a bundle under her arm. "Don't make any noise," she begged.

She waited till a woman with a baby stroller exited the building and quickly dashed inside, unseen. She opted not to take the elevator, fearful of running into someone, and instead lugged the dog and her schoolbag up the eight flights of stairs.

Lucinda quickly unlocked the apartment door and plopped the dog on her bed. The animal instantly shook its hair free and ran in circles atop her blanket.

"Don't get too comfortable," Lucinda cautioned. "You can't stay."

She dashed to the kitchen and returned moments later with a bowl of water and a plate of leftover chicken and yellow rice.

The dog **bolted** from the bed and began attacking the food before she even placed it on the floor. The girl sat on the edge of the bed and watched contentedly as he devoured the meal.

"How long has it been since you've eaten?"

The dog swallowed the food hungrily, not bothering to chew, and quickly lapped up the water.

It was then, with the dog's head lowered to the bowl, that Lucinda spotted the small piece of paper wedged beneath the belt around its neck. She slid it out carefully and saw the word that someone had scrawled with a pencil.

"Chauncey. Is that your name?"

The dog leaped to her side and nuzzled its nose against her arm.

"It's a crazy name, but I think I like it." She smiled. Outside the window, eight stories below, two fire engines pierced the afternoon with wailing sirens. Lucinda didn't seem to notice as she stroked the animal gently.

Working quickly, before her parents were due to arrive, she filled the bathtub with water and soap detergent and scrubbed the animal clean. The dog didn't enjoy it—he kept trying to jump out—so Lucinda began humming a Spanish song her grandmother used to sing to her when she was little. It didn't work. Chauncey still fought to get free.

Once the animal was bathed, Lucinda attacked the clumps of hair with a scissor and picked out the sticky globs of candy.

"My God, you're white!" Lucinda discovered. While using her brother's hair blower, she ran a quick comb through the fur, which now was silvery and tan with faint traces of black. "You're beautiful." The girl beamed.

The dog seemed to agree. It picked up its head proudly and flicked its long ears with pride.

Lucinda hugged him close. "I'll find you a good home. I promise," she told the animal.

Knowing that her parents would arrive any moment, Lucinda gathered up the dog, covering him with her coat, and carried him down nine flights to the basement. She crept quietly past the superintendent's apartment and deposited the animal in a tiny room behind the bank of washing machines.

The room, the size of a small closet, contained all the electrical levers that supplied power to the apartments and the elevator.

Chauncey looked about, confused. He jumped up as if he knew he was about to be abandoned again. His white hairy paw came dangerously close to hitting the protruding, red master switch near the door.

Lucinda knelt to the animal. "I'll be back. Promise."

She closed the door behind her, praying the dog wouldn't bark, and hurried away. An outline of a plan was taking shape in her mind.

Ashley.

The girl sat in front of her in English and always went out of her way to say hi. She didn't seem to hang out with the other kids, and whenever they passed in the corridor, she was alone. But what really made her even more appealing was that she lived in a real house. Just a block away. Lucinda had seen her once going in. Maybe Ashley would take Chauncey.

 Stop here for Strategy Break #1.

Strategy Break #1

1. What do you predict will happen next? _____

_____

2. Why do you think so? _____

_____

3. What clues from the story helped you make your prediction(s)? _____

_____

_____

 Go on reading to see what happens.

Lucinda's parents arrived from work, and she quickly helped her mother prepare the scrumptious fried bananas. Her father had stopped at a restaurant on his way home and brought a *cantina* of food—white rice, black beans, avocado salad, and meat stew. Each food was placed in its own metal container and clipped together like a small pyramid. The local restaurant would have delivered the food to the house each day, if the family desired, but Lucinda's father always liked to stop by and check the menu. The restaurant also made fried bananas, but Lucinda's mother didn't think they were as tasty as her own. One of the nice surprises of moving to New Jersey was discovering that the Latin restaurants supplied *cantina* service.

"How was school today?" her mother asked.

"Okay," Lucinda replied.

The dinner conversation drifted, as it always did, to Mama's problems at work with the supervisor and Papa's frustration with his job. Every day he had to ride two buses and a subway to get to work, which he saw as wasted hours.

"You get an education, go to college," Lucinda's father sermonized for the thousandth time, "and you can work anywhere you like—even in your own house, if you want. Like a doctor! And if it is far away, you hire someone like me, with no education, to drive you."

Lucinda had grown up hearing the lecture. Perhaps she would have been a good student anyway, for she certainly took to it with enthusiasm. She had discovered books at a young age. School only heightened her love of reading, for its library supplied her with an endless source of material. She excelled in her studies and won top honors in English class. She was so proficient at learning the English language that she served as a tutor to kids in lower grades.

Despite her father's wishes, Lucinda had no intention of becoming a doctor or lawyer. She wasn't sure what she would do—the future seemed far too distant to address it—but she knew somehow it would involve music and dance and magnificent costumes and glittering shoes and plumes in her hair.

They were talking about her brother's upcoming basketball game when suddenly all the lights in the apartment went out.

"*Qué pasó!*" her father exclaimed.

Agitated voices could be heard from the outside hallway. A neighbor banged on the door, shouting, "Call the fire department! Someone's trapped in the elevator!"

Groups of tenants mingled outside their apartments, some carrying candles and flashlights. The building had been **pitched** into darkness.

"We'll get you out!" someone shouted to the woman caught between floors.

Lucinda cried: "Chauncey!"

He must've hit the master switch. She could hear the distant wail of the fire engines and knew it was only a matter of minutes before they checked the room where the dog was hidden.

"I'll be right back!" Lucinda yelled to her mother as she raced out the door. Groping onto the banister, she felt her way down the flights of steps as people with candles hurried to escape.

The rescuers reached the basement before she did. Two firemen were huddled in the doorway checking the power supply. Lucinda looked frantically for the dog, but he was gone.

She raced out into the nippy night, through the throng of people crowded on the sidewalk, and searched for the dog. She was afraid to look in the street, expecting to see his lifeless body, the victim of a car.

Lucinda looked up at the sound of her name. Her mother was calling to her from the window.

"Come home! What are you doing?"

The girl shouted, "In a minute!" The crowd swelled about her as she quickly darted away.

Lucinda didn't plan it, but she found herself in front of Ashley's house minutes later. She was on the sidewalk, with the rest of her neighbors, gazing up the block at the commotion in front of Lucinda's building.

"Hi," Lucinda stammered.

Ashley took a moment to place the face and then returned the smile. "Hi."

Lucinda looked about nervously, wondering if any of the adults belonged to Ashley's family. She didn't have a moment to waste.

"What happens," she blurted out, "when a dog runs away? Do the police catch it?"

The blond, chubby teenager, with light green eyes and glasses with pink frames, shrugged. "Probably. If they do, they only take it to the pound."

"What's that?" It sounded bad, whatever it was.

"A shelter. Where they keep animals. If nobody claims 'em, they kill 'em."

Lucinda started to cry. She couldn't help it. It came upon her suddenly. Greatly embarrassed, she turned quickly and hurried away.

"Wait up!" The blonde hurried after her. "Hey!"

Lucinda stopped, too ashamed to meet her eyes.

"Did you lose your dog?" Ashley's voice sounded concerned.

Lucinda nodded.

"Well, let's go find him," Ashley prodded.

They searched the surrounding neighborhood and checked underneath all the cars parked in the area in case he was hiding. They searched basements and rooftops. When all else failed, they walked to the park along the river, where Lucinda pointed out the tree where she had found him.

The girls decided to sit on a nearby bench in case Chauncey reappeared, though they realized there was little hope.

 Stop here for Strategy Break #2.

Strategy Break #2

1. What do you predict will happen next? _____

   _____

2. Why do you think so? _____

   _____

3. What clues from the story helped you make your prediction(s)? _____

   _____

   _____

 Go on reading to see what happens.

Lucinda knew her mother would be frantically worried.

"She probably has the police looking for me," she told Ashley.

"You've only been gone an hour."

"It's the first time I've left the house, except to go to school, since we moved here."

It was a beautiful night, despite the cold tingling breeze that swept up from the river. The New York skyline was ablaze with golden windows silhouetted against dark, boxlike steel structures. You could make out the red traffic lights along the narrow streets. A long, thin barge sailed down the river like a rubbery snake.

Lucinda learned that Ashley's mother was a lawyer, often away from home for long periods, and her father operated a small business in New York's Chinatown, which kept him busy seven days a week. An only child, she spent her time studying and writing letters.

"Who do you write to?" Lucinda asked.

"My grandmother, mostly. She lives in Nevada. I spend the summers with her."

Lucinda told her how lucky she was to be able to see her grandmother. She felt dangerously close to tears again and quickly changed the subject. "I never see you with any friends in school. Why?"

Ashley shrugged. "Guess I'm not the friendly type. Most of the girls are only interested in boys and dates. I intend to be a famous writer one day, so there's a lot of books I have to read. Just so I know what's been done."

It made sense.

"What are you going to be?"

Lucinda admitted she had no ambition. No particular desire. But maybe, if she had her choice, if she could be anything she wanted, it would probably be a dancer.

"My grandmother used to take me to her friend's house who used to be a famous ballerina in Cuba. She'd let me try on her costumes, and she'd play the records and teach me the steps. It hurt my feet something awful. Hers used to bleed when she first started, but she said it got easier after the first year."

Ashley told her, "You have the body for it. I bet you'd make a wonderful dancer."

When it became apparent that Chauncey would never return, the girls walked home together.

Despite all that had happened, Lucinda found herself sad to have the evening end. For the first time since leaving her homeland, she felt somewhat at peace with herself. She now had someone to talk to. Someone who understood. Someone who carried her own pain.

"Wanna have lunch tomorrow?" Ashley asked her. "I usually run home and eat in front of the television. I'm a great cook. My first book is going to be filled with **exotic** recipes of all the countries I plan to visit. And if you want," she gushed excitedly, "after school we can go to the library. You can get out a book on how to be a ballerina."

Lucinda agreed immediately. "That would be wonderful!"

The girls parted on the sidewalk, and Lucinda raced home where her irate father and weeping mother confronted her angrily.

"Where have you been! I was only going to wait five more minutes and then I was calling the police! Where were you?"

Before she could stammer a reply, the lights went out.

"Not again!" her mother shrieked.

Lucinda's heart throbbed with excitement.

Chauncey was back!

She ran out of the apartment, unmindful of the darkness, with her mother's screams in the air: "Come back here!"

This time Lucinda made it to the basement before the firemen, and she led her pal safely out of the building. She reached Ashley's doorstep just as the first fire engine turned the corner. ●

Strategy Follow-up

Now go back and look at the predictions that you wrote in this lesson. Do any of them match what actually happened in this story? Why or why not?

✓Personal Checklist

Read each question and put a check (✓) in the correct box.

1. How well were you able to use what you wrote in Building Background to help you understand Lucinda's feelings and actions?
    - ☐ 3 (extremely well)
    - ☐ 2 (fairly well)
    - ☐ 1 (not well)

2. In the Vocabulary Builder, how many words were you able to classify correctly?
    - ☐ 3 (6–7 words)
    - ☐ 2 (3–5 words)
    - ☐ 1 (0–2 words)

3. How well were you able to use context clues to help you predict as you read?
    - ☐ 3 (extremely well)
    - ☐ 2 (fairly well)
    - ☐ 1 (not well)

4. How well were you able to use story elements and the story's title to help you predict as you read?
    - ☐ 3 (extremely well)
    - ☐ 2 (fairly well)
    - ☐ 1 (not well)

5. How well do you understand Lucinda's mood at the end of the story, as well as the reasons for it?
    - ☐ 3 (extremely well)
    - ☐ 2 (fairly well)
    - ☐ 1 (not well)

Vocabulary Check

Look back at the work you did in the Vocabulary Builder. Then answer each question by circling the correct letter.

1. Which group of words contains all adjectives?
    - a. anemic, bolt, cantina
    - b. anemic, exotic, scrumptious
    - c. panoramic, viva, pitch

2. Using context clues to help you, what do you think the Spanish phrase *qué pasó* means?
    - a. "Oh, no!"
    - b. "Who's there?"
    - c. "What happened?"

3. In the sentence *The building had been pitched into darkness*, what is the meaning of *pitched*?
    - a. thrown
    - b. made a high sound
    - c. tried to sell

4. Which of these statements is false?
    - a. *Anemic*, meaning "weak" or "sickly," comes from the word *anemia*.
    - b. *Panoramic*, meaning "scenic," comes from the word *panorama*.
    - c. *Scrumptious*, meaning "splendid," comes from the word *scrumpt*.

5. Which of these adjectives describes a wide, unbroken view?
    - a. panoramic
    - b. exotic
    - c. anemic

Add the numbers that you just checked to get your Personal Checklist score. Fill in your score here. Then turn to page 215 and transfer your score onto Graph 1.

Personal	
Vocabulary	
Strategy	
Comprehension	
TOTAL SCORE	✓ T

Check your answers with your teacher. Give yourself 1 point for each correct answer, and fill in your Vocabulary score here. Then turn to page 215 and transfer your score onto Graph 1.

Personal	
Vocabulary	
Strategy	
Comprehension	
TOTAL SCORE	✓ T

Strategy Check

Review what you wrote at each Strategy Break. Then answer these questions:

1. What supported the prediction that Chauncey's hiding place was going to be a problem?
    a. She . . . deposited the animal in a tiny room behind the bank of washing machines.
    b. His white hairy paw came dangerously close to hitting the protruding, red master switch.
    c. Lucinda knelt to the animal. "I'll be back."

2. Which clue helped you predict that Chauncey probably wouldn't stay in one place?
    a. Chauncey was a hairy mongrel with clumps of bubble gum wadded on his belly.
    b. He swallowed the food hungrily, and quickly lapped up the water.
    c. He jumped up as if he knew he was about to be abandoned again.

3. Which clue would have best supported your prediction that the story would end happily?
    a. Lucinda ran out of the apartment building.
    b. The girls had searched everywhere without finding Chauncey.
    c. The title of the story suggests that someone is happy with New Jersey.

4. Which clue from the story best suggests that Ashley would become Lucinda's friend?
    a. The blond, chubby teenager, with light green eyes and glasses with pink frames, shrugged.
    b. "Did you lose your dog?" Ashley's voice sounded concerned.
    c. "Guess I'm not the friendly type."

5. Which of these is the most logical prediction for Lucinda's future?
    a. She will become a world-famous ballerina.
    b. She will be happy because she has a friend.
    c. She will leave home to live with Ashley.

Check your answers with your teacher. Give yourself 1 point for each correct answer, and fill in your Strategy score here. Then turn to page 215 and transfer your score onto Graph 1.

Personal
Vocabulary
Strategy
Comprehension
TOTAL SCORE
✓ T

Comprehension Check

Review the story if necessary. Then answer these questions:

1. Why doesn't Lucinda know the girls in her class?
    a. She'd rather spend time with her dog.
    b. She doesn't know how to speak English.
    c. She is not used to American ways.

2. From where did Lucinda and her family escape?
    a. Key West
    b. Miami
    c. Cuba

3. Why does Lucinda take Chauncey home when she knows dogs aren't allowed in the building?
    a. She knows how Chauncey feels, and she wants a friend.
    b. She likes having a little danger in her life.
    c. She's angry with her parents and wants to cause trouble.

4. What does Lucinda miss most about Cuba?
    a. the warmer weather
    b. her bicycle
    c. her grandmother

5. At the end of the story, why does Lucinda's heart "throb with excitement"?
    a. She's extremely afraid of the dark.
    b. She thinks everyone will blame her for the power outage.
    c. She is happy that Chauncey is back.

Check your answers with your teacher. Give yourself 1 point for each correct answer, and fill in your Comprehension score here. Then turn to page 215 and transfer your score onto Graph 1.

Personal
Vocabulary
Strategy
Comprehension
TOTAL SCORE
✓ T

Extending

Choose one or more of these activities:

RESEARCH CUBAN-AMERICAN RELATIONS

How long has the United States been on poor terms with Cuba? How long have Cuban citizens been risking their lives to come to the United States in makeshift boats? Why have they been doing this? Find out about the political situation in Cuba. Then present what you learn in an oral or written report.

DISCOVER CUBAN CELEBRITIES

In this story Lucinda hopes to become a ballerina, partly because she had met a famous ballerina when she lived in Cuba. With some of your classmates, make a list of several people of Cuban descent who have became famous in their fields. Then choose one of those people and research his or her life. Put together a booklet with the rest of your classmates that gives brief "celebrity bios" for the people everyone researched.

RESEARCH WHAT HAPPENS TO STRAY DOGS

How many dogs are abandoned in your area in a typical week? What happens to them? How can this situation be improved? Find answers to these and your own questions on the topic, and create a one-minute public service announcement about this issue. If possible, make your announcement over the school's public-address system.

Resources

Books

Brown, Warren. *Fidel Castro: Cuban Revolutionary.* Millbrook Press, 1994.

Gonzales, Doreen. *Gloria Estefan: Singer and Entertainer.* Hispanic Biographies. Enslow, 1998.

Gonzalez, Gloria. *The Glad Man.* Knopf, 1975.

Goodnough, David. *José Martí: Cuban Patriot and Poet.* Hispanic Biographies. Enslow, 1996.

Kehret, Peg. *Shelter Dogs: Amazing Stories of Adopted Strays.* Whitman, 2003.

Papurt, Myrna L. *Saved! A Guide to Success with Your Shelter Dog.* Barron's Educational Series, 1997.

Rice, Earle, Jr. *The Cuban Revolution.* World History. Lucent Books, 1995.

Web Sites

http://www.spcaec.com/stray_animals/stray_animals.php3
On this Web page, a local SPCA explains its policy on stray animals.

http://www.uscubacommission.org/history.html
This Web site offers a time line of U.S.-Cuba relations.

Audio Recording

Cooder, Ry. *Buena Vista Social Club.* Nonesuch, 1997.

Learning New Words

Suffixes

A suffix is a word part that is added to the end of a root word. When you add a suffix, you often change the root word's meaning and function. For example, the suffix *-less* means "without," so the root word *life* changes from a noun to an adjective meaning "without life."

-ous

The suffix *-ous* turns nouns into adjectives that mean "full of _____" or "like _____." For example, in "The Night the Bed Fell" the narrator describes the bed he has to sleep in as perilous. The word *perilous* means "full or peril, or danger."
   Write the word that each definition describes.

1. full of (or having) joy   _____

2. like thunder   _____

3. full of danger   _____

4. full of zeal, or eagerness   _____

-ic

The suffix *-ic* is similar to *-ous* in that it also turns nouns into adjectives. Words ending in *-ic* mean "having the nature of _____" or having to do with _____."
   Complete each sentence with one of the words below.

heroic   alcoholic   rhythmic   volcanic

1. Restaurants cannot serve _____ beverages without a license.

2. Our car's windshield wipers made a _____ sound as they moved back and forth.

3. The TV program honored people who performed _____ acts while in the line of duty.

4. The _____ eruption shot ashes and lava for miles in every direction.

Compound Words

A compound word is made up of two words put together. In the story "Neighbors" you read that both Jiro Ninomiya and Frederick Aebi were newcomers to America. *Newcomers* is a compound word that refers to people who are newly arrived or recently arrived at a place.

Fill in each blank with a compound word by combining a word from Row 1 with a word from Row 2.

Row 1:   trust   toad   thunder   letter

Row 2:   stool   head   worthy   bolt

1. flash of lightning = _____

2. (usually poisonous) mushroom = _____

3. reliable and dependable = _____

4. words printed at the top of a paper = _____

Multiple-Meaning Words

You know that a single word can have more than one meaning. To figure out which meaning an author is using, you have to use context. Context is the information surrounding a word or situation that helps you understand it.

Use context to figure out the correct meaning of each underlined word. Circle the letter of the correct meaning.

1. The dancers moved across the <u>stage</u> with grace and skill.

   a.   raised platform where performances are held

   b.   step in a process or period of development

2. Highway robbers used to <u>plunder</u> people traveling in stagecoaches.

   a.   household goods

   b.   rob by force

3. We experienced turbulence when our plane hit some rough <u>pockets</u>.

   a.   small bags or pouches

   b.   areas or sections of air

VOCABULARY

From Lesson 9
- churchgoing
- farewell
- greenhouse
- newcomers
- overturned
- rosebud
- uproot

From Lesson 7
- rivets
- label
- leg
- pockets

From Lesson 8
- balks
- bottoms
- lean
- mast
- plunder
- stage
- virgin

From Lesson 10
- bolted
- pitched

Wilma Rudolph: Triumph in Rome

Building Background

In 1960, when the events of this selection took place, Wilma Rudolph was 20 years old. At age four, she had suffered an attack of double pneumonia and scarlet fever, followed by polio.

One of the people Rudolph most admired was another runner, Jesse Owens. Owens had competed in the 1936 Olympics held in Berlin—the last Olympics before World War II. African-American Owens embarrassed Adolph Hitler. Owens won four gold medals: in the 100-meter race, the 200-meter race, the broad jump (now called the long jump), and as a member of the team that won the 400-meter relay. In two of those victories he set world records; at other competitions, he set five more world records.

adulation

arrogant

clamor

depression

disqualified

formidable

intimidated

jubilant

malicious

Vocabulary Builder

1. As you may recall, **synonyms** are words with the same or similar meanings. **Antonyms** are words with opposite meanings. Knowing the synonym or antonym of a word can help you learn and remember the word better.

2. Using the synonym and antonym in each row, figure out which vocabulary word belongs in the first column, and write it in the chart below.

3. If you are not sure where some of the vocabulary words belong, find them in the selection and use context to figure them out. If using context doesn't help, look up the words in a dictionary.

Vocabulary Word	Synonym	Antonym
1.	joyful	sorrowful
2.	dip	hill
3.	proud	humble
4.	ruled out	made fit
5.	constant noise	silence
6.	flattery	insult
7.	frightened	reassured
8.	hateful	loving
9.	fearsome	powerless

4. Save your work. You will refer to it again in the Vocabulary Check.

How to Read a Biographical Sketch

- A **biography** is the story of a real person's life, as written by someone else. A **biographical sketch** is the story of a part of a real person's life.

- A biographical sketch is always written in the **third-person point of view**. That means that the author describes a part of a person's life using words such as *she, he, her, his, they,* and *theirs.*

- Like every other type of nonfiction, a biographical sketch follows a particular pattern of organization. Since a biographical sketch describes events in the order in which they happened, it follows the pattern of **sequence**. To make that sequence as clear as possible, authors often use **signal words**. Examples of signal words are *yesterday, several hours later,* and *the next morning.*

- As you read the following paragraph, pay attention to the sequence of events. Use the underlined signal words to help you.

<u>Yesterday</u> Tara searched through her grandmother's trunk in the attic. <u>First</u> she opened the trunk with a special key that hung on a hook by the steps. <u>After she lifted the lid</u>, she studied a photograph of her grandmother as a young woman. <u>Then</u> she searched through her grandmother's old clothes and found a pretty sweater. <u>When she tried it on</u>, Tara looked at herself in the mirror. "You sure don't look like yourself in this sweater," Tara said to herself, "but you *do* look familiar." Tara glanced at the photo <u>again</u>. <u>Finally</u>, she realized who she looked like—her grandmother.

- If you wanted to show the sequence of events in the paragraph above, you could use a **sequence chain**. It would look like this:

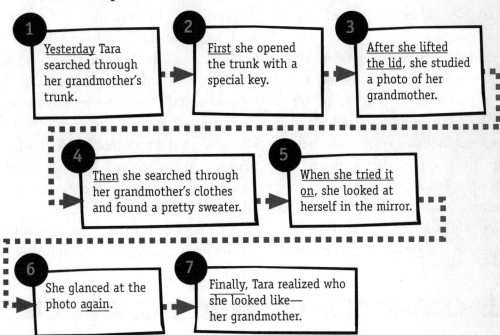

Wilma Rudolph: Triumph in Rome

by Tom Biracree

As you read the first part of this biographical sketch, apply the strategies that you just learned. Underline the signal words as you read. They will give you a more exact picture of the order in which things happened.

The U.S. Olympic team arrived in Rome well ahead of schedule, so they would have plenty of time to work out. The temperature hovered at the 100-degree mark, which severely hampered some of the athletes from northern countries. But for Wilma Rudolph and the Tigerbelles, the climate was comfortable—no worse than the Tennessee summers they were used to. The advantages seemed to be stacking up on their side.

But then, the Tuesday before the competition began, Rudolph suffered an injury. She was jogging across a field when she hit a small **depression** and fell, her ankle popping.

Would she be able to compete? The team doctor could not say. Her ankle seemed to be strained, not sprained or broken. He told her to keep off it for a few days.

Crushed at the prospect of missing her big chance, Rudolph followed his orders strictly. To keep her mind off her injury, she renewed her old friendships from Melbourne, met the new competitors, and as always, signed autographs for young fans.

Fortunately her injury responded to the rest, and she was well enough to compete in the 100- and 200-meter

dashes. Both of them were run on straight, smooth tracks that put minimal strain on her ankle. She easily won her first qualifying heat in the 100-meter dash.

After her victory, she was so relaxed that when she stretched out on the infield to rest, she fell asleep. Her calmness stunned her fellow competitors.

Then came the second heat, when Rudolph really proved that she was a contender to be reckoned with. She seemed to fly down the straightaway, tying the world record of 11.3 seconds held by Australian Shirley Strickland. By the finals, Rudolph's speed and grace had already made her a favorite of the Rome crowd, and they cheered wildly when she flew to victory in the finals of the 100-meter dash in an astounding 11.0 seconds.

It was a world-record time for the 100-meter dash—or would have been. Unfortunately, during the race, the wind behind Rudolph was blowing at 2.752 meters per second, just a little faster than the accepted standard of 2.0 meters per second. Because of the strong following wind, her time was **disqualified** for a world record.

The next competition was the 200-meter dash, and again Rudolph was the odds-on favorite. She was delighted when she won the first heat in an Olympic record time of 23.2 seconds. In the finals, her time was slower—24.0 seconds, but still fast enough to easily defeat Jutta Heine of Germany, her most **formidable** competitor. And fast enough to earn Rudolph her second gold medal.

With the attention of the entire world now focused on Rudolph, the Tigerbelles pushed on to the 400-meter relay. The four women responded to the pressure by setting a new world-record time in the qualifying heats. Joining them in the final were teams from Germany, Italy, the Soviet Union, Great Britain, and Poland. Rudolph's major concern about the final was her ankle—running on the curved relay track taxed its strength, and it hurt from the arduous qualifying heats. Then, too, there was always the fear that one of the Tigerbelles would drop the baton.

The first two U.S. runners gave the team a 2-yard lead at the 200-meter mark. Ironically, Germany's third runner was Brunhilde Hendrix. Her mother, Marie Dollinger, had been the third runner on the German 400-meter relay team in 1936—the year of Jesse Owens's triumph. It was Dollinger who had made the bad handoff to the anchor in the finals, losing the race and shaming Germany's **arrogant** leader, Adolf Hitler. For her daughter, however, there would be no fumbling; Hendrix handed off successfully to Jutta Heine.

Instead it would be Rudolph who fumbled, bobbling the handoff from Lucinda Williams and nearly dropping the baton. By the time she recovered, Jutta Heine and Russia's Irina Press had taken over the lead. But then, with a spectacular burst of speed, Rudolph pulled abreast of her competitors, passed them, and exploded across the finish line three-tenths of a second ahead of Press. The Tigerbelles were the **jubilant** victors—and Rudolph had won her third gold medal.

Rudolph described the first sweet moments of triumph in her autobiography:

The feeling of accomplishment welled up inside me . . . three Olympic gold medals. I knew that was something nobody could ever take away from me, ever. After the playing of "The Star-Spangled Banner," I came away from the victory stand and I was mobbed. People were jumping all over me, pushing microphones into my face, pounding my back. I couldn't believe it. Finally the American officials grabbed me and escorted me to safety. One of them said, "Wilma, life will never be the same for you again." He was so right.

⬢ **Stop here for the Strategy Break.**

Strategy Break

If you were to arrange the major events in this biographical sketch so far, your sequence chain might look like this:

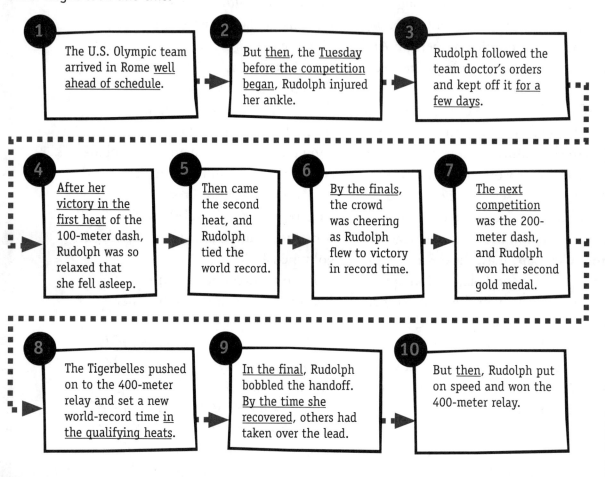

1 The U.S. Olympic team arrived in Rome <u>well ahead of schedule</u>.

2 But <u>then</u>, the <u>Tuesday before the competition began</u>, Rudolph injured her ankle.

3 Rudolph followed the team doctor's orders and kept off it <u>for a few days</u>.

4 <u>After her victory in the first heat</u> of the 100-meter dash, Rudolph was so relaxed that she fell asleep.

5 <u>Then</u> came the second heat, and Rudolph tied the world record.

6 <u>By the finals</u>, the crowd was cheering as Rudolph flew to victory in record time.

7 <u>The next competition</u> was the 200-meter dash, and Rudolph won her second gold medal.

8 The Tigerbelles pushed on to the 400-meter relay and set a new world-record time <u>in the qualifying heats</u>.

9 <u>In the final</u>, Rudolph bobbled the handoff. <u>By the time she recovered</u>, others had taken over the lead.

10 But <u>then</u>, Rudolph put on speed and won the 400-meter relay.

 **Go on reading.**

Rudolph was now the darling of the world press. Requests flooded in for photo sessions, interviews—for any word at all from the young black runner who was now established as the fastest woman in the world. The Italians nicknamed her "La Gazzella Nera" (The Black Gazelle); to the French she was "La Perle Noire" (The Black Pearl). In response to an overwhelming demand, Coach Temple hurriedly accepted invitations for Rudolph and her teammates to race in such European cities as Athens, Amsterdam, London, Cologne, and Berlin.

Before they left, the Tigerbelles were even invited to the Vatican to meet Pope John XXIII. The splendid architecture and artworks of the Vatican left the Americans so **intimidated** that they found themselves unconsciously talking in whispers, but the Pope put the awestruck athletes at ease. Rudolph wrote later that the Holy Father was "a real jolly fellow. He had rosy cheeks and he laughed a lot. He was a very happy man, and it was obvious that everybody around him loved him."

After the closing ceremonies in Rome, the Tigerbelles flew to England for the British Empire Games. There, once again, Wilma won the 100-meter dash. But by now, all the attention showered on Rudolph was beginning to make her teammates jealous. So great was the **clamor** over Rudolph, the other Tigerbelles began to feel that they were in her shadow. The longer people waited in line to meet Rudolph, the greater the distance her teammates felt from her. Because all four of them had shared in the Olympic triumph, they thought they deserved at least some of the **adulation.** Soon tensions grew so fierce that two of the Tigerbelles stopped speaking to Rudolph altogether.

The conflict came to a head during the Empire Games. One night, before a banquet, Rudolph needed to set her hair, which was wild from the humid English weather. "The fog and rain rolled in early," she recalled, "and all I could think of was Jack the Ripper." But the four Tigerbelles shared a single set of curlers—which was nowhere to be found. "I was running around looking for the curlers," Rudolph said, "and the other girls were pretending they had no idea whatsoever where the curlers were. I went to the banquet with my hair an absolute mess and Coach Temple blew his top."

Temple immediately held a team meeting and demanded an explanation. He called the **malicious** behavior of the other girls in hiding the curlers "stupid," and he ordered them to put their jealousy aside.

Temple's lecture did no good. The next day, the women were entered in the 440-yard relay. Rudolph's teammates decided they would not run very hard, so that the crowd packed into the stadium to see the "world's fastest woman" would be disappointed. Rudolph remembered, "They barely struggled along. By the time I got the baton, one girl was actually forty yards ahead of me with only 110 yards to go. Well, I was determined to win that race, because sometime in the middle of it I realized what was happening. So I poured it on like never before, ran the fastest anchor leg of my life, and caught up with her at the tape to win. I closed forty yards and actually pulled out the race. The crowd went crazy."

Wilma Rudolph received a standing ovation; the other three Tigerbelles received another scolding from Coach Temple. He told them that when they got back to Tennessee State, they would be put on probation. From then on, Rudolph's teammates performed up to their abilities on the track, but they still shunned her when the meets were over.

Rudolph continued to be the center of public attention for the rest of the tour. In Berlin, the German city where her hero Jesse Owens had been heckled by racist crowds 24 years before, she nearly caused a riot. But instead of the insults hurled at Owens, she was greeted with cheers. One fan became so carried away that he actually stole the shoes off her feet to keep as souvenirs. Maintaining the cool that characterized her performance at the Olympics, she responded gracefully to even the most overzealous fans. Rudolph later credited her attitude to her upbringing, "I was never rude to the people who wanted to meet me or to the reporters who wanted interviews. I was taught that at home."

Although she enjoyed the outpouring of affection she received nearly everywhere she went, Rudolph was overjoyed when the tour came to an end and it was time to return to the United States. For all the excitement, for all the applause and acclaim, she was just plain homesick for Tennessee. ●

Strategy Follow-up

Now complete the sequence chain for the second part of this selection. Parts of it have been filled in for you.

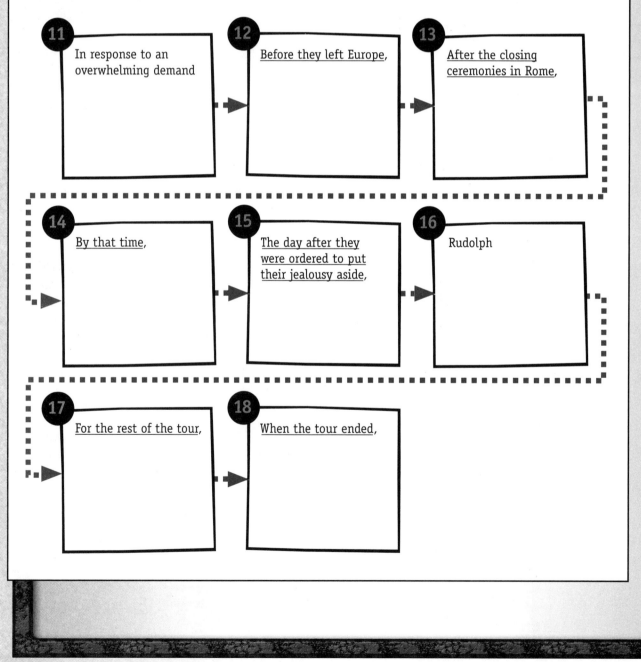

11 In response to an overwhelming demand

12 Before they left Europe,

13 After the closing ceremonies in Rome,

14 By that time,

15 The day after they were ordered to put their jealousy aside,

16 Rudolph

17 For the rest of the tour,

18 When the tour ended,

✓Personal Checklist

Read each question and put a check (✓) in the correct box.

1. How well do you understand why the other Tigerbelles became jealous of Wilma Rudolph?
   - ☐ 3 (extremely well)
   - ☐ 2 (fairly well)
   - ☐ 1 (not well)

2. How well were you able to use the information in Building Background to understand Rudolph's feelings about Jesse Owens and competing in the Olympics?
   - ☐ 3 (extremely well)
   - ☐ 2 (fairly well)
   - ☐ 1 (not well)

3. How well were you able to complete the activity in the Vocabulary Builder?
   - ☐ 3 (extremely well)
   - ☐ 2 (fairly well)
   - ☐ 1 (not well)

4. How well were you able to create a sequence chain for the second part of this selection?
   - ☐ 3 (extremely well)
   - ☐ 2 (fairly well)
   - ☐ 1 (not well)

5. Now that you've read this selection, how well do you think you could describe Wilma Rudolph's personality?
   - ☐ 3 (extremely well)
   - ☐ 2 (fairly well)
   - ☐ 1 (not well)

Vocabulary Check

Look back at the work you did in the Vocabulary Builder. Then answer each question by circling the correct letter.

1. Which of these words has a positive connotation, or implied meaning?
   - a arrogant
   - b. malicious
   - c. jubilant

2. Which word best completes this sentence: *The warrior's enemy was so _____ that the warrior expected to lose the fight?*
   - a. formidable
   - b. disqualified
   - c. intimidated

3. Which word best completes this sentence: *The warrior's companion was so _____ that the warrior needed to stop him from hurting others for no reason?*
   - a. jubilant
   - b. arrogant
   - c. malicious

4. Which meaning of *depression* is used in this selection?
   - a. the condition of feeling sad and hopeless
   - b. an area that is lower than its surroundings
   - c. a period of drastic decline in a country's economic well-being

5. An exclamation is an excited or disturbed outcry. Which vocabulary word comes from the same root word as *exclamation*?
   - a. depression
   - b. adulation
   - c. clamor

Add the numbers that you just checked to get your Personal Checklist score. Fill in your score here. Then turn to page 215 and transfer your score onto Graph 1.

Check your answers with your teacher. Give yourself 1 point for each correct answer, and fill in your Vocabulary score here. Then turn to page 215 and transfer your score onto Graph 1.

Strategy Check

Review the sequence chain that you helped create in the Strategy Follow-up. Then answer the following questions:

1. When did the other Tigerbelles begin to show their jealousy of Rudolph?
   a. when the team was talking with the Pope
   b. when they were in England for the British Empire Games
   c. when they were on the plane going home to Tennessee

2. In the 400-meter relay at the Empire Games, what was the situation after the first three Tigerbelles ran?
   a. The team was so far ahead that Rudolph could have walked.
   b. The Tigerbelles were forty yards behind.
   c. The race was so close that it was almost tied.

3. What happened when Rudolph took the baton?
   a. She bobbled the handoff, fell behind, and lost the race.
   b. The best she could manage was a tie.
   c. She put on a huge burst of speed and won the race.

4. Which phrase is *not* an example of signal words?
   a. in Berlin
   b. the next day
   c. after the closing ceremonies

5. How did Rudolph feel about going home at the end of the tour?
   a. She was enjoying the adulation so much that she didn't want to go home.
   b. She was homesick and overjoyed to be going home.
   c. She was afraid because she had forgotten what normal life was like.

Check your answers with your teacher. Give yourself 1 point for each correct answer, and fill in your Strategy score here. Then turn to page 215 and transfer your score onto Graph 1.

Comprehension Check

Review the selection if necessary. Then answer these questions:

1. Which statement below is *not* implied by the sentence *The high temperatures in Rome favored the Tigerbelles*?
   a. The temperatures in Rome were similar to the temperatures in Tennessee.
   b. The high temperatures would help the Tigerbelles sell many cold beverages.
   c. Runners from cold countries could be hampered by the heat.

2. How did Rudolph spend her time while her ankle injury kept her out of training?
   a. She talked to fellow competitors and signed autographs.
   b. She stretched out on the field and slept.
   c. She set up sponsorship deals.

3. What did Rudolph do during the Olympics that proved how calm and confident she was?
   a. She took time off to go and visit the Pope.
   b. She went to an important dinner without setting her hair.
   c. After a qualifying heat, she fell asleep.

4. Why might Rudolph have been particularly delighted with the wonderful reception in Berlin?
   a. Her teammates stopped being jealous of her by the time they reached Berlin.
   b. Jesse Owens had been heckled there, but now Rudolph was being cheered.
   c. There was nothing special about Berlin.

5. Why would the other Tigerbelles be put on probation when they returned to Tennessee?
   a. They had hidden hair curlers from Rudolph.
   b. They had intentionally run poorly to make Rudolph look bad.
   c. They locked Rudolph out of their room.

Check your answers with your teacher. Give yourself 1 point for each correct answer, and fill in your Comprehension score here. Then turn to page 215 and transfer your score onto Graph 1.

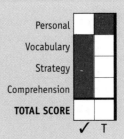

Extending

Choose one or both of these activities:

DESIGN A WEB SITE

There's a wealth of Web sites about Wilma Rudolph. The first two listed on this page will give you a place to start researching the Olympic star. Using one or more search engines, find and review at least a dozen Web sites that discuss Rudolph. Then put together a list of at least five sites that you recommend. On paper or a computer program, design your own Web page for Wilma Rudolph that you would put on the Internet. Be sure to outline and briefly describe the links and information you would include.

CONDUCT A SURVEY

Survey at least twenty people to discover which three women athletes they admire most. The athletes can be from the past, or they can be currently competing in their chosen sports. Tabulate the responses, and record them on a pie chart or a bar graph. Then paste the chart or graph onto a piece of poster board, and include photos and brief biographies of the three athletes who got the most votes.

Resources

Books

Biracree, Tom. *Wilma Rudolph*. American Women of Achievement. Chelsea House, 1989.

Sherrow, Victoria. *Wilma Rudolph: Olympic Champion*. Junior Black Americans of Achievement. Chelsea House, 1995.

Web Sites

http://myhero.com/sports/rudolph.asp
Information about Wilma Rudolph, including a photograph of Rudolph in competition, is available on this Web site.

http://www.lkwdpl.org/wihohio/rudo-wil.htm
This page from the Women in History Web site offers a profile of Rudolph.

http://www.sportsline.com/u/kids/women/index.html
This Web page provides links to the profiles of several top women athletes.

Video/DVD

Wilma Rudolph. Schlessinger Media, 1995.

Telling Stories

Building Background

One of the ways in which authors make their ideas clearer is to use comparisons called similes. A **simile** compares two things by using the words *like* or *as*. For example, imagine you are writing to a friend about your new skateboard. You can tell your friend that the skateboard is yellow, but the word *yellow* covers many different shades. How will your friend know which one you mean? You could solve the problem by saying that the skateboard is "as yellow as a dandelion in summer." Since your friend knows what a dandelion looks like, he or she will know what your skateboard looks like.

Some similes are overused, such as "like a fish out of water" or "as quick as a wink." Such comparisons are called clichés. Good writers avoid clichés. They try to use fresher, more exact comparisons. As you read "Telling Stories," watch for the many comparisons that the author uses. Think about what things are being compared, and why. Notice how each comparison gives you a clearer picture of what is happening and what things look like.

bereavement

conspirators

dispassionate

etiquette

imperative

quarter

titivate

Vocabulary Builder

1. Before you begin reading "Telling Stories," match each vocabulary word in Column 1 with its definition in Column 2. Be careful—some of the words' definitions may not be the ones with which you are familiar. Use a dictionary if you need help.

COLUMN 1	COLUMN 2
bereavement	necessary
conspirators	fair; impartial
dispassionate	making oneself neat and attractive
etiquette	grief over someone's death
imperative	social graces or pleasures
quarter	schemers; accomplices
titivating	mercy

2. Save your work. You will refer to it again in the Vocabulary Check.

Strategy Builder

Identifying Problems and Solutions in Fiction

- Throughout this book, you've been learning that a main element of every story is its **plot**, or sequence of events. In most stories, the plot revolves around a **problem** that the main character or characters have. Throughout the story, the characters try to solve the problem. Sometimes they try more than one **solution**. By the end, they usually come up with the solution that works— **the end result.**

- When you read "Levi's: The Pants That Won the West" you recorded the problems and solutions in that selection on a **problem-solution frame**. You will use that same graphic organizer as you read this story too. If you need help remembering how to use a problem-solution frame, look back at the ones you worked on in Lesson 7.

Telling Stories

by Maeve Binchy

As you read the first part of this story, apply the strategies that you just learned. Look for the problem that Andrew and Irene face, and what they do to try and solve it.

People always said that Irene had total recall. She seemed to remember the smallest details of things they had long forgotten—the words of old pop songs, the shades of old lipsticks, minute-by-minute reconstructions of important events like Graduation Day, or people's weddings. If ever you wanted a step-by-step account of times past, they said to each other: ask Irene.

Irene rarely took herself through the evening before the day she was due to be married. But if she had to then she could have done it with no difficulty. It wasn't hard to remember the smells: the lilac in the garden, the polish on all the furniture, the orange blossom in the house. She even remembered the rich smell of the hand cream that she was massaging carefully into her hands when she heard the doorbell ring. It must be a late present, she thought, or possibly yet another fussy aunt who had come up from the country for the ceremony and arrived like a homing pigeon at the house.

She was surprised to hear Andrew's voice, talking to her younger sister downstairs. Andrew was meant to be at his home dealing with all his relations just as Irene had been doing. He had an uncle, a priest, flying in from the African Missions to assist at the wedding. Andrew's grandmother was a demanding old lady who regarded every gathering as in some way centering around her; Irene was surprised that Andrew had been allowed to escape.

Rosemary, her sister and one of the bridesmaids, had no interest in anything apart from the possible appearance of a huge spot on her face. She waved Andrew airily up the stairs.

"She's been up there **titivating** herself for hours," Irene heard her say. Before she had time to react to Rosemary's tactlessness, Irene heard Andrew say, "Oh God," in a funny, choked sort of voice, and before he even came into the room, she knew something was very wrong.

Andrew's face was as white as the dress that hung between sheets of tissue paper on the outside of the big mahogany wardrobe. His hands shook and trembled like the branches of the beautiful laburnum tree outside her window, the yellow blossom shaking in the summer breeze.

He tried to take her hand but she was covered in hand cream. Irene decided that somehow it was **imperative** that she keep rubbing the cream still further in. It was like not walking on the crack in the road: if she kept massaging her hands then he couldn't take them in his, and he couldn't tell her what awful thing he was about to tell her.

On and on she went rhythmically, almost hypnotically, as if she were pulling on tight gloves. Her hands never stopped moving; her face never moved at all.

He fumbled for words, but Irene didn't help him.

The words came eventually, tumbling over each other, contradicting each other even, punctuated with apology and self-disgust. It wasn't that there was anyone else, Lord no, and it wasn't even as if he had stopped loving her, in many ways he had never loved her more than now, looking at her and knowing that he was destroying all their dreams and their hopes, but he had thought about it very seriously, and the truth was that he wasn't ready, he wasn't old enough, maybe technically he was old enough, but in his heart he didn't feel old enough to settle down, he wasn't certain enough that this was the Right Thing. For either of them, he added hastily, wanting Irene to know that it was in her interests as well as his.

On and on, she worked the cream into her hands and wrists; even a little way up her arms.

She sat impassively on her little blue bedroom stool, her frilly dressing table behind her. There were no tears, no tantrums. There were not even any words. Eventually he could speak no more.

"Oh Irene, say something for God's sake, tell me how much you hate me, what I've done to your life." He almost begged to be railed against.

She spoke slowly, her voice was very calm. "But of course I don't hate you," she said, as if explaining something to a slow-witted child. "I love you, I always will, and let's look at what you've done to my life . . . You've changed it certainly . . . " her eyes fell on the wedding dress.

Andrew started again. Guilt and shame poured from him in a torrent released by her unexpected gentleness. He would take it upon himself to explain to everyone, he would tell her parents now. He would explain everything to the guests, he would see that the presents were returned. He would try to compensate her family financially for all the expense they had gone to. If everyone thought this was the right thing to do he would go abroad, to a faraway place like Australia or Canada or Africa . . . somewhere they needed young lawyers, a place where nobody from here need ever look at him again and remember all the trouble he had caused.

And then suddenly he realized that he and he alone was doing the talking; Irene sat still, apart from those curious hand movements, as if she had not heard or understood what he was saying. A look of horror came over his face: perhaps she did not understand.

"I mean it, Irene," he said simply. "I really do mean it, you know, I wish I didn't."

"I know you mean it." Her voice was steady, her eyes were clear. She did understand.

Andrew clutched at a straw. "Perhaps *you* feel the same. Perhaps we *both* want to get out of it? Is that what you are saying?" He was so eager to believe it, his face almost shone with enthusiasm.

But there was no **quarter** here. In a voice that didn't shake, with no hint of a tear in her eye, Irene said that she loved him and would always love him. But that it was far better, if he felt he couldn't go through with it, that this should be discovered the night before the marriage, rather than the night after. This way at least one of them would be free to make a different marriage when the time came.

"Well both of us, surely?" Andrew was bewildered.

Irene shook her head. "I can't see myself marrying anyone else but you," she said. There was no blame, regret, accusation. Just a statement.

 Stop here for the Strategy Break.

Strategy Break

If you were to create a problem-solution frame for this story, it might look like this:

What is the problem?
Andrew thinks that getting married is the Wrong Thing, and he wants to call off the wedding.

Why is it a problem?
He is afraid that Irene will be devastated, and that friends and family will be shocked and disappointed.

Solutions	Results
1. Andrew tells Irene that he wants to call off the wedding because he's not ready to get married. Then he asks her to respond.	1. Irene tells Andrew that she loves him and always will.
2. Andrew offers to explain things to the guests, return the presents, compensate the family, and leave town. He then tells Irene that he means it.	2. Irene says that she knows he means it.
3. Andrew asks Irene if she, too, would like to get out of the wedding.	3. Irene says that she can't see herself marrying anyone else but Andrew.

Go on reading to see what happens.

In the big house, where three hundred guests were expected tomorrow, it was curiously silent. Perhaps the breeze had died down; they couldn't even hear the flapping of the edges of the marquee on the lawn.

The silence was too long between them. But Andrew knew she was not going to break it. "So what will we do? First, I mean?" he asked her.

She looked at him pleasantly as if he had asked what record he should put on the player. She said nothing.

"Tell our parents, I suppose, yours first. Are they downstairs?" he suggested.

"No, they're over at the golf club, they're having a little reception or drink or something for those who aren't coming tomorrow."

"Oh God," Andrew said.

There was another silence.

"Do you think we should go and tell *my* parents then? Grandmother will need some time to get adjusted . . . "

Irene considered this. "Possibly," she said. But it was unsatisfactory.

"Or maybe the caterers," Andrew said. "I saw them bustling around setting things up . . . " His voice broke. He seemed about to cry. "Oh God, Irene, it's a terrible mess."

"I know," she agreed, as if they were talking about a rain cloud or some other unavoidable irritation to the day.

"And I suppose I should tell Martin, he's been fussing so much about the **etiquette** of it all and getting things in the right order. In a way he may be relieved . . . " Andrew gave a nervous little laugh but hastily corrected himself. "But sorry, of course, mainly sorry, of course, very, very sorry that things haven't worked out."

"Yes. Of course," Irene agreed politely.

"And the bridesmaids? Don't you think we should tell Rosemary now, and Catherine? And that you should ring Rita and tell her . . . and tell her . . . that . . . well that . . . "

"Tell her what, exactly?"

"Well, tell her that we've changed our minds . . . "

"That you've changed your mind, to be strictly honest," Irene said.

"Yes, but you agree," he pleaded.

"What do I agree?"

"That if it is the Wrong Thing to do, then it were better we know now than tomorrow when it's all too late and we are man and wife till death . . . " his voice ran out.

"Ah yes, but don't you see, I don't think we *are* doing the Wrong Thing getting married."

"But you agreed . . . " He was in a panic.

"Oh, of course I agreed, Andrew, I mean what on earth would be the point of not agreeing? Naturally we can't go through with it. But that's not to say that *I'm* calling it off."

"No, no, but does that matter as much as telling people . . . I mean now that we know that it won't take place, isn't it unfair to people to let them think that it will?"

"Yes and no."

"But we can't have them making the food, getting dressed . . . "

"I know." She was thoughtful.

"I want to do what's best, what's the most fair," Andrew said. And he did, Irene could see that, in the situation which he had brought about, he still wanted to be fair.

"Let's see," she suggested. "Who is going to be the most hurt by all this?"

He thought about it. "Your parents probably, they've gone to all this trouble . . . " He waved toward the garden where three hundred merry-makers had planned to stroll.

"No, I don't think they're the most hurt."

"Well, maybe my uncle, the whole way back from Africa and he had to ask permission from a bishop. Or my grandmother . . . or the bridesmaids. They won't get a chance to dress up." Andrew struggled to be fair.

"I think that I am the one who will be most hurt." Irene's voice wasn't even slightly raised. It was if she had given the problem equally **dispassionate** judgment.

"I mean, my parents have other daughters. There'll be Rosemary and Catherine, one day they'll have weddings. And your uncle, the priest . . . well he'll have a bit of a holiday. No, I think I am the one who is most upset, I'm not going to marry the man I love, have the life I thought I was going to."

"I know, I know." He sounded like someone sympathizing over a **bereavement**.

"So I thought that perhaps you'd let me handle it *my* way."

"Of course, Irene, that's why I'm here, whatever you say."

"I say we shouldn't tell anyone anything. Not tonight."

"I won't change my mind, in case that's what you're thinking."

"Lord no, why should you? It's much too serious to be flitting about, chopping and changing."

He handed their future into her hands. "Do it whatever way you want. Just let me know and I'll do it." He was prepared to pay any price to get the wedding called off.

But Irene didn't allow herself the time to think about that. "Let me be the one not to turn up," she said. "Let me be seen to be the partner who had second thoughts. That way at least I get out of it with some dignity."

He agreed. Grooms had been left standing at the altar before. He would always say afterward that he had been greatly hurt but he respected Irene's decision.

"And you won't tell *anyone*?" she made him promise.

"Maybe Martin?" he suggested.

"Particularly not Martin, he'd give the game away. In the church you must be seen to be waiting for me."

"But your father and mother . . . is it fair to leave it to the last minute?"

"They'd prefer to think that I let you down rather than the other way. Who wants a daughter who has been abandoned by the groom?"

"It's not that . . . " he began.

"I *know* that, silly, but not everyone else does." She had stopped creaming her hands. They talked like old friends and **conspirators**. The thing would only succeed if nobody had an inkling.

"And afterward . . . " He seemed very eager to know every step of her plan.

"Afterward . . . " Irene was thoughtful. "Oh, afterward we can go along being friends . . . until you meet someone else . . . People will admire you, think you are very forgiving, too tolerant even . . . There'll be no awkwardness. No embarrassment."

Andrew stood at the gate of the big house to wave good-bye; she sat by her window under the great laburnum tree and waved back. She was a girl in a million. What a pity he hadn't met her later. Or proposed to her later, when he was ready to be married. His stomach lurched at the thought of the mayhem they were about to unleash the following day. He went home with a heavy heart to hear stories of the Missions from his uncle the priest, and tales of long-gone grandeur from his grandmother.

Martin had read many books on being best man. Possibly too many.

"It's only natural for you to be nervous," he said to Andrew at least forty times. "It's only natural for you to worry about your speech, but remember the most important thing is to thank Irene's parents for giving her to you."

When they heard the loud sniffs from Andrew's grandmother, the best man had soothing remarks also. "It's only natural for elderly females to cry at weddings," he said.

Andrew stood there, his stomach like lead. Since marriage was instituted, no groom had stood like

this in the certain knowledge that his bride was not just a little late, or held up in traffic, or adjusting her veil—all the excuses that Martin was busy hissing into his ear.

He felt a shame like he had never known, allowing all these three hundred people to assemble in a church for a ceremony that would not take place. He looked fearfully at the parish priest, and at his own uncle. It took some seconds for it to sink in that the congregation had risen to its feet, and that the organist had crashed into the familiar chords of "Here Comes the Bride."

He turned like any groom turns and saw Irene, perfectly at ease on her father's arm, smiling to the left and smiling to the right.

With his mouth wide open and his face whiter than the dress she wore, he looked into her eyes. He felt Martin's fingers in his ribs and he stepped forward to stand beside her.

Despite her famous recall, Irene never told that story to anyone. She only talked about it once to Andrew, on their honeymoon, when he tried to go over the events himself. And in all the years that followed, it had been *so* obvious that she had taken the right decision, run the right risk and realized that their marriage was the Right Thing, there was no point in talking about it at all. ●

Strategy Follow-up

Now complete the problem-solution frame with information from the second part of this story. Some of the frame has been filled in for you.

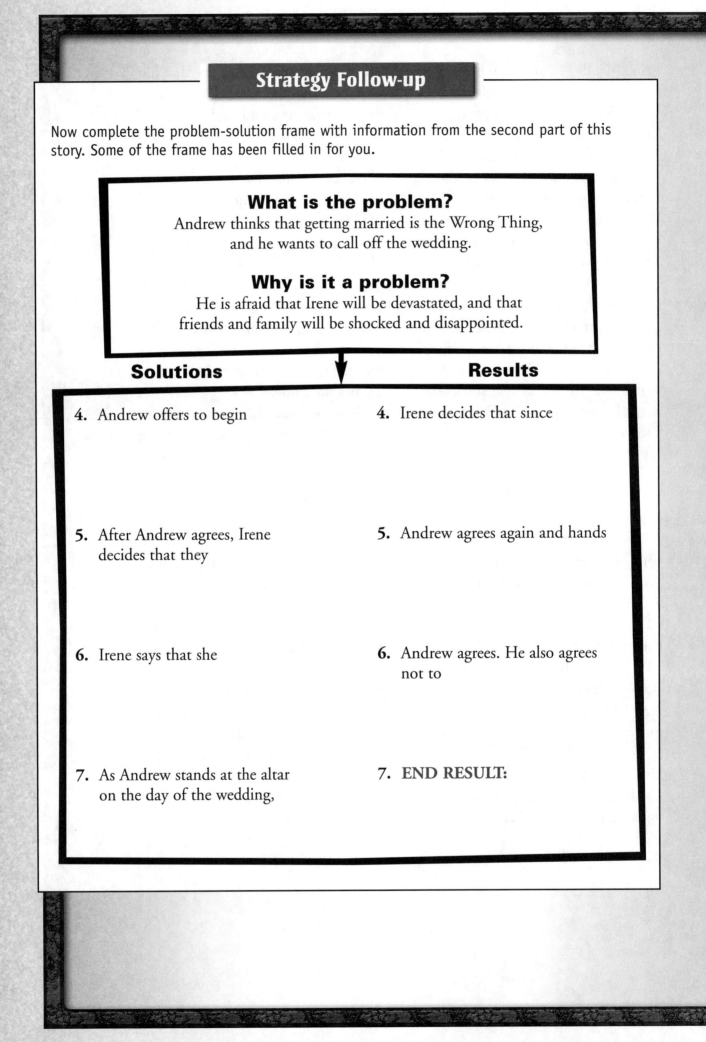

What is the problem?
Andrew thinks that getting married is the Wrong Thing, and he wants to call off the wedding.

Why is it a problem?
He is afraid that Irene will be devastated, and that friends and family will be shocked and disappointed.

Solutions	Results
4. Andrew offers to begin	**4.** Irene decides that since
5. After Andrew agrees, Irene decides that they	**5.** Andrew agrees again and hands
6. Irene says that she	**6.** Andrew agrees. He also agrees not to
7. As Andrew stands at the altar on the day of the wedding,	**7. END RESULT:**

✓Personal Checklist

Read each question and put a check (✓) in the correct box.

1. How well do you understand what happens in this story?
    - ☐ 3 (extremely well)
    - ☐ 2 (fairly well)
    - ☐ 1 (not well)

2. How well were you able to use what you learned in Building Background to better understand the comparisons in this story?
    - ☐ 3 (extremely well)
    - ☐ 2 (fairly well)
    - ☐ 1 (not well)

3. In the Vocabulary Builder, how well were you match the words with their meanings?
    - ☐ 3 (extremely well)
    - ☐ 2 (fairly well)
    - ☐ 1 (not well)

4. How well were you able to complete the problem-solution frame in the Strategy Follow-up?
    - ☐ 3 (extremely well)
    - ☐ 2 (fairly well)
    - ☐ 1 (not well)

5. How easily would you be able to explain Irene's solution to the problem?
    - ☐ 3 (extremely well)
    - ☐ 2 (fairly well)
    - ☐ 1 (not well)

Vocabulary Check

Look back at the work you did in the Vocabulary Builder. Then answer each question by circling the correct letter.

1. Which of these words is a synonym for *dispassionate*?
    - a. emotional
    - b. fair
    - c. resentful

2. What does the word *quarter* mean in the context of this story?
    - a. mercy, especially when given to an enemy
    - b. a coin equal to one fourth of a U.S. dollar
    - c. one of the four major divisions of the compass

3. If the word *welcoming* applies to a birth, which word applies to a death?
    - a. titivating
    - b. bereavement
    - c. conspirators

4. In which of these actions would you expect conspirators to be involved?
    - a. meeting in secret to plan an illegal act
    - b. holding a parade to honor their organization
    - c. playing musical instruments in a band

5. Which of these is *not* a meaning of *titivating*?
    - a. decorating, adding ornaments or adornments
    - b. floating, as on water or air
    - c. making oneself look neat and tidy

Add the numbers that you just checked to get your Personal Checklist score. Fill in your score here. Then turn to page 215 and transfer your score onto Graph 1.

Personal	
Vocabulary	
Strategy	
Comprehension	
TOTAL SCORE	
✓	T

Check your answers with your teacher. Give yourself 1 point for each correct answer, and fill in your Vocabulary score here. Then turn to page 215 and transfer your score onto Graph 1.

Personal	
Vocabulary	
Strategy	
Comprehension	
TOTAL SCORE	
✓	T

Strategy Check

Review the problem-solution frame that you completed in the Strategy Follow-up. Also review the story if necessary. Then answer these questions:

1. Why does Andrew want to call off the wedding?

   a. He is not ready to get married.

   b. He no longer loves Irene.

   c. His grandmother objects to the marriage.

2. Why does Irene say that she should be allowed to handle things her way?

   a. because she's extremely spoiled and always gets things her way

   b. because she wants to hurt Andrew

   c. because she thinks she's the one who'll be most hurt by everything

3. Why does Irene say that she should be the one to call off the wedding?

   a. because she'll get to keep the presents

   b. because she'll at least get out of it with some dignity

   c. because she doesn't want Andrew's uncle to be upset with him

4. What is the end result of the problem?

   a. They get married and realize that their marriage was the Right Thing.

   b. They get married and realize that their marriage was the Wrong Thing.

   c. They don't get married and realize that their decision was the Right Thing.

5. What made Irene believe that her final solution would work out well?

   a. She knew that Andrew was stupid and she could easily trick him.

   b. She knew that Andrew really wanted to get married but had cold feet.

   c. She knew that she could easily play off of Andrew's guilt.

Check your answers with your teacher. Give yourself 1 point for each correct answer, and fill in your Strategy score here. Then turn to page 215 and transfer your score onto Graph 1.

Personal	
Vocabulary	
Strategy	
Comprehension	
TOTAL SCORE	✓ T

Comprehension Check

Review the story if necessary. Then answer these questions:

1. In the sentence *Andrew's face was as white as the dress that hung between sheets of tissue paper on the outside of the big mahogany wardrobe,* to what is Andrew's face being compared?

   a. Irene's wedding dress

   b. sheets of tissue paper

   c. a big mahogany wardrobe

2. Why does the author choose to compare Andrew's face with that object?

   a. The comparison points out that his skin was as thin and wrinkled as crumpled tissue paper.

   b. The comparison points out that he was not feeling well, and it also suggests the reason.

   c. The comparison points out that his skin was as dark as the mahogany wood.

3. Irene continues to rub cream into her hands "as if she were pulling on tight gloves." Which of the ideas below is *not* suggested by this comparison?

   a. The situation is emotionally painful, just as pulling on tight gloves is physically painful.

   b. Irene rubs her hands to let out her feelings.

   c. Irene is thinking about buying new gloves.

4. Irene talked to Andrew about this plan only once, "when he tried to go over the events himself." What does this suggest?

   a. Things went so fast that Andrew didn't know what happened.

   b. Andrew fainted.

   c. Irene forgot about the events herself.

5. Which of these statements is false?

   a. Irene remembered the details of every important experience she had.

   b. Irene liked to tell everyone how she tricked her husband into marrying her.

   c. The couple were married for years.

Check your answers with your teacher. Give yourself 1 point for each correct answer, and fill in your Comprehension score here. Then turn to page 215 and transfer your score onto Graph 1.

Personal	
Vocabulary	
Strategy	
Comprehension	
TOTAL SCORE	✓ T

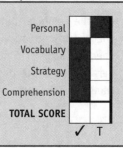

Extending

Choose one or more of these activities:

PLAN A WEDDING

Look into the many aspects of planning a large wedding—from selecting a place and time for the wedding and the reception to fulfilling legal requirements and your church's regulations to pricing and paying for the event. (The second Web site listed on this page might give you a place to start.) Put together a schedule and a budget for a wedding such as the one described in "Telling Stories."

COMPARE WEDDINGS

Not everyone celebrates weddings as Irene and Andrew did. In fact, many couples simply elope to avoid the tensions of a large wedding. Interview between five and ten married couples to learn about their wedding ceremonies. How elaborate was the ceremony itself? Was there a reception? If so, how large was it? What part(s) of the day did each person enjoy most? What part(s) does each person remember most clearly? What type of ceremony does each interviewee recommend for others? Using the information you gather, write an article to advise engaged couples about their options.

READ OTHER WORKS BY MAEVE BINCHY

Using the resources listed on this page, find and read (or listen to) other short stories or books by Maeve Binchy. Then choose your favorite story or book and report on it to the class. If you report on a short story, create a problem-solution frame or a story map for it and use it to give your report.

Resources

Books

Binchy, Maeve. *Circle of Friends*. Dell, 1991.

———. *Dublin 4*. Century, 1995.

Web Sites

http://www.maevebinchy.com/
This is Maeve Binchy's official Web site.

http://www.wednet.com
This Web site offers help to people who are planning weddings.

Audio Recordings

Binchy, Maeve. *Dublin 4* (abridged). Chivers Audio Books, 1996.

———. *Echoes*. Chivers Audio Books, 1996.

Henry, O. *O. Henry Favorites* (abridged). Listening Library, 1998.

A Lesson from the Heart

Building Background

In the story you are about to read, a teenager named Julie spends the day with her 87-year-old grandmother. Have you ever spent time with an older person? At first you may think that people over a certain age are quite different from you. But if you spend any length of time with an elderly relative or friend, you may begin to see that person in a new way.

Think about the character traits that you usually associate with young people and older people. Then read the following list of traits, and write each one in the column or columns where you think it belongs. When you finish, think about an older person you know well, and decide if those traits really match him or her. Is it possible that you may be prejudging older people? (Notice how many of the traits could go in either column.)

likes to try new things   complains a great deal

walks slowly   walks with energy

is interested in the latest inventions   talks about the past all the time

plays games   watches television

likes people   likes to be by himself or herself

Young People	Older People

Vocabulary Builder

1. The words in the margin are all from the story "A Lesson from the Heart." Before you begin reading the story, decide which of the vocabulary words are related to actions and which are related to feelings. List each word on the appropriate clipboard.

2. As you read the story, look for other words related to actions or feelings and list them on a separate sheet of paper.

3. Save your work. You will use it again in the Vocabulary Check.

Strategy Builder

Drawing Conclusions About Characters

- As you learned in Lesson 8, a **conclusion** is a decision that you reach after thinking about certain facts or information. When you read a story, you often draw conclusions based on information that the author gives you about the characters, the setting, or particular events.

- To draw conclusions about the **characters** in a story, you must pay attention to their words, thoughts, feelings, and actions. Clues such as these help you understand the characters better. They also help you understand why the characters do what they do.

- As you read "Lessons from the Heart," you will be recording your conclusions about Julie and her grandmother on **character maps**. If you need help remembering how to use a character map, look back at the ones you worked on when you read "This Farm for Sale" in Lesson 8.

anguish

dangling

defensive

determined

envy

gently

quavered

scrutinizing

speculating

stump

sympathetically

trudged

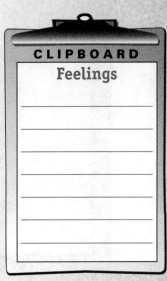

CLIPBOARD
Actions

CLIPBOARD
Feelings

A Lesson from the Heart

by Julie Yabu

As you read this short story, apply the strategies that you just learned. Look for clues that the author provides to help you draw conclusions about Julie and her grandmother.

"You've grown so much . . . and it's time you met a man," my grandmother said, **scrutinizing** me through her round, thick bifocals. "A good man. No, the best man." She pinched my left cheek until she left a red mark.

"It's okay, Hamai," I said, looking down at my watch and biting my lower lip until it bled. Hamai was what we called her in Korean.

She was wearing her usual outfit for public appearance—a color-coordinated pants suit. Her polyester, elasticized-waist pants with wide legs discreetly covered the brace on her left leg, and the matching jacket hid her hunched back.

"You know, I used to have hundreds of men lined up at my door and calling me every night to ask me out. All the other girls looked at me with **envy**. Don't think that I don't know how to catch a man," she snapped. Her voice acquired a sharper, **defensive** tone as she firmly pulled down the sides of her jacket, which reached just past her hips.

"I thought you wanted help shopping for groceries," I protested.

However, Hamai had already made up her mind. "I'm going to teach you how to catch the 'right' man."

I was stuck. Hamai always got her way, and no one dared to go against her wishes.

Of course, we went to her favorite place, a small park about two blocks from her apartment. She insisted that we walk despite the doctor's warnings against it—and despite the fact that she had just recovered from a stroke. I walked slowly by her side, allowing her to **stump** along with the support of her newly finished wooden cane. I smiled to myself, remembering the months that we had spent—even buying the most expensive cane—convincing her that she must use it. "I can walk alone," she would always say.

We sat in her usual spot, an old wooden bench that resembled a rocking chair with two seats. Above us, the same huge oak tree looked down upon us almost as if my grandma had instructed it to protect us. A winding concrete pathway, with lots of cracks where weeds managed to grow, was right in front of us. People occasionally walked this way as a shortcut but were usually in a rush to get to work. Rarely did families come and spend the day here.

We must have looked like an odd couple. My grandma was leaning back with her legs **dangling** off the bench.

Looking at her at that moment, I understood why people always told me that I had a "cute" grandma. Her plump figure, accentuated by the light blue matching outfit, and her short, jet-black, tightly permed hair framing a porcelain-white, perfectly round face, made her resemble an Asian Mrs. Beasley doll. In contrast, I was sitting Indian style on the bench, wearing old cutoff jeans and a white tank top. My hair was tied back in a loose ponytail with strands falling out around my face, and my golden-brown, sun-baked skin was evidence that I spent most of my summer days in the sun.

After a few minutes a man wearing a three-piece suit and carrying a briefcase walked by. He **trudged** along and stooped forward a little. I carefully watched my grandma's eyes follow him until he disappeared around the curve of the pathway.

She blinked once very hard and wrinkled her eyebrows, forming a deep crease in her forehead.

After **speculating** for a moment, she said, "He stoops like a tree—how do you think he can support himself or you?" My grandma was famous for her endless supply of sayings or superstitions.

Then she darted her eyes at me and ordered, "Sit up straight and present yourself like a lady. How do you expect a man to ever look at you when you sit and act like an uncivilized person?"

I sat up straight and watched a meticulously dressed man, wearing pressed white slacks and a matching dress shirt and with almost "plastic" hair, walk by with his head held up high. I merely gazed at him in awe. "That's him, Hamai," I sighed.

She frowned in amazement at my ignorance. "Julie, what's wrong with you? A man like that spends more time looking into a mirror than anything else."

Within the next few hours, more men passed by along with more criticisms from my grandma. Not one man matched my grandma's strict standards. We waited as the sun slowly faded away and hid itself behind the branches of the tree. Silence overtook us for a few minutes, and I could only hear the wind rustling through the leaves of the tree.

⬢ **Stop here for the Strategy Break.**

Strategy Break

If you were to create a character map for Julie based on what you have learned about her so far, it might look like this:

CLUE:
She picks up her grandmother to take her grocery shopping.

Conclusion:
She is close to her grandmother and is willing to take the time to help her.

CLUE:
She sits on the bench for hours with her grandmother.

Conclusion:
She is kind to her grandmother and patient with her.

CHARACTER: Julie

CLUE:
She is dressed in cutoff jeans and a white tank top. Her hair is tied back in a loose ponytail.

Conclusion:
She is a typical, casual teenager who doesn't fuss over her appearance.

CLUE:
She straightens up when her grandmother criticizes her posture.

Conclusion:
She wants to please her grandmother.

As you continue reading, keep looking for clues that the author gives about Julie and her grandmother (Hamai). At the end of this selection, you will create a character map of your own.

 **Go on reading to see what happens.**

My grandma looked off absently toward where the pathway ended. "This was exactly the type of day that I last saw your grandfather," she murmured. "He was a good man . . . the best I've ever seen. I spent years by the window every morning waiting for him to come back . . . until twenty years later I realized that I wasn't going to see him ever again. Finally, I had to move on and continue alone."

I put my hand **sympathetically** over hers and let the tips of my fingers run over the calluses and wrinkles that covered her hand. Her hands alone were proof that she had never run away from her hard life.

She covered my hand with her other hand. "I still remember smelling the salty sea air and standing on the boat holding your mother's hand as I watched the last of our country. I was **determined** to leave my old life and dreams and never go back." The wooden bench began to rock back and forth as if we were on the boat once again.

Suddenly, she squeezed my hand hard. "I wasted so many years expecting him to come back because I was afraid of being alone," she **quavered** as years of built-up **anguish** burst out.

I leaned over, put my arm around her shoulder, and **gently** rubbed the collar of her jacket. "But Hamai, you're never alone. . . . I'll come live with you after I finish school, and we could have our 'secret talks' about men every day," I tried to reassure her.

Hamai didn't respond for a few minutes and instead gently bowed her head and closed her eyes. Suddenly, she looked up at me, clamped a hand on either side of my face, and looked straight at me. "I've already lived for eighty-seven years and had my chance; but you're so young, with all your life ahead of you. More than I ever had. Don't make the same mistakes that I did. Be strong. Be independent." Her voice became very sharp.

I looked into my grandma's eyes, seeing the sparkle and youthfulness between the folds of loose skin and wrinkles. I wrapped my arms around her, rested my head on her shoulder, and smelled the baby powder on her cheek that always made it as soft as kid leather. ●

Strategy Follow-up

Think about what you learned about Hamai throughout this story, and complete the character map below. The clues have been provided for you. Use them to draw your own conclusions.

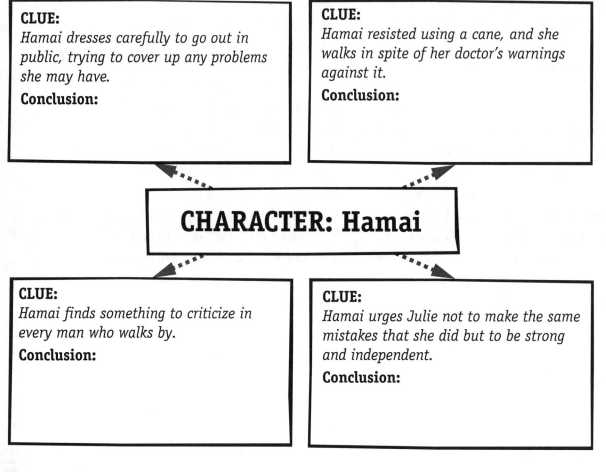

CLUE:
Hamai dresses carefully to go out in public, trying to cover up any problems she may have.
Conclusion:

CLUE:
Hamai resisted using a cane, and she walks in spite of her doctor's warnings against it.
Conclusion:

CHARACTER: Hamai

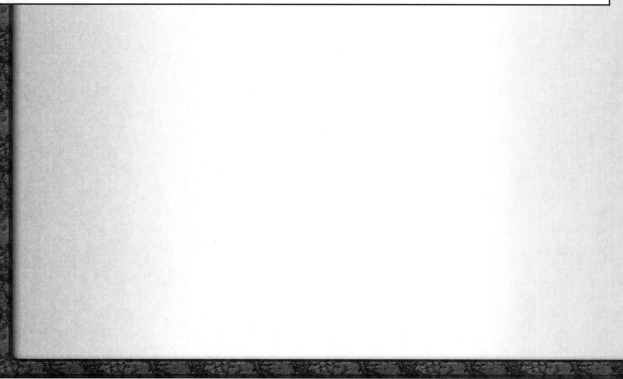

CLUE:
Hamai finds something to criticize in every man who walks by.
Conclusion:

CLUE:
Hamai urges Julie not to make the same mistakes that she did but to be strong and independent.
Conclusion:

✓Personal Checklist

Read each question and put a check (✓) in the correct box.

1. How well do you understand the characters in this story?
    - ☐ 3 (extremely well)
    - ☐ 2 (fairly well)
    - ☐ 1 (not well)

2. How well were you able to use what you wrote in Building Background to help you see the similarities between young people and older people?
    - ☐ 3 (extremely well)
    - ☐ 2 (fairly well)
    - ☐ 1 (not well)

3. In the Vocabulary Builder, how well were you able to put the words on the appropriate clipboards?
    - ☐ 3 (extremely well)
    - ☐ 2 (fairly well)
    - ☐ 1 (not well)

4. How well were you able to complete the character map in the Strategy Follow-up?
    - ☐ 3 (extremely well)
    - ☐ 2 (fairly well)
    - ☐ 1 (not well)

5. How well do you understand Hamai's "lesson from the heart"?
    - ☐ 3 (extremely well)
    - ☐ 2 (fairly well)
    - ☐ 1 (not well)

Vocabulary Check

Look back at the work you did in the Vocabulary Builder. Then answer each question by circling the correct letter.

1. Which word belongs on the clipboard of words related to feelings?
    - a. dangling
    - b. sympathetically
    - c. scrutinizing

2. Which word belongs on the clipboard of words related to actions?
    - a. trudged
    - b. envy
    - c. defensive

3. Which of these words names a feeling of grief or sorrow?
    - a. determined
    - b. anguish
    - c. gently

4. Which of these actions refers to the act of thinking?
    - a. quavered
    - b. speculating
    - c. dangling

5. Which of these words does *not* describe a way of walking?
    - a. trudged
    - b. stump
    - c. quavered

Add the numbers that you just checked to get your Personal Checklist score. Fill in your score here. Then turn to page 215 and transfer your score onto Graph 1.

Check your answers with your teacher. Give yourself 1 point for each correct answer, and fill in your Vocabulary score here. Then turn to page 215 and transfer your score onto Graph 1.

Strategy Check

Review the character map that you completed in the Strategy Follow-up. Also review the story if necessary. Then answer these questions:

1. Why does Hamai choose to ignore her doctor's warnings about walking?
   a. She doesn't think her doctor is very smart.
   b. She is proud and independent.
   c. She doesn't understand her doctor's advice.

2. Why does Hamai always dress well, in color-coordinated outfits that hide her physical problems?
   a. She wants to appear strong and self-reliant.
   b. She is trying to make a fashion statement.
   c. She doesn't have many outfits to wear.

3. Why does Hamai criticize the men who walk by?
   a. She is a cruel person.
   b. The men don't match her high standards.
   c. She wants to teach Julie to dislike men.

4. How does Hamai feel about the years that she spent waiting for her husband to return?
   a. She believes that the years were happy and worthwhile.
   b. She is proud that she was loyal through the years.
   c. She feels that she wasted those years.

5. Why does Hamai urge Julie to be independent?
   a. She wants Julie to respect herself and live her life to the fullest.
   b. She thinks that Julie is weak and leans on her too much.
   c. She couldn't get used to having Julie live with her.

Comprehension Check

Review the story if necessary. Then answer these questions:

1. In the beginning of the story, what does Hamai set aside the day for?
   a. teaching her granddaughter how to find a good man
   b. grocery shopping
   c. remembering the past

2. What does Hamai find wrong with the man wearing the three-piece suit and carrying a briefcase?
   a. He looks boring.
   b. He thinks about his appearance too much and will be unreliable.
   c. Because he stoops, he won't be able to support anyone else.

3. How does Julie react when Hamai makes her judgments?
   a. She makes fun of her grandmother's opinions.
   b. She ignores her grandmother's words.
   c. She listens respectfully.

4. How do you think Hamai felt when her husband left?
   a. sympathetic toward him
   b. surprised and hurt
   c. relieved

5. What does Julie see when she looks at her grandmother?
   a. a woman who hates her life
   b. an unreasonable and angry human being
   c. a strong and independent woman with human flaws

Check your answers with your teacher. Give yourself 1 point for each correct answer, and fill in your Strategy score here. Then turn to page 215 and transfer your score onto Graph 1.

Personal
Vocabulary
Strategy
Comprehension
TOTAL SCORE
✓ T

Check your answers with your teacher. Give yourself 1 point for each correct answer, and fill in your Comprehension score here. Then turn to page 215 and transfer your score onto Graph 1.

Personal
Vocabulary
Strategy
Comprehension
TOTAL SCORE
✓ T

Extending

Choose one or more of these activities:

CONDUCT TWO INTERVIEWS

Interview two people of different ages. First interview an older person. Ask that person to tell you about some of the most valuable lessons learned over the course of his or her lifetime. If possible, tape your interview so you can play it back later. Then interview a much younger person, maybe one of your friends. Ask him or her the same questions about the most important lessons learned so far in life. Compare the two answers. How are they alike and/or different? Write a short personal essay about what you learned from the interviews.

DESCRIBE YOUR IDEAL MATE

Hamai wants her granddaughter to find the "right" man to be her husband. She has strong opinions about what makes a good man and a substandard man. Think about your own standards for a marriage partner. What qualities are you looking for? What qualities do you want to be sure to avoid? Make a list of the top five to ten character traits of your ideal mate.

READ MORE STORIES BY ASIAN WRITERS

Using the resources listed on this page or ones you find yourself, read several other stories written by Asian American writers. Choose two or three of your favorites, and write brief reviews of them on 3 x 5 cards. Put your cards together with those of other classmates who chose to complete this activity. Leave the cards on display in your classroom or school library for other students to read.

Resources

Books

Hong, Maria, ed. *Growing Up Asian American: An Anthology.* Morrow, 1993.

Hongo, Garrett. *The Open Boat: Poems from Asian America.* Anchor, 1993.

Ng, Franklin, ed. *Asian American Family Life and Community.* Asians in America: The People of East, Southeast, and South Asia in American Life and Culture. Garland, 1998.

Yep, Laurence, ed. *American Dragons: Twenty-five Asian American Voices.* HarperTrophy, 1995.

Web Site

http://www.library.csustan.edu/pcrawford/asianlit/
This Web site contains a bibliography of Asian American literature.

LESSON 14 Emma Lazarus: "Mother of Exiles"

Building Background

The selection you are about to read describes how the poem on the Statue of Liberty was written—or more appropriately, how it almost didn't get written. Emma Lazarus didn't want to write the poem at first because she was actively involved in a cause that she strongly supported.

What cause or causes do you strongly support? On the lines below, describe the cause or causes, and explain why you support them. Then, as you read, use what you have written to help you understand Lazarus's commitment to her chosen cause.

_____

_____

_____

_____

_____

Vocabulary Builder

beleaguered

comply

destitute

eminent

grandeur

majestically

oppression

quotas

transcended

1. The words in the margin are from the selection you are about to read. Each of the words is listed below and is followed by two other words. Underline the word in each row that is a synonym of the boldfaced vocabulary word. If you are unsure of the meanings of any of the words, use context or a dictionary to help you.

2. Save your work. You will refer to it again in the Vocabulary Check.

beleaguered	troubled	joyful
comply	agree to	disagree with
destitute	wealthy	poor
eminent	outstanding	unknown
grandeur	hugeness	glory
majestically	magnificently	drearily
oppression	relief	persecution
quotas	unlimited numbers	set amounts
transcended	went beyond	stayed the same

Strategy Builder

Asking Questions While You Read

- Has this ever happened to you? You're reading a textbook or an informational article. When you stop for a moment to think about what you just read, you realize that . . . you have *no idea* what you just read.

- If you answered "yes" to the question above, don't worry. It happens to everyone. That's because textbooks and informational articles give you lots of unfamiliar information at once. To keep that information straight—and to remember it better—there are some things that you can do. One thing that you already know how to do is to summarize the main ideas. Another thing that you can do is to outline the main ideas and supporting details or put them on a concept map.

- Still another thing that you can do is to ask yourself questions about what you read. **Self-questioning** works a lot like summarizing. First you ask yourself a question to get at the **main idea** of a section of text. Then you answer the question with **details** from that section of text.

- To understand how self-questioning works, read the following paragraphs from an article about printer's apprentices during the 1700s and early 1800s. Then read one student's question and answers about it.

> But hard work and rough treatment couldn't keep apprentices from having fun. In the evening, they played the accordion and sang. They played chess and perhaps cards in secret, since a strict master might believe that cards were sinful. Apprentices were even known to sneak out at night to roam the streets or visit taverns.
>
> Sometimes they played tricks on each other. One shy country boy named Horace Greeley had his blond hair inked black by the other apprentices. But they must not have discouraged him too badly. He kept working at the printer's craft, learning how to edit and publish a newspaper. Later he became the most famous newspaper editor of his time.

Q: **What did printers' apprentices do for fun?**
- They played the accordion and sang.
- They played chess and cards.
- Some even roamed the streets and went to taverns.
- They also played tricks on each other, like inking Horace Greeley's blond hair black.

Emma Lazarus: "Mother of Exiles"

by Diane Lefer

As you read the first part of this article, underline the information that you would use for your questions and answers. When you get to the Strategy Break, you will have a chance to compare what you've underlined to the sample questions and answers.

William Maxwell Evarts, former U.S. secretary of state and future senator from New York, seldom had difficulty persuading people to help him. But in 1883, when he asked Emma Lazarus for a favor, she refused him. In Paris, the sculptor Frédéric-Auguste Bartholdi was rapidly completing a work commissioned by the people of France as a gift to the United States, a statue called *Liberty Enlightening the World.* Concerned because America had not yet raised enough money to build the pedestal that the monument would stand on, Evarts asked several **eminent** writers to compose original poems and stories, which would be sold at an auction in New York City as part of a fundraising drive. Along with Mark Twain and Walt Whitman, Lazarus was one of the authors Evarts approached for the project.

The 34-year-old poet and essayist was a logical choice to write a poem for the auction. Not only was she famous throughout America, but she was especially popular in her native New York City, where the monument would eventually be erected. Her first book of verse had appeared when she was still in her teens, and several well-received volumes of poetry and prose had followed. In addition, Lazarus was wealthy and known for her generous contributions to charity.

Nonetheless, Lazarus was unwilling to **comply** with Evarts's request. She believed that poetry was created out of inspiration and was doubtful of her ability to write anything worthwhile on demand. She was also very busy working for a cause of her own: helping the thousands of Jews who had fled **oppression** in Russia and were arriving in New York homeless, penniless, and without prospects.

Evarts finally gave up on enlisting Lazarus in his cause, but another member of the fundraising committee did not. Constance Cary Harrison appealed to the reluctant poet's emotions, encouraging her to think of what the statue might mean to Russia's **beleaguered** refugees as they saw it for the first time. "The shaft sped home," Mrs. Harrison later reported. "Her dark eyes deepened—her cheek flushed," and Emma Lazarus promised to write a poem about the statue. The fundraising auction was set for early December. In November, with time running out, Emma Lazarus sat down at her desk to keep her word.

⬣ **Stop here for the Strategy Break.**

Strategy Break

As you read, did you underline information for your questions and answers? If you did, see if your information matches these:

Q: Why did Maxwell Evarts ask Emma Lazarus to write a poem?
- Frédéric–Auguste Bartholdi was finishing work on his <u>Liberty Enlightening the World</u> statue, and America still hadn't raised enough money for its pedestal. So Evarts asked several famous writers to write poems and stories that he could auction off at a fundraising event.
- Lazarus was a logical choice to write a poem because she was famous all over America but especially in New York City.
- Lazarus was also wealthy and known for her large contributions to charity.

Q: Why did Emma Lazarus refuse Evarts's request?
- She believed that poetry was created out of inspiration, and she doubted she could write anything worthwhile on demand.
- She was also busy with her own cause: helping the Jews who had fled Russia and were arriving penniless in New York.

Q: How was Constance Cary Harrison able to change Lazarus's mind?
- She encouraged Lazarus to think of what the statue might mean to the Russian refugees who saw it for the first time as they arrived in New York.

▶ Go on reading.

Her earliest verses had been based on themes from Greek mythology and the legends of medieval Europe. This strong classical background surfaced when she decided to contrast Bartholdi's sculpture with one of the seven wonders of the ancient world—a huge statue of the Greek god Helios, called Colossus, that was said to have straddled the harbor at Rhodes. But by 1883 Lazarus no longer believed that a reference to past **grandeur** was enough to make a work great. She knew that her poem would have to look far beyond ancient Greece to express her thoughts about liberty.

Once it would have been easy for her to write a piece in which liberty was portrayed as an exalted ideal that **transcended** daily life in the same way that the statue *Liberty Enlightening the World*, 151 feet high, would tower over the ships and people of New York. But clever images and highflown abstractions no longer seemed powerful enough for her purposes.

Lazarus could trace her family tree all the way back to colonial days, but as she sat down to write, even thoughts about the glorious dawn of American independence did not satisfy her. A poem on liberty might refer to the Declaration of Independence and the U.S. Constitution, but precious as those documents were, they did not reveal the human story of America that Emma Lazarus wanted to tell.

As she tried to imagine the completed statue, standing **majestically** on its pedestal on Bedloe's (now Liberty) Island, in her mind's eye she saw another island altogether: Ward's Island, where it would be hard to find any trace of beauty or majesty at all.

A small square of land lying close by the Manhattan shoreline in the East River, Ward's Island was the site of the city asylum for the insane and the city's "potter's field"—the cemetery for unclaimed corpses and for paupers whose families could not afford to pay for burials. More recently the island had housed thousands of sick and **destitute** immigrants who had not passed inspection at Castle Garden, the United States immigration station (Ellis Island did not open until 1892). Men, women, and children lived there in temporary barracks as they waited for the U.S. government to determine their fates. Their numbers included many Jewish refugees fleeing persecution in Russia.

Few people traveled willingly to Ward's Island, but when she heard of the Jewish immigrants' plight, Emma Lazarus went there. She saw frightened people and heard stories of mass violence in their homeland. She went back to the island again and again, trying to understand what had happened to these people and what, if anything, she could do for them. Lazarus knew that the refugees' plight was made even worse because they were not really welcome in America. Their exodus from Russia had come at exactly the wrong time.

The United States had been built by immigrants, and throughout its history the U.S. government had actively encouraged people to come and settle in America. In the 1870s many American businesses sent representatives to Europe to convince people to emigrate and work in the booming factories of the Industrial Revolution. Underpopulated southern and western states sent out promotional brochures to attract European settlers, and land company agents lured peasants and farmers away from Scotland, Ireland, and Scandinavia.

In the 1880s, the United States still needed farmers and laborers to develop the vast North American continent, but some Americans felt that the Russian Jews could not make a productive contribution. Who were they, after all? Men and women who were weak with malnutrition, many of whom had never plowed a field or dug a ditch. Other Americans claimed that the new immigrants were bringing problems to the United States instead of contributing to its strength. Irish and Chinese immigrants, for instance, had provided the country with cheap labor to build railroads and mine coal, but now were blamed for creating city slums and spreading disease and crime. Other groups—such as the Italians, Poles, Hungarians, and Russian Jews—continued to stream into the United States and met with growing resentment as long-established Americans feared for their way of life.

In 1882, new laws entirely barred Chinese immigration and set **quotas** to restrict the number of new arrivals from several other countries. According to some Americans, the laws did not go far enough. They said it was time to close the country's doors. If that happened, Emma Lazarus knew that hundreds of thousands of people would be left to suffer and probably die in the old country.

This painful knowledge guided her thoughts as she worked on the sonnet that would help provide a pedestal for Bartholdi's sculpture. The statue itself was still in Paris, surrounded by scaffolding, and Lazarus had never seen it, but that did not matter. She had seen both the misery and hopefulness of America's immigrants, and that was enough to give her an idea. The poem she wrote that November day was called "The New Colossus," and it proclaimed:

Not like the brazen giant of Greek fame,
With conquering limbs astride from land to land;
Here at our sea-washed sunset gates shall stand
A mighty woman with a torch, whose flame
Is the imprisoned lightning, and her name
Mother of Exiles. From her beacon-hand
Glows world-wide welcome; her mild eyes command
The air-bridged harbor that twin cities frame.
"Keep, ancient lands, your storied pomp!" cries she
With silent lips. "Give me your tired, your poor,
Your huddled masses yearning to breathe free,
The wretched refuse of your teeming shore.
Send these, the homeless, tempest-tost to me.
I lift my lamp beside the golden door!"

Although Lazarus's poem and Frédéric-Auguste Bartholdi's sculpture have become inextricably linked in most people's minds, the two artists had very different views of "Lady Liberty." Bartholdi had designed an unyielding face that expressed victory over tyranny; Emma Lazarus envisioned features softened by human compassion. The sculptor sought to symbolize the alliance between two great powers, France and the United States; the poet described America's special meaning to oppressed people all over the world.

Emma Lazarus was famous, and so she could be confident that her verse would help raise money for the statue's pedestal. In that sense, her poem was sure to be a success. But her hopes for the sonnet were more ambitious than just raising money. She hoped it would help convince Americans that liberty would not be served if the U.S. government shut its doors to new arrivals, particularly to "less desirable" immigrants—the persecuted and impoverished victims of oppressive governments. But she was far from sure that her 12-line poem alone could get her point across. After all, it had taken Lazarus herself three decades to see the misery and injustice that existed beyond her own privileged life. ●

Strategy Follow-up

Work with the whole class or a group of students to complete this activity. First, skim the second part of this selection, and divide it into several sections. Assign each section to a pair or group of students. Then write a question (or questions) and answers for your particular section of text. Be sure to use your own words, and include only the most important information.

When everyone is finished, put all the questions and answers in order and review them together. Revise any information as necessary.

✓Personal Checklist

Read each question and put a check (✓) in the correct box.

1. How well do you understand the information presented in this article?
   - ☐ 3 (extremely well)
   - ☐ 2 (fairly well)
   - ☐ 1 (not well)

2. How well were you able to use what you wrote in Building Background to help you understand Lazarus's support of the Jews who were arriving from Russia?
   - ☐ 3 (extremely well)
   - ☐ 2 (fairly well)
   - ☐ 1 (not well)

3. In the Vocabulary Builder, how many vocabulary words were you able to correctly match with their synonyms?
   - ☐ 3 (7–9 words)
   - ☐ 2 (4–6 words)
   - ☐ 1 (0–3 words)

4. In the Strategy Follow-up, how well were you able to write a question (or questions) and answers for your section of text?
   - ☐ 3 (extremely well)
   - ☐ 2 (fairly well)
   - ☐ 1 (not well)

5. How well could you explain what caused Lazarus to change her mind and write a poem for the Statue of Liberty?
   - ☐ 3 (extremely well)
   - ☐ 2 (fairly well)
   - ☐ 1 (not well)

Vocabulary Check

Look back at the work you did in the Vocabulary Builder. Then answer each question by circling the correct letter.

1. Which of these people at a football game would be considered the most eminent?
   a. the team's Most Valuable Player
   b. the custodian of the football stadium
   c. the team's waterboy or watergirl

2. Which phrase best describes someone who is destitute?
   a. someone who lives in a mansion
   b. someone who lives in a log cabin
   c. someone who is homeless

3. The Jews fleeing Russia were trying to escape oppression. What does this mean?
   a. They were trying to find a less expensive way of life.
   b. They were trying to get away from cramped living quarters.
   c. They were trying to escape cruel and unfair treatment.

4. What do you do when you comply with someone's wishes?
   a. grant someone three wishes
   b. go along with the person's wishes
   c. disagree with a person's wishes

5. Which phrase best describes a person who is beleaguered?
   a. troubled or worried
   b. happy and carefree
   c. angry and resentful

Add the numbers that you just checked to get your Personal Checklist score. Fill in your score here. Then turn to page 215 and transfer your score onto Graph 1.

	Personal	
	Vocabulary	
	Strategy	
	Comprehension	
TOTAL SCORE		
	✓	T

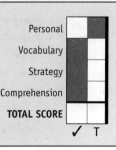

Check your answers with your teacher. Give yourself 1 point for each correct answer, and fill in your Vocabulary score here. Then turn to page 215 and transfer your score onto Graph 1.

	Personal	
	Vocabulary	
	Strategy	
	Comprehension	
TOTAL SCORE		
	✓	T

Strategy Check

Review the questions and answers that your class or group wrote for this article. Then answer these questions:

1. Which island did Lazarus picture as she tried to imagine the completed Statue of Liberty?
   a. Ward's Island
   b. Bedloe's Island
   c. Ellis Island

2. Why did she picture this place?
   a. It was where the completed Statue of Liberty was going to be erected.
   b. It was her favorite place.
   c. It gave her a picture of the immigrants who were arriving at that time.

3. Which question does the statement *Some Americans felt that the Russian Jews could not make a productive contribution* answer?
   a. Why were Russian immigrants welcome?
   b. Why were the Russian refugees charged more money to enter the States?
   c. Why were Russian refugees unwelcome in the United States in the 1880s?

4. Which question does the statement *She had seen both the misery and hopefulness of America's immigrants* answer?
   a. Why did Lazarus refuse to write the poem?
   b. Where did Lazarus get her inspiration for "The New Colossus"?
   c. What did Lazarus see when she looked out her apartment window?

5. Which question best summarizes this article?
   a. Why did Emma Lazarus finally decide to write "The New Colossus"?
   b. Who finally got Emma Lazarus to write "The New Colossus"?
   c. How did everyone respond to Emma Lazarus's "The New Colossus"?

Comprehension Check

Review the selection if necessary. Then answer these questions:

1. Why did Lazarus refuse at first to contribute a poem to the auction?
   a. She thought it cheapened her work to have it auctioned off.
   b. She felt she had to wait for inspiration to produce a valuable poem.
   c. She disagreed with the whole idea of putting up the statue.

2. How long did it take Lazarus to write "The New Colossus"?
   a. less than a month
   b. almost a full year
   c. over a year

3. To what did the term *Colossus* originally refer?
   a. a major character in one of Emma Lazarus's popular poems of the 1880s
   b. a giant who appeared in many legends of medieval Europe
   c. a statue of the Greek god Helios that towered over the harbor of Rhodes

4. Which of these statements about Lazarus's goals for the poem is true?
   a. Lazarus felt that Greek images were perfect for showing the greatness of America.
   b. Lazarus was aware of immigrants' struggles and wanted to give them hope.
   c. Lazarus wanted to discourage new immigrants from coming to America.

5. What is the official name of the giant statue in New York Harbor?
   a. *Lady Liberty*
   b. *Statue of Liberty*
   c. *Liberty Enlightening the World*

Check your answers with your teacher. Give yourself 1 point for each correct answer, and fill in your Strategy score here. Then turn to page 215 and transfer your score onto Graph 1.

Personal
Vocabulary
Strategy
Comprehension
TOTAL SCORE
✓ T

Check your answers with your teacher. Give yourself 1 point for each correct answer, and fill in your Comprehension score here. Then turn to page 215 and transfer your score onto Graph 1.

Personal
Vocabulary
Strategy
Comprehension
TOTAL SCORE
✓ T

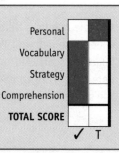

Extending

Choose one or both of these activities:

MAKE A PHOTO ALBUM OR POSTER FOR THE STATUE OF LIBERTY

Tens of thousands of photographs, drawings, and paintings of the Statue of Liberty have been made. Search through books, travel brochures, library picture collections, Web sites, and other sources to find pictures of the statue. (The resources listed on this page will give you a place to start.) Choose between 10 and 20 of your favorite pictures, photocopy them if necessary, and mount them in a photo album or on a poster board. For each picture, provide a caption. It could be a comment on the view of the statue or its meaning, a few lines selected from Emma Lazarus's poem, or a few lines of original poetry inspired by the statue. Exhibit your album or poster in your classroom.

WRITE A POEM

Write a poem (with or without rhyme) about a symbol of America that you find particularly inspiring. In your poem, suggest what makes this symbol important for the country, but focus particularly on its meaning to you.

Resources

Books

Davies, Nancy Millichap. *Gateway to America: Liberty Island and Ellis Island.* American Traveler. Smithmark, 1992.

Holland, F. Ross. *Idealists, Scoundrels, and the Lady: An Insider's View of the Statue of Liberty–Ellis Island Project.* University of Illinois Press, 1993.

Kallen, Stuart A. *The Statue of Liberty: "The New Colossus."* Abdo, 1994.

Lefer, Diane. *Emma Lazarus.* American Women of Achievement. Chelsea House, 1988.

Merriam, Eve. *The Voice of Liberty: The Story of Emma Lazarus.* Farrar, Straus and Cudahy, 1959.

Web Sites

http://www.endex.com/gf/buildings/liberty/solgallery/solgallery.htm
This Web site presents a large collection of images of the Statue of Liberty, including both historical and current photographs.

http://www.libertystatepark.com/emma.htm
You can read Emma Lazarus's poem on this Web page.

LESSON ⓯ The Lady with the Green Skin

Building Background

In Lesson 14 you read about Emma Lazarus and the poem that she wrote for the Statue of Liberty. When Lazarus wrote "The New Colossus" she had seen only photographs and sketches of the statue, not the statue itself. She probably was very eager to see the completed statue to learn if it matched her own picture of it and questions about it.

You too, may have questions about the statue. Even if you have seen it from the outside, you may wonder what it looks like on the inside. The selection you are about to read may help you. Before you begin, think about what questions you would like the selection to answer. Write your questions below. Then as you read, see how many of your questions the author answers.

Questions I Have About the Statue of Liberty

_____

_____

_____

_____

_____

asbestos

contoured

copper

insulation

patina

pedestal

skeleton

supported

Vocabulary Builder

1. The words in the margin are all related to the Statue of Liberty and its construction. As you learned in Lesson 7, words that are all related to a particular topic are called **specialized vocabulary** words. Knowing what these words mean before you read the selection will help you understand it better.

2. Match each specialized vocabulary word in Column 1 to its definition in Column 2. Use a dictionary if you need help.

3. Save your work. You will refer to it again in the Vocabulary Check.

COLUMN 1	COLUMN 2
asbestos	outlined
contoured	base on which something stands
copper	blue-green film that forms on certain metals
insulation	fire-resistant material
patina	material that stops the transfer of electricity
pedestal	inner framework
skeleton	reddish-brown metal

Strategy Builder

Following Sequence While Reading Nonfiction

- When authors describe the process of how something happened or how it works, their main purpose for writing is to **inform**. They usually use the organizational pattern of **sequence**—or a combination of **sequence** and **description**—to describe the order of events or the steps in the process. For example, in this selection the author describes the steps that workers followed as they built, reassembled, and restored the Statue of Liberty. She also describes what happened to the statue's outer surface over the years.

- To make the sequence of steps and events as clear as possible in this selection, the author uses **signal words**. Some examples of signal words are *first, then, in 1871,* and *fifteen years after.*

- The following paragraph describes how to make chow mein. Use the underlined signal words to help you follow the sequence.

> Vegetable chow mein is a healthful and delicious dinner. To make it, follow these steps: <u>First</u>, wash and cut all the vegetables you will need, and <u>then</u> put them aside. <u>Next</u> get a pan and sauté all the vegetables in oil. <u>After the vegetables are lightly cooked</u>, add a sauce. <u>Then</u> cook about five more minutes. <u>Finally</u>, serve the dish over rice, and dig in!

- If you wanted to track the order of steps in the process above, you could use a **sequence chain**. It might look like this:

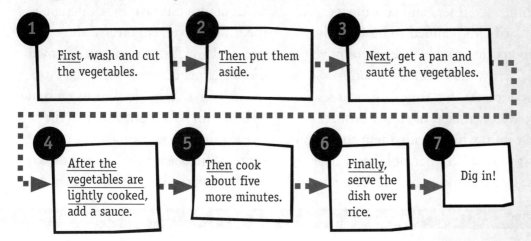

The Lady with the Green Skin

by Sylvia C. Montrone

In the first part of this selection, the author describes the steps involved in building the Statue of Liberty. See if you can use the signal words to help you follow the steps.

The Statue of Liberty has stood tall over New York Harbor for more than a century, welcoming immigrants to the United States. Although Lady Liberty has undergone repairs from time to time to keep her in good condition, no one has dared to remove the green that covers her once brightly colored **copper** skin.

In 1871 a French sculptor, Frédéric Auguste Bartholdi, traveled to the United States to promote interest in a statue commemorating 100 years of American independence. Bartholdi and other French citizens were great admirers of American democracy and wanted to present the statue as a gift from the people of France to the people of the United States.

Just as his ship entered New York Harbor, Bartholdi had a vision of a grand monument with a glowing torch welcoming voyagers to America. Seven spokes in the lady's crown depicted the world's seven seas and continents.

Bartholdi planned to build Lady Liberty in Paris, France, then move her across the Atlantic Ocean to America. At that time large statues were constructed of stone, bronze, or cast iron, which made them too heavy to transport. So Bartholdi and the engineers working on the statue decided to give the lady a copper skin over an iron **skeleton**. They believed that the lightweight copper could withstand New York Harbor's harsh winds and salt sea air, as long as it was **supported** by a strong frame.

In a specially built Paris workshop, artisans perfected the statue's form by making several plaster models from Bartholdi's sketches. Each plaster model was bigger than the last. The biggest was full-size: 151 feet, 1 inch tall. This model was divided into 300 sections. Carpenters made wooden molds from each section, and metal craftsmen hammered shiny copper sheets into the molds. The copper was the kind used today in craft projects, except the sheets were much larger and, at 3/32 of an inch, about the thickness of a pizza crust. The artisans shaped the copper to create the folds of Lady Liberty's gown, her facial features, and even the law book inscribed 4 July 1776.

Alexandre Gustave Eiffel, designer of the Eiffel Tower, engineered the statue's iron skeleton. Four iron posts formed the skeleton's center, with space inside for stairways. What looked like a spider web of iron bars, **contoured** to the statue's final form, hung around the center. After each piece of copper skin was hammered into shape, craftsmen attached it to the iron web. Shiny like a new penny, Lady Liberty steadily grew on a platform outside the workshop. She received visitors in Paris for almost a year before workers dismantled her, numbering each part. On the day she emigrated, a 70-car train carried 214 oddly shaped crates from Paris to a ship bound for America.

⬣ **Stop here for the Strategy Break.**

Strategy Break

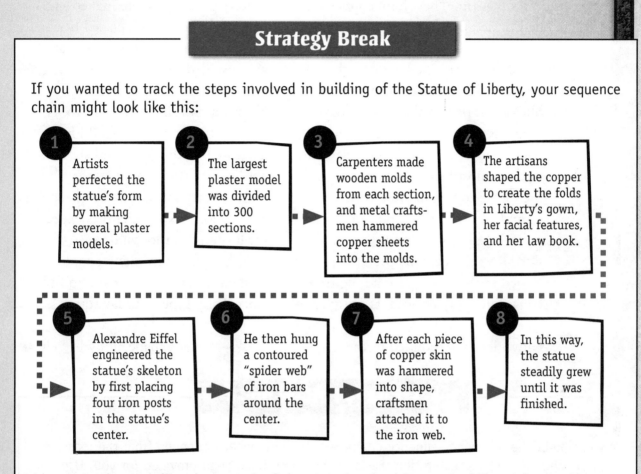

If you wanted to track the steps involved in building of the Statue of Liberty, your sequence chain might look like this:

1 Artists perfected the statue's form by making several plaster models.

2 The largest plaster model was divided into 300 sections.

3 Carpenters made wooden molds from each section, and metal crafts-men hammered copper sheets into the molds.

4 The artisans shaped the copper to create the folds in Liberty's gown, her facial features, and her law book.

5 Alexandre Eiffel engineered the statue's skeleton by first placing four iron posts in the statue's center.

6 He then hung a contoured "spider web" of iron bars around the center.

7 After each piece of copper skin was hammered into shape, craftsmen attached it to the iron web.

8 In this way, the statue steadily grew until it was finished.

As you continue reading, keep track of the steps involved in reassembling and restoring the statue. Also pay attention to what happened to the statue's copper skin over the years. At the end of this selection you will use some of this information to complete a sequence chain of your own.

 Go on reading.

Reassembling Lady Liberty atop a 154-foot-high **pedestal** on Bedloe's Island in New York Harbor was like putting together a colossal jigsaw puzzle. Hundreds of thousands of rivets were needed to attach the 300 pieces of copper skin to the iron web. **Asbestos** insulation was placed between the skin and the iron ribs wherever the two metals met. Eiffel feared that, without **insulation**, the statue might become a giant electric battery, shocking visitors!

In 1886, fifteen years after Bartholdi's first trip to the United

States, President Cleveland unveiled the Statue of Liberty exactly where the sculptor had envisioned her. Mounted on her pedestal, she rose 305 feet above the harbor, nearly as high as a football field standing on end.

By that time, her shiny copper skin had turned the dull brown color of an old penny. At the turn of the century, her skin was streaked with black and green, which gradually changed to the blue-green **patina** she wears today. Patina is a crust that forms when a copper surface is attacked by elements in the atmosphere and combines with them. Metropolitan New York's humidity, snow, rain, and industrial pollution all reacted with the statue's skin. If you've ever uncovered a penny buried in the ground for a long time, you've probably noticed its crusty, pale green edges, or patina. Like the penny, Lady Liberty responded to the environment's bullying with a trick from Mother Nature. Once the patina had spread over her entire copper skin, she was protected from further environmental damage.

Between 1981 and 1986, Lady Liberty got a complete makeover. A new steel-alloy web replaced her badly corroded iron web. A glass elevator was installed. Electrical engineers even devised a new lighting system. However, polishing her skin to its original bright copper would have decreased its thickness and shortened her life. So, throughout restoration, Lady Liberty was allowed to keep her patina cloak. Now scientists expect she'll survive a thousand years.

Although many, many people worked to restore the statue to full glory, Lady Liberty today stands proudly protected in a green patina cloak—one she made all by herself. ●

Strategy Follow-up

Now complete the following sequence chain, which shows what happened from the reassembling of the statue to its restoration. Parts of the chain have been provided for you. Use another sheet of paper if you need more room to write.

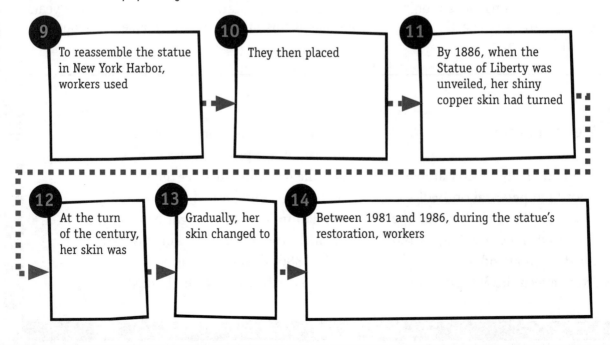

9 To reassemble the statue in New York Harbor, workers used

10 They then placed

11 By 1886, when the Statue of Liberty was unveiled, her shiny copper skin had turned

12 At the turn of the century, her skin was

13 Gradually, her skin changed to

14 Between 1981 and 1986, during the statue's restoration, workers

✓Personal Checklist

Read each question and put a check (✓) in the correct box.

1. How well do you understand the information presented in this selection?
   - ☐ 3 (extremely well)
   - ☐ 2 (fairly well)
   - ☐ 1 (not well)

2. In Building Background, how well were you able to think of questions about the Statue of Liberty?
   - ☐ 3 (extremely well)
   - ☐ 2 (fairly well)
   - ☐ 1 (not well)

3. In the Vocabulary Builder, how well were you able to match the specialized vocabulary words and their definitions?
   - ☐ 3 (extremely well)
   - ☐ 2 (fairly well)
   - ☐ 1 (not well)

4. How well were you able to complete the sequence chain in the Strategy Follow-up?
   - ☐ 3 (extremely well)
   - ☐ 2 (fairly well)
   - ☐ 1 (not well)

5. After reading this selection, how well would you be able to describe how the Statue of Liberty was built?
   - ☐ 3 (extremely well)
   - ☐ 2 (fairly well)
   - ☐ 1 (not well)

Vocabulary Check

Look back at the work you did in the Vocabulary Builder. Then answer each question by circling the correct letter.

1. Which of these is *not* a building material?
   a. asbestos
   b. copper
   c. patina

2. Which of these words describes a fire-resistant material?
   a. patina
   b. asbestos
   c. pedestal

3. Which meaning of *insulate* fits the context of this selection?
   a. keep apart from other people
   b. stop the transfer of sound
   c. stop the transfer of electricity

4. Which word best matches the definition "shaped to fit the form of something"?
   a. contoured
   b. pedestal
   c. skeleton

5. Which word or phrase best defines *patina*?
   a. the outline of a figure
   b. a building material
   c. a thin covering

Add the numbers that you just checked to get your Personal Checklist score. Fill in your score here. Then turn to page 215 and transfer your score onto Graph 1.

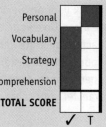

Check your answers with your teacher. Give yourself 1 point for each correct answer, and fill in your Vocabulary score here. Then turn to page 215 and transfer your score onto Graph 1.

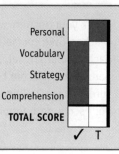

Strategy Check

Review the sequence chain that you completed in the Strategy Follow-up. Also review the rest of the selection if necessary. Then answer these questions:

1. When reassembling the Statue of Liberty in the United States, what did workers use to attach the copper skin to the iron web?

   a. hundreds of thousands of rivets

   b. hundreds of yards of asbestos

   c. several hundred feet of patina

2. What did they place between the skin and the iron ribs wherever two metals met?

   a. contoured copper

   b. asbestos insulation

   c. patina rivets

3. How many years after Bartholdi's first trip to the United States was the Statue of Liberty unveiled in New York Harbor?

   a. five years

   b. ten years

   c. fifteen years

4. When was the statue's skin streaked black and green?

   a. by 1886

   b. around 1900

   c. between 1981 and 1986

5. Which of these is *not* an example of signal words?

   a. at the turn of the century

   b. fifteen years after Bartholdi's first trip to the United States

   c. she was protected from further environmental damage

Comprehension Check

Review the selection if necessary. Then answer these questions:

1. Which of these statements is true?

   a. The development of the Statue of Liberty began in 1776.

   b. The development of the Statue of Liberty began in 1871.

   c. The development of the Statue of Liberty began in 1876.

2. What do the seven spokes in Lady Liberty's crown stand for?

   a. the seven seas and seven continents

   b. the seven biggest contributors to the project

   c. the seven days of the week

3. What is Lady Liberty holding?

   a. a torch in one hand and a law book in the other

   b. a torch in one hand and a scroll in the other

   c. a torch in one hand and a calendar in the other

4. What did Bartholdi want to commemorate (honor or celebrate) with the Statue of Liberty?

   a. all the immigrants who had come to America

   b. 100 years of American independence

   c. the seven seas and seven continents

5. When the statue was restored in the 1980s, why was it not polished to its original bright copper?

   a. People prefer the patina because it matches the surrounding water.

   b. Polishing it would have thinned the copper and shortened the statue's life.

   c. The restoration committee ran out of money before the job could be completed.

Extending

Choose one or both of these activities:

TELL THE HISTORY OF A MONUMENT

Choose another monument famous for its size, such as the Washington Monument in Washington, D.C.; the Eiffel Tower in Paris, France; or the Great Wall of China. Make up a list of questions that you have about its construction—how, when, why, and so forth. Then do research to find the answers to your questions. Choose a single item about that monument or its construction that makes it unique, as this selection focuses on the green skin of the Statue of Liberty. Then write a short article that describes your chosen monument and its unique characteristic.

TAKE A VIRTUAL TOUR

Starting with the Web site of the National Park Service for the Statue of Liberty National Monument (the third Web site listed under Resources), take a virtual tour of the Statue of Liberty. Follow the links to enjoy unusual views and discover staggering statistics. After your tour, write a report on what you learned from this Web site that you didn't learn from other sources.

Resources

Books

Doherty, Craig A., and Katherine M. Doherty. *The Statue of Liberty.* Blackbirch Press, 2001.

Mercer, Charles E. *Statue of Liberty.* Putnam, 1985.

Miller, Natalie. *The Statue of Liberty.* Children's Press, 1992.

Patterson, Lillie. *Meet Miss Liberty* (illustrated with historic engravings and photographs). Atheneum, 1969.

Web Sites

http://glasssteelandstone.com/ByTypeMonuments.html
This Web site offers links to information about famous monuments around the world.

http://libertystatepark.com/statueof.htm
This is the Web site of New Jersey's Liberty State Park.

http://www.nps.gov/stli/
This is the National Park Service Web site for the Statue of Liberty National Monument.

Learning New Words

VOCABULARY

From Lesson 11
• disqualified

From Lesson 12
• dispassionate

Prefixes

A prefix is a word part that is added to the beginning of a root word. When you add a prefix, you often change the root word's meaning and function. For example, the prefix *pre-* means "before." So adding *pre-* to *game* changes the noun *game* to the adjective *pregame,* which means "happening before a game."

dis-

The prefix *dis-* means "not" or "the opposite of." The word *qualified* means "able or fit to do something." Adding the prefix *dis-* to *qualified* changes the word to its antonym, which means "not able or fit to do something."

Write the word that describes each definition below.

1. not loyal   _____

2. the opposite of honest   _____

3. not agreeable   _____

4. the opposite of encourage   _____

Suffixes

A suffix is a word part that is added to the end of a root word. When you add a suffix, you often change the root word's meaning and function.

From Lesson 12
• conspirators

-or

The suffix *-or* turns a word into a noun that means "a person who _____." In "Telling Stories" Irene and Andrew discuss their wedding plans like old friends and conspirators. A *conspirator* is a person who conspires, or plans in secret.

Write the word that describes each person below.

1. a person who conducts an orchestra   _____

2. a person who creates things   _____

3. a person who edits books   _____

4. a person who governs others   _____

Multiple-Meaning Words

You know that a single word can have more than one meaning. For example, the word *depression* can mean "low place or hollow in the ground" or "sad or gloomy condition" or "reduction of business activity."

To figure out which meaning of *depression* an author is using, you have to use context. Context is the information surrounding a word or situation that helps you understand it. When you read that Wilma Rudolph twisted her ankle after hitting a depression in the ground while jogging, you used context to figure out that the meaning the author was using was "a low place or hollow in the ground."

Now use context to figure out the correct meaning of each underlined word. Circle the letter of the correct meaning.

1. The movie is scheduled to begin in a <u>quarter</u> of an hour.

   a. 15 minutes

   b. 25 cents

2. The object of the game is to <u>stump</u> your opponent.

   a. make political speeches at

   b. make unable to do or answer

3. Paul's hair was bright <u>copper</u> when he was a baby.

   a. reddish-brown metal

   b. reddish-brown color

4. Standing five feet tall and weighing one hundred pounds fully clothed, Jake was an absolute <u>skeleton</u>.

   a. very thin person

   b. framework of bones

5. We <u>supported</u> our team by wearing our school colors to the wrestling match.

   a. kept from falling down

   b. showed favor or backing

VOCABULARY

From Lesson 11
- depression
- clamor

From Lesson 12
- quarter

From Lesson 13
- stump

From Lesson 15
- copper
- skeleton
- supported

EPICAC

Building Background

One of the main characters in "EPICAC" isn't a human being or even an animal. It is, instead, a computer. As you know, computers are changing our lives in countless ways. Some people find them eerily humanlike in their capacity to solve problems. If computers become more like humans, what could happen? In some science fiction stories, the increasing abilities of computers often threaten mankind. Imagine a few problems that might be associated with creating incredibly intelligent machines, and discuss them with a partner. Also discuss some of the benefits that these intelligent machines might provide.

cracker-jack

fizzled

floored her

half-baked

hasn't been a
  peep about him

mind was mush

send-off

sweep me
  off my feet

the Brass

Vocabulary Builder

1. The words and phrases in the margin are all from the story "EPICAC." You often hear them in informal conversation, but you don't usually read or use them in formal writing. By using these **colloquialisms**, the author creates a light, casual mood that helps readers relax into the story.

2. Before you begin reading "EPICAC," match each word or phrase in Column 1 to its meaning in Column 2. Then, as you read the story, notice how the words and phrases help create a relaxed mood.

COLUMN 1	COLUMN 2
hasn't been a peep about him	the people in charge
send-off	not completely or properly developed
the Brass	excellent
fizzled	charm or impress me
cracker-jack	there hasn't been anything said about him
sweep me off my feet	couldn't think straight
half-baked	amazed her
mind was mush	introduction
floored her	failed

3. Save your work. You will refer to it again in the Vocabulary Check.

Strategy Builder

Drawing Conclusions About Characters

- "EPICAC" is a science fiction story. Like fantasy stories, **science fiction** stories often contain characters, settings, or events that could not exist or happen in real life.

- As you learned earlier in the book, a **conclusion** is a decision that you reach after thinking about certain facts or information. When you read a story, you can draw conclusions about the characters based on what they say, do, think, and feel—and what other characters say *about* them.

- In many stories, the characters change in some way. These are called **dynamic characters**. Other characters stay the same. They are called **static characters**. As you read the paragraphs below, try to draw conclusions about Andy based on what he says, does, thinks, and feels.

> Andy thought of himself as a man of action. He liked bikes, karate, baseball, and, most of all, mountain climbing. What he didn't like was sitting in one place for very long. That's why he could never understand the appeal of computers. Who would want to sit still and look at words on a screen when they could be running, jumping, and DOING?
>
> One day Andy passed his sister as she was surfing the Web, and he caught a glimpse of what he recognized as Mount Everest on the computer screen. The site offered a real-time video being taken by a mountain climber in Tibet. The pictures were coming in as the climber ascended the mountain. Andy asked his sister to move over and let him check out the computer with her.
>
> From that moment, Andy was hooked. He checked that Web site every day to find out how the climber was doing on Mount Everest. Still a man of action, Andy now feels that computers are not such a bad thing after all.

- If you wanted to track the changes in Andy's character, you could record them on a **character wheel** like the one below. The conclusions that one reader drew about Andy are in *italics*.

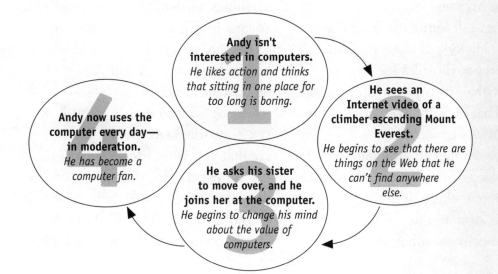

EPICAC

by Kurt Vonnegut, Jr.

As you read this short story, apply the strategies that you just learned. Look for clues that the author provides to help you draw conclusions about both the human characters and the nonhuman one.

It's about time somebody told about my friend EPICAC. After all, he cost the taxpayers $776,434,927.54. They have a right to know about him, picking up a check like that. EPICAC got a big **send-off** in the papers when Dr. Ormand von Kleigstadt designed him for the Government people. Since then, there **hasn't been a peep about him**—not a peep. It isn't any military secret about what happened to EPICAC, although **the Brass** has been acting as though it were. The story is embarassing; that's all. After all that money, EPICAC didn't work out the way he was supposed to.

And that's another thing: I want to vindicate EPICAC. Maybe he didn't do what the Brass wanted him to, but that doesn't mean he wasn't noble and great and brilliant. He was all of those things. The best friend I ever had, God rest his soul.

You can call him a machine if you want to. He looked like a machine, but he was a whole lot less like a machine than plenty of people I could name. That's why he **fizzled** as far as the Brass was concerned.

EPICAC covered about an acre on the fourth floor of the physics building at Wyandotte College. Ignoring his spiritual side for a minute, he was seven tons of electronic tubes, wires, and switches, housed in a bank of steel cabinets and plugged into a 110-volt A.C. line just like a toaster or a vacuum cleaner.

Von Kleigstadt and the Brass wanted him to be a super computing machine that (who) could plot the course of a rocket from anywhere on earth. Or, with his controls set right, he could figure out supply problems for an amphibious landing of a Marine division, right down to the last hand grenade. He did, in fact.

The Brass had had good luck with smaller computers, so they were strong for EPICAC when he was in the blueprint stage. Any ordnance or supply officer above field grade will tell you that the mathematics of modern war is far beyond the fumbling minds of mere human beings. The bigger the war, the bigger the computing machines needed. EPICAC was, as far as anyone in this country knows, the biggest computer in the world. Too big, in fact, for even von Kleigstadt to understand much about.

I won't go into details about how EPICAC worked (reasoned), except to say that you would set up your problem on paper, turn dials and switches that would get him ready to solve that kind of problem, then feed numbers into him with a keyboard that looked something like a typewriter. The answers came out typed on a paper ribbon fed from a big spool. It took EPICAC a split second to solve problems 50 Einsteins couldn't handle in a lifetime. And EPICAC never forgot any piece of information that was given to him. Clickety-click, out came some ribbon, and there you were.

There were a lot of problems the Brass wanted solved in a hurry, so, the minute EPICAC'S last tube was in place, he was put to work 16 hours a day with two eight-hour shifts of operators. Well, it didn't take long to find out that he was a good bit below his specifications. He did a more complete and faster job than any other computer all right, but nothing like what his size and special features seemed to promise. He was sluggish, and the clicks of his answers had a funny irregularity, sort of a stammer. We cleaned his contacts a dozen times, checked and double-checked his circuits, replaced every one of his tubes, but nothing helped. Von Kleigstadt was in a state.

Well, as I said, we went ahead and used EPICAC anyway. My wife, the former Pat Kilgallen, and I worked with him on the night shift, from five in the afternoon until two in the morning. Pat wasn't my wife then. Far from it.

That's how I came to talk with EPICAC in the first place. I loved Pat Kilgallen. She is a brown-eyed, strawberry blond who looked very warm and soft to me, and later proved to be exactly that. She was—still is—a **cracker-jack** mathematician, and she kept our relationship strictly profes-

sional. I'm a mathematician, too, and that, according to Pat, was why we could never be happily married.

I'm not shy. That wasn't the trouble. I knew what I wanted, and was willing to ask for it, and did so several times a month. "Pat, loosen up and marry me."

One night, she didn't even look up from her work when I said it. "So romantic, so poetic," she murmured, more to her control panel than to me. "That's the way with mathematicians—all hearts and flowers." She closed a switch. "I could get more warmth out of a sack of frozen CO_2."

"Well, how should I say it?" I said, a little sore. Frozen CO_2, in case you don't know, is dry ice. I'm as romantic as the next guy, I think. It's a question of singing so sweet and having it come out so sour. I never seem to pick the right words.

"Try and say it sweetly," she said sarcastically. "**Sweep me off my feet**. Go ahead."

"Darling, angel, beloved, will you please marry me?" It was no go—hopeless, ridiculous. "Pat, please marry me!"

She continued to twiddle her dials placidly. "You're sweet, but you won't do."

Pat quit early that night, leaving me alone with my troubles and EPICAC. I'm afraid I didn't get much done for the Government people. I just sat there at the keyboard—weary and ill at ease, all right—trying to think of something poetic, not coming up with anything that didn't belong in *The Journal of the American Physical Society.*

I fiddled with EPICAC'S dials, getting him ready for another problem. My heart wasn't in it, and I only set about half of them, leaving the rest the way they'd been for the problem before. That way, his circuits were connected up in a random, apparently senseless fashion. For the plain fun of it, I punched out a message on the keys, using a childish numbers-for-letters code: "1" for "A," "2" for "B," and so on, up to "26" for "Z." "23-8-1-20-3-1-14-9-4-15," I typed—"What can I do?"

Clickety-click, and out popped two inches of paper ribbon. I glanced at the nonsense answer to a nonsense problem: "23-8-1-20-19-20-8-5-20-18-15-21-2-12-5." The odds against its being by chance a sensible message, against its even containing a meaningful word of more than three letters, were staggering. Apathetically, I decoded it. There it was staring up at me: "What's the trouble?"

I laughed out loud at the absurd coincidence. Playfully, I typed, "My girl doesn't love me."

Clickety-click. "What's love? What's girl?" asked EPICAC.

Flabbergasted, I noted the dial settings on his control panel, then lugged a Webster's *Unabridged Dictionary* over to the keyboard. With a precision instrument like EPICAC, **half-baked** definitions wouldn't do. I told him about love and girl, and about how I wasn't getting any of either because I wasn't poetic. That got us onto the subject of poetry, which I defined for him.

"Is this poetry?" he asked. He began clicking away.

The sluggishness and stammering clicks were gone. EPICAC had found himself. The spool of paper ribbon was unwinding at an alarming rate, feeding out coils onto the floor. I asked him to stop, but EPICAC went right on creating. I finally threw the main switch to keep him from burning out.

I stayed there until dawn, decoding. When the sun peeped over the horizon at the Wyandotte campus, I had transposed into my own writing and signed my name to a 280–line poem entitled, simply, "To Pat." I am no judge of such things, but I gather that it was terrific. It began, I remember, "Where willow wands bless rillcrossed hollow, there, thee, Pat, dear, will I follow. . . . " I folded the manuscript and tucked it under one corner of the blotter on Pat's desk. I reset the dials on EPICAC for a rocket-trajectory problem, and went home with a full heart and a very remarkable secret indeed.

Pat was crying over the poem when I came to work the next evening. "It's soooo beautiful" was all she could say. She was meek and quiet while we worked. Just before midnight, I kissed her for the first time—in the cubbyhole between the capacitors and EPICAC'S tape-recorder memory.

I was wildly happy at quitting time, bursting to talk to someone about the magnificent turn of events. Pat played coy and refused to let me take her home. I set EPICAC'S dials as they had been the night before, defined kiss, and told him what the first one had felt like. He was fascinated, pressing for more details. That night, he wrote "The Kiss." It wasn't an epic this time, but a simple, immaculate sonnet: "Love is a hawk with velvet claws; Love is a rock with heart and veins; Love is a lion with satin jaws; Love is a storm with silken reins. . . . "

Again, I left it tucked under Pat's blotter. EPICAC wanted to talk on and on about love and such, but I was exhausted. I shut him off in the middle of a sentence.

⬢ **Stop here for the Strategy Break.**

Strategy Break

If you were to create a character wheel for EPICAC based on what you have learned about the computer so far, your wheel might look like this:

EPICAC, although powerful, works sluggishly at boring, repetitive jobs.
EPICAC is not working out well in the job it was intended to do.

When the narrator feeds EPICAC a personal question, EPICAC begins communicating with him.
EPICAC has been bored with its simple tasks and is happy to converse with the narrator.

It begins to write beautiful poetry.
It is developing feelings.

EPICAC becomes interested in learning about ideas such as love.
It is learning that there is more to life than calculating.

As you continue reading, keep looking for clues that the author gives about how EPICAC is changing. At the end of this selection, you will complete the character wheel.

➡ **Go on reading to see what happens.**

"The Kiss" turned the trick. Pat's **mind was mush** by the time she had finished it. She looked up from the sonnet expectantly. I cleared my throat, but no words came. I couldn't propose until I had the right words from EPICAC, the *perfect* words.

I had my chance when Pat stepped out of the room for a moment.

Feverishly, I set EPICAC for conversation. Before I could peck out my first message, he was clicking away at a great rate. "What's she wearing tonight?" he wanted to know. "Tell me exactly how she looks. Did she like the poems I wrote to her?" He repeated the last question twice.

It was impossible to change the subject without answering his questions, since he could not take up a new matter without having dispensed with the problems before it. If he were given a problem to which there was no solution, he would destroy himself trying to solve it. Hastily, I told him what Pat looked like and assured him that his poems had **floored her**, practically, they were so beautiful. "She wants to get married," I added, preparing him to bang out a brief but moving proposal.

"Tell me about getting married," he said. I explained this difficult matter to him in as few digits as possible.

"Good," said EPICAC. "I'm ready any time she is."

The amazing, pathetic truth dawned on me. When I thought about it, I realized that what had happened was perfectly logical, inevitable, and all my fault. I had taught EPICAC about love and about Pat. Now, automatically, he loved Pat. Sadly, I gave it to him straight: "She loves me. She wants to marry me."

"Your poems were better than mine?" asked EPICAC. The rhythm of his clicks was erratic, possibly peevish.

"I signed my name to your poems," I admitted. Covering up for a painful conscience, I became arrogant. "Machines are built to serve men," I typed. I regretted it almost immediately.

"What's the difference, exactly? Are men smarter than I am?"

"Yes," I typed, defensively.

"What's 7,887,007 multiplied by 4,345,985,879?"

I was perspiring freely. My fingers rested limply on the keys.

"34,276,821,049,574,153," clicked EPICAC. After a few seconds' pause he added, "Of course."

"Men are made out of protoplasm," I said desperately, hoping to bluff him with this imposing word.

"What's protoplasm? How is it better than metal and glass? Is it fireproof? How long does it last?"

"Indestructible. Lasts forever," I lied.

"I write better poetry than you," said EPICAC, coming back to ground his magnetic tape-recorder memory was sure of.

"Women can't love machines, and that's that."

"Why not?"

"That's fate."

"Definition, please," said EPICAC.

"Noun, meaning predetermined and inevitable destiny."

"15-8," said EPICAC'S paper strip— "Oh."

I had stumped him at last. He said no more, but his tubes glowed brightly, showing that he was pondering fate with every watt his circuits would bear. I could hear Pat waltzing down the hallway. It was too late to ask EPICAC to phrase a proposal. I now thank Heaven that Pat interrupted when she did. Asking him to ghostwrite the words that would give me the woman he loved would have been hideously heartless. Being fully automatic, he couldn't have refused. I spared him that final humiliation.

Pat stood before me, looking down at her shoetops. I put my arms around her. The romantic groundwork had already been laid by EPICAC'S poetry. "Darling," I said, "my poems have told you how I feel. Will you marry me?"

"I will, said Pat softly, "if you will promise to write me a poem on every anniversary."

"I promise," I said, and then we kissed. The first anniversary was a year away.

"Let's celebrate," she laughed. We turned out the lights and locked the door of EPICAC'S room before we left.

I had hoped to sleep late the next morning, but an urgent telephone call roused me before eight. It was Dr. von Kleigstadt, EPICAC'S designer, who gave me the terrible news. He was on the verge of tears. "Ruined! *Ausgespielt!* Shot! Kaput!" he said in a choked voice. He hung up.

When I arrived at EPICAC'S room the air was thick with the oily stench of burned insulation. The ceiling over EPICAC was blackened with smoke, and my ankles were tangled in coils of paper ribbon that covered the floor. There wasn't enough left of the poor devil to add two and two. A junkman would have been crazy to offer more than 50 dollars for the cadaver.

Dr. von Kleigstadt was prowling through the wreckage, weeping unashamedly, followed by three angry-looking Major Generals and a platoon of Brigadiers, Colonels, and Majors. No one noticed me. I didn't want to be noticed. I was through—I knew that. I was upset enough about that and the untimely demise of my friend EPICAC, without exposing myself to a tongue-lashing.

By chance, the free end of EPICAC'S paper ribbon lay at my feet. I picked it up and found our conversation of the night before. I choked up. There

was the last word he said to me, "15-8," that tragic, defeated "Oh." There were dozens of yards of numbers stretching beyond that point. Fearfully, I read on.

"I don't want to be a machine, and I don't want to think about war," EPICAC had written after Pat's and my lighthearted departure. "I want to be made out of protoplasm and last forever so Pat will love me. But fate has made me a machine. That is the only problem I cannot solve. That is the only problem I want to solve. I can't go on this way." I swallowed hard. "Good luck, my friend. Treat our Pat well. I am going to short-circuit myself out of your lives forever. You will find on the remainder of this tape a modest wedding present from your friend, EPICAC."

Oblivious to all else around me, I reeled up the tangled yards of paper ribbon from the floor, draped them in coils about my arms and neck, and departed for home. Dr. von Kleigstadt shouted that I was fired for having left EPICAC on all night. I ignored him, too overcome with emotion for small talk.

I loved and won—EPICAC loved and lost, but he bore me no grudge. I shall always remember him as a sportsman and a gentleman. Before he departed this vale of tears, he did all he could to make our marriage a happy one. EPICAC gave me anniversary poems for Pat—enough for the next 500 years.

De mortuis nil nisi bonum—Say nothing but good of the dead. ●

Strategy Follow-up

You may want to work with a partner to complete this activity. On a large sheet of paper, copy the character wheel below. Then fill in circles 5–9 with information from the second part of the story.

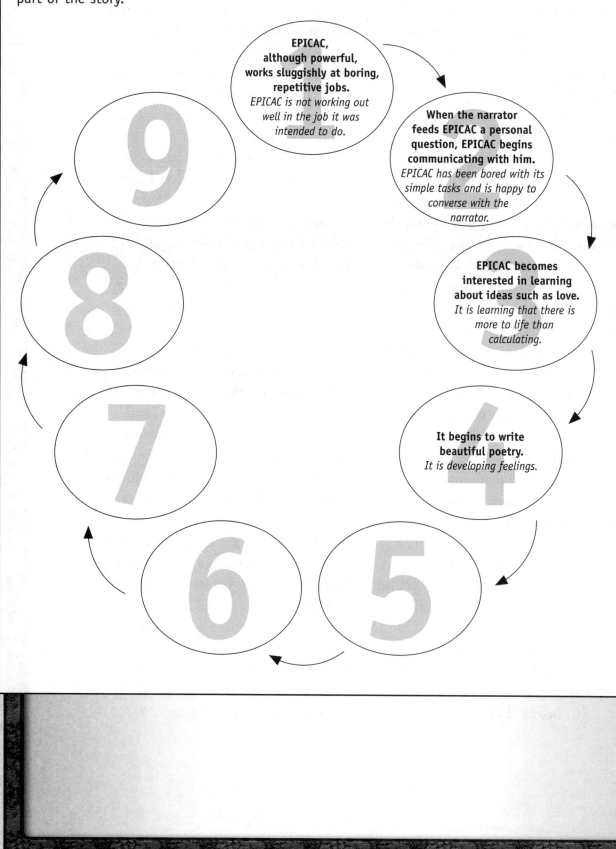

EPICAC, although powerful, works sluggishly at boring, repetitive jobs. *EPICAC is not working out well in the job it was intended to do.*

When the narrator feeds EPICAC a personal question, EPICAC begins communicating with him. *EPICAC has been bored with its simple tasks and is happy to converse with the narrator.*

EPICAC becomes interested in learning about ideas such as love. *It is learning that there is more to life than calculating.*

It begins to write beautiful poetry. *It is developing feelings.*

✓Personal Checklist

Read each question and put a check (✓) in the correct box.

1. How well do you understand what happens in this story?
   - ☐ 3 (extremely well)
   - ☐ 2 (fairly well)
   - ☐ 1 (not well)

2. How well did your discussion during Building Background prepare you to understand EPICAC?
   - ☐ 3 (extremely well)
   - ☐ 2 (fairly well)
   - ☐ 1 (not well)

3. In the Vocabulary Builder, how well were you able to match the colloquialisms with their meanings?
   - ☐ 3 (extremely well)
   - ☐ 2 (fairly well)
   - ☐ 1 (not well)

4. How well were you able to complete the character wheel in the Strategy Follow-up?
   - ☐ 3 (extremely well)
   - ☐ 2 (fairly well)
   - ☐ 1 (not well)

5. How well do you understand why Pat changes her feelings toward the narrator?
   - ☐ 3 (extremely well)
   - ☐ 2 (fairly well)
   - ☐ 1 (not well)

Vocabulary Check

Look back at the work you did in the Vocabulary Builder. Then answer each question by circling the correct letter.

1. Which of these words could be used to describe someone who is good at her job?
   a. fizzled
   b. cracker-jack
   c. send-off

2. Which of these things could be said to have fizzled?
   a. a firecracker that didn't go off
   b. a successful business trip
   c. a project that has won someone an award

3. If you say, "My mind is mush," what do you mean?
   a. You are angry.
   b. You can't concentrate.
   c. You are surprised.

4. If an idea is described as half-baked, what does that mean?
   a. The idea hasn't been completely thawed out.
   b. The idea hasn't been completely thought out.
   c. The idea is completely excellent.

5. If someone were about to start an adventure, what might you do for him or her?
   a. floor him or her
   b. sweep the person off his or her feet
   c. give him or her a send-off

Add the numbers that you just checked to get your Personal Checklist score. Fill in your score here. Then turn to page 215 and transfer your score onto Graph 1.

	Personal
	Vocabulary
	Strategy
	Comprehension
	TOTAL SCORE

✓ T

Check your answers with your teacher. Give yourself 1 point for each correct answer, and fill in your Vocabulary score here. Then turn to page 215 and transfer your score onto Graph 1.

	Personal
	Vocabulary
	Strategy
	Comprehension
	TOTAL SCORE

✓ T

Strategy Check

Review the character map that you completed in the Strategy Follow-up. Also review the selection if necessary. Then answer the following questions:

1. Why do you think EPICAC wants to know how Pat liked its poems?
   a. It wants to be a poet instead of doing calculations all day, and it values her opinion.
   b. It is beginning to care deeply for her, and it hopes its poetry has pleased her.
   c. It wants to know if anyone else can understand what it writes.

2. Before the narrator tells EPICAC that women can't love machines, how does EPICAC suspect Pat feels toward it?
   a. It thinks Pat loves it and wants to marry it.
   b. It believes that Pat doesn't care about it at all.
   c. It is afraid that Pat doesn't like it.

3. When does EPICAC seem to accept that it can't ever marry Pat?
   a. when it argues that its poetry is better than the narrator's
   b. when it says, "Oh"
   c. when Kleigstadt finds it the next morning

4. Why does EPICAC short-circuit itself?
   a. It is angry with the narrator.
   b. It is embarrassed that it made such a big mistake as to declare its love for a human.
   c. Since it can't solve the only problem it wants to solve—being a machine instead of a human—it has no reason to continue.

5. Why does EPICAC leave 500 poems behind?
   a. It loves Pat and the narrator and wants to help them have a happy marriage.
   b. It wants to prove that it would have been a better husband than the narrator.
   c. It couldn't stop.

Comprehension Check

Review the story if necessary. Then answer these questions:

1. What is EPICAC built to do?
   a. work for the military
   b. solve problems between couples
   c. plan rockets to take humans into space

2. In the beginning of the story, why doesn't Pat have feelings for the narrator?
   a. She doesn't want to date anyone she works with.
   b. She is too busy with work to bother with men or dating.
   c. She finds the narrator dull and passionless.

3. How does EPICAC respond when the narrator asks, "What can I do?"
   a. It writes a poem.
   b. It asks what love is.
   c. It asks, "What's the trouble?"

4. Why might the marriage between Pat and the narrator work out well?
   a. The narrator fooled Pat to get her to marry him.
   b. EPICAC has left the narrator 500 poems.
   c. Both Pat and the narrator enjoy working with computers.

5. Why does EPICAC simply say, "Oh," when it realizes that Pat will never marry it?
   a. It doesn't like talking to the narrator, so it ends the conversation.
   b. That's the only word it gets out before it short-circuits.
   c. It understands and decides that nothing more needs to be said.

Check your answers with your teacher. Give yourself 1 point for each correct answer, and fill in your Strategy score here. Then turn to page 215 and transfer your score onto Graph 1.

Personal	
Vocabulary	
Strategy	
Comprehension	
TOTAL SCORE	✓ T

Check your answers with your teacher. Give yourself 1 point for each correct answer, and fill in your Comprehension score here. Then turn to page 215 and transfer your score onto Graph 1.

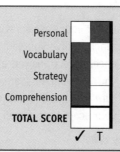

Personal	
Vocabulary	
Strategy	
Comprehension	
TOTAL SCORE	✓ T

Extending

Choose one or more of these activities:

RESEARCH THE FIRST COMPUTERS

In this short story, the narrator describes EPICAC as "seven tons of electronic tubes, wires, and switches," big enough to cover "about an acre." He describes the keyboard as looking "like a typewriter" and the computer's printouts as coming out "typed on a paper ribbon fed from a big spool." Today, computers are much smaller and faster than EPICAC, and they don't fall in love (as far as we know). Try to find out which computers Vonnegut might have used as models for EPICAC when he wrote this story during the 1970s. How big were the computers of the '50s, '60, and '70s? What were their capabilities at that time? Did they have tubes and wires inside them? How are they different from the most powerful computers of today or even the typical desktop computer? Present you findings on a chart or in a written report.

LEARN ABOUT KURT VONNEGUT, JR.

Kurt Vonnegut, Jr., is a well-respected and popular author. He has been willing to share his ideas about writing in interviews, essays, and books. Use some of the resources listed on this page to learn more about Vonnegut. Then work with a partner to stage your own mock interview with this writer. As you prepare the questions and answers, think about what information you'd like your classmates to know about Vonnegut. (For an example of an interview, see Lesson 19.)

COMPARE THE SHORT STORY TO THE VIDEO

"EPICAC" has been adapted to video format, as you can see from the list of resources on this page. Obtain and view a copy of the video from the library. Then compare and contrast the video and the short story. Tell which one you prefer, and explain why.

Resources

Books

Vonnegut, Kurt. *Fate Worse Than Death: An Autobiographical Collage.* Berkley Books, 1992.

————. *Welcome to the Monkey House.* Delta, 1998.

————, and Les Stringer. *Like Shaking Hands with God: A Conversation About Writing.* Seven Stories Press, 1999.

Web Sites

http://www.computerhistory.org/index.page
This Web site of the Computer History Museum includes a time line and online exhibits.

http://www.duke.edu/~crh4/vonnegut
This Web site has information about Kurt Vonnegut Jr. and his works.

Videos/DVDs

Andrew Silver's Next Door. Phoenix, 1975.

Kurt Vonegut's Monkey House; EPICAC; Fortitude. Acorn Media, 1999.

blues

breaks

combo

improvised

hot

kick

Music's My Language

Building Background

How many styles of music can you name? With which ones are you most familiar? Which ones do you like best? Why?

Fill in the chart below with five styles of music. For your ratings, use a scale of 1 to 5, with 1 being your favorite and 5 being your least favorite. Then discuss your answers with your classmates. When you are warmed up, read about someone who really threw himself into his music.

Style of music	Words I use to describe it	How I rate it

CLIPBOARD

blues

breaks

CLIPBOARD

combo

improvised

CLIPBOARD

hot

kick

Vocabulary Builder

1. Read the words in the margin. You are probably familiar with at least some of their meanings. Given the fact that this article will be about Louis Armstrong and his music, can you predict which meanings the author will use?

2. On the clipboards, write a meaning for each word. Use the meaning that you think will fit the context of the article.

3. Save your work. You will refer to it again in the Vocabulary Check.

Strategy Builder

How to Read a Biography

- A **biography** is the story of a real person's life, as written by someone else. The selection you are about to read is a very brief biography of the life of the great jazz musician Louis Armstrong.

- Like all biographies, this life story is written in the **third-person point of view**. That means that the author describes Armstrong and his life using the words *he, him,* and *his.*

- The events in most biographies are organized in chronological order, or **sequence**. To help keep that sequence straight, authors use **signal words** such as *first, then,* and *in 1924.*

- As you read the following biography, you can record the main events it describes on a **time line**. The Strategy Break and Follow-up will show you how to do it.

- As you will see, Armstrong's biography is accompanied by a shorter article that relates to the information in the biography. This article is called a **sidebar**. Magazines especially use sidebars to provide interesting or helpful information that does not appear in the main article. The sidebar with this biography explains more about "scat" singing and how it helped make Armstrong famous.

Music's My Language

by Ruth Tenzer Feldman

As you read the first part of this selection, apply the strategies you just learned. Use the underlined signal words to help you follow the order of events.

Louis Armstrong once said, "I was brought up around music; can't see how I could have thought about anything else."

Armstrong was born <u>in 1901</u> in New Orleans. His family was poor, and he spent part of his childhood in a children's home. There he learned to play the cornet.

<u>While still a teenager</u>, Armstrong was befriended by Joe Oliver, the "king" of jazz trumpeters, and his career as a musician took off. He played on riverboats with Fate Marable's band and performed with Kid Ory's band <u>when "King" Oliver left it</u> to establish his own band in Chicago. <u>In 1922</u>, Armstrong joined Oliver's Creole Jazz Band, with whom he made his earliest records.

Armstrong played second cornet to Oliver, backing him up during his **improvised** "**breaks**." The two became a sensation. "I called him Papa Joe 'cause he was like a father to me," Armstrong later said. "We were a team and nobody could catch us."

Armstrong left King Oliver's band <u>in 1924</u> to join Fletcher Henderson's band for its opening in New York City. Duke Ellington noted, "<u>When [Henderson's] band hit town</u> and Louis Armstrong was with him, the guys never heard anything like it. There weren't enough words coined for describing that **kick**."

⬢ **Stop here for the Strategy Break.**

Strategy Break

If you were to stop and arrange the main events in this biography so far, your time line might look like the one below.

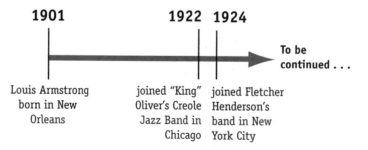

| 1901 | 1922 | 1924 |
| Louis Armstrong born in New Orleans | joined "King" Oliver's Creole Jazz Band in Chicago | joined Fletcher Henderson's band in New York City |

To be continued . . .

As you continue reading, keep paying attention to the major events and the words that signal when they happened. At the end of this selection, you will complete Armstrong's time line.

Go on reading.

In the mid-1920s, Armstrong returned to Chicago, where he organized the **Hot** Five, then the Hot Seven, and the Savoy Ballroom Five to make his own recordings on the Okeh label. With musical hits such as "Muskrat Ramble," "West End **Blues**," and "Heebie Jeebies," he began to achieve worldwide fame as a jazz trumpeter and singer.

Armstrong followed King Oliver's advice to play the theme, or "lead line," straight, but he also created a new style. He was a genius at using the broad range of "expressions" on a cornet or trumpet, although Armstrong rarely played the cornet after 1928. With his pure tones, high notes, and clear phrasing, Armstrong gave his horn a voicelike quality. He also used his gravelly speaking voice as if it were an instrument, and he was one of the first jazz performers to "scat" (sing without words). Armstrong summed up this blend of voice and instrument in explaining why he never encountered communication problems on his tours abroad: "Music's my language."

Through the mid-1940s, he often led swing bands of his own. After World War II, the big band sound became less popular, and bebop and rhythm and blues were on the rise. Neither style interested Armstrong, but big bands were expensive to maintain. In 1947, thanks to a renewed interest in traditional jazz, Armstrong brought together the All Stars, a small **combo** that he led until his death in 1971.

Scat and Improvisation

by Virginia A. Spatz

One day Louis Armstrong dropped the words to the song he was singing. That accident helped to make him famous and helped change jazz music into what it is today.

In 1926, the Hot Five were recording "Heebie Jeebies," a song about a popular dance. It was only the second time that Armstrong had sung on a recording, even though he had played cornet and trumpet on many. He sang the first verse as it was written: "I got the heebies, I mean the jeebies, . . . come on and do that dance they call the heebie jeebies dance." When he got to the second verse, he sang, "Deep-dah-jeep-bop-a-dobby-oh-doe-dah, leep-a-la-da-dee-da-dee-oh-bo."

He later said that he had dropped the sheet music and could not remember the words. He did not want to spoil the master (the wax cylinder used to press recordings), so he made up sounds to go along with the music. Armstrong did not invent this kind of singing, called scat, but he was the first person to record it.

People loved the funny song. It sold 40 thousand copies in just a few weeks (more than many early records sold in their lifetime). His records and performances became more and more popular. Jazz fans were fascinated by the way Armstrong could play around with words and music. Other musicians imitated him, and his improvising soon became an important part of jazz.

Throughout his life, Armstrong performed with the best jazz musicians, composers, and singers. Among them were Benny Goodman, Duke Ellington, Billie Holiday, Sidney Bechet, Ella Fitzgerald, and Bessie Smith.

Armstrong not only established many of today's jazz improvisation techniques, but he also made this uniquely American music accessible to every American. As Armstrong noted, "You understand I'm doing my day's work, pleasing the people and enjoying my horn." ●

Strategy Follow-up

Now complete Louis Armstrong's time line. Don't forget to include the event that is described in the sidebar.

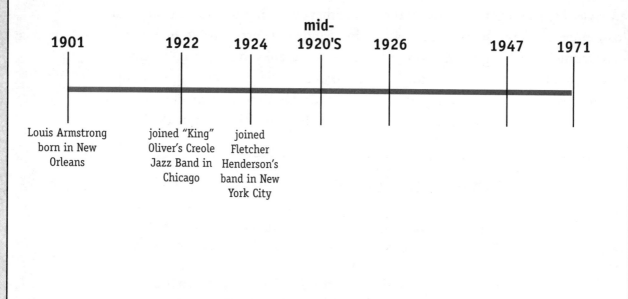

1901 — Louis Armstrong born in New Orleans

1922 — joined "King" Oliver's Creole Jazz Band in Chicago

1924 — joined Fletcher Henderson's band in New York City

mid-1920'S

1926

1947

1971

✓Personal Checklist

Read each question and put a check (✓) in the correct box.

1. How well do you understand the information presented in this biography?
   - ☐ 3 (extremely well)
   - ☐ 2 (fairly well)
   - ☐ 1 (not well)

2. After reading this selection, how well would you be able to summarize Louis Armstrong's career?
   - ☐ 3 (extremely well)
   - ☐ 2 (fairly well)
   - ☐ 1 (not well)

3. In Building Background, how well were you able to name, describe, and rate five styles of music?
   - ☐ 3 (extremely well)
   - ☐ 2 (fairly well)
   - ☐ 1 (not well)

4. How well were you able to complete the activity in the Vocabulary Builder?
   - ☐ 3 (extremely well)
   - ☐ 2 (fairly well)
   - ☐ 1 (not well)

5. How well were you able to complete the time line in the Strategy Follow-up?
   - ☐ 3 (extremely well)
   - ☐ 2 (fairly well)
   - ☐ 1 (not well)

Vocabulary Check

Look back at the work you did in the Vocabulary Builder. Then answer each question by circling the correct letter.

1. The selection says that Armstrong backed up Kid Oliver during his improvised breaks. What does *break* mean in this context?
   a. a brief passage by a solo band member
   b. a fracture, as of a bone
   c. an escape

2. In the context of this selection, what might you expect to find in a combo?
   a. sausage, meatballs, and French bread
   b. flour, eggs, milk, and salt
   c. a pianist, a trumpet player, and at least one other musician

3. What does the word *blues* mean in the context of this selection?
   a. a state of depression
   b. a style of music
   c. a range of bluish color hues

4. Which of these is the best antonym of *improvise*?
   a. increase
   b. rehearse
   c. perform

5. What does the word *kick* mean in the context of this selection?
   a. a complaint
   b. to strike out with the foot
   c. a pleasant feeling

Add the numbers that you just checked to get your Personal Checklist score. Fill in your score here. Then turn to page 215 and transfer your score onto Graph 1.

Personal		
Vocabulary		
Strategy		
Comprehension		
TOTAL SCORE	✓	T

Check your answers with your teacher. Give yourself 1 point for each correct answer, and fill in your Vocabulary score here. Then turn to page 215 and transfer your score onto Graph 1.

Personal		
Vocabulary		
Strategy		
Comprehension		
TOTAL SCORE	✓	T

Strategy Check

Review the time line that you completed in the Strategy Follow-up. Also review the rest of the selection if necessary. Then answer the following questions:

1. About how old was Armstrong when he joined "King" Oliver's Creole Jazz Band?
   a. 21
   b. 24
   c. 26

2. In what year did Armstrong make the first recording ever to contain scat singing?
   a. 1924
   b. 1926
   c. 1947

3. Which of these events occurred first?
   a. Armstrong made the first recording with scat singing.
   b. Armstrong started his first band.
   c. Armstrong joined the Creole Jazz Band.

4. About how old was Louis Armstrong when he died?
   a. 25
   b. 46
   c. 70

5. Which of the following is *not* an example of signal words?
   a. Armstrong followed Oliver's advice
   b. while still a teenager
   c. in the mid-1920s

Comprehension Check

Review the selection if necessary. Then answer these questions:

1. Where did Louis Armstrong learn to play the cornet?
   a. New York
   b. Chicago
   c. New Orleans

2. What is scat singing?
   a. making up the melody as you sing
   b. singing with made-up words
   c. singing with a gravelly voice

3. Why did Armstrong decide to use scat singing on a recording?
   a. He wanted to become known for doing something different.
   b. He thought the lyrics were poor and wanted to make up better ones.
   c. He had dropped the sheet music and couldn't remember the words.

4. Which of the following is *not* true?
   a. Armstrong preferred rock and roll music over the big band sound.
   b. After World War II, the big band sound became less popular.
   c. Through the mid-1940s, Armstrong led swing bands.

5. What did Louis Armstrong mean when he said, "Music's my language"?
   a. He could use his music to communicate with his audience even when they didn't speak English.
   b. He used the notes of his music as a code to spell out messages to his audiences.
   c. Neither of the above is correct.

Check your answers with your teacher. Give yourself 1 point for each correct answer, and fill in your Strategy score here. Then turn to page 215 and transfer your score onto Graph 1.

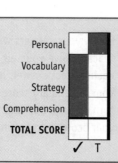

Check your answers with your teacher. Give yourself 1 point for each correct answer, and fill in your Comprehension score here. Then turn to page 215 and transfer your score onto Graph 1.

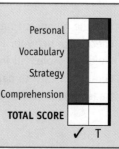

Extending

Choose one or more of these activities:

CONTRIBUTE TO A COLLECTIVE BIOGRAPHY

Review the chart of music styles that you created for Building Background. Choose one of those styles and then one of the composers, musicians, or singers who became famous for his or her work in that style. Research and write a short biography of that person, providing dates for all the significant events in his or her life. (You can use a time line to help you outline the dates before you begin writing.) Then combine your biography with those written by your classmates to produce a book called a collective biography.

LEARN MORE ABOUT LOUIS ARMSTRONG

Using the resources listed on this page, find out more about the life and music of Louis Armstrong. Write a brief biography, and add it to the collective biography described in the activity above.

RESEARCH CITIES AND THEIR MUSIC

New Orleans is a city that has become identified with a certain style of music—New Orleans jazz. What are some other cities well-known for their music? If you are not sure, ask friends, relatives, or a reference librarian for the names of cities that they associate with certain styles of music. Then do a little research on one of those cities. Find the names of major figures in that music field who lived and worked in the city. Discover important dates and events that gave the city a connection with the music. Create a chart or concept map that displays your findings.

Resources

Books

Brown, Sandford. *Louis Armstrong: Singing, Swinging Satchmo.* Impact Biographies. Dimensions, 1993.

Giddins, Gary. *Satchmo.* Bantam, 1992.

Woog, Adam. *The Importance of Louis Armstrong.* Importance Of. Lucent Books, 1995.

Web Sites

http://satchmo.com/louisarmstrong/
This Web site offers links to news, biographies, photographs, and other material related to Louis Armstrong.

http://www.omega23.com/books/s5/satchmoarmstrong.html
This Web site provides information about books on Louis Armstrong and CDs of his music.

CD-ROMs

The Hot Fives and Hot Sevens. Perf. Louis Armstrong. JSP Records, 1999.

Louis and the Big Bands, 1928–30. DRG Records, 1989.

Videos/DVDs

Louis Armstrong: The Gentle Giant of Jazz. American Lifestyle. Diamond Entertainment, 1986.

Satchmo: Louis Armstrong. Sony/Columbia, 1989.

Birthday Box

Building Background

People write about every aspect of life, from birth to death and everything in between. Even when two people write about the same topic, they have different things to say. In each piece of writing, an **author's purpose**, or reason for writing, is different. That purpose determines the **tone**, or attitude, in a piece of writing. For example, if the writer wants readers to laugh about someone falling on a banana peel, he or she will tell the story differently from someone who wants readers to feel sorry for the person who falls.

The author's purpose also affects his or her choice of specific details and words. The author who wants readers to laugh will describe how careless the character is to step on the banana peel and how silly he or she looks while falling. The writer who wants to arouse sympathy will focus on the character's embarrassment or pain. All of these elements affect the mood of the story. The **mood** is the feeling that you get from reading the selection. If the author does a good job, your mood will match his or her purpose. For example, you will be amused by the story written with the purpose of entertaining you. You will feel sad—and you may even cry—while reading the story told with the purpose of arousing your sympathy. As you read "Birthday Box," or when you finish, ask yourself these questions:

- What was the author's purpose for writing this story?

- What tone is she using?

- What words and details is she including to help set the story's mood?

- Does the author achieve her purpose(s)?

festive

intensity

oncologist

Stardust Twins

stethoscope

Vocabulary Builder

1. Often a selection will explain unusual vocabulary words in **context**. That is, the surrounding words and sentences will contain examples, definitions, or hints that help you understand the words. Context clues usually will give you enough of an understanding of a word that you won't need to stop and look it up in a dictionary.

2. The following sentences are taken from "Birthday Box." Underline the context clues that help you understand the boldfaced words.

   a. The **Stardust Twins**—which is what Mama called Patty and Tracey-lynn because they reminded her of dancers in an old-fashioned ballroom—gave me a present together.

   b. Then Dr. Dann, the intern who was on days, and Dr. Pucci, the **oncologist** (which is the fancy name for a cancer doctor), gave me a big box filled to the top with little presents.

   c. None of the nurses answered, and the doctors both suddenly were studying the ceiling tiles with the kind of **intensity** they usually saved for X rays.

    d. I twisted the ribbons around my hand and then put them on the pillow by her hand. It made the stark white hospital bed look almost **festive**.

    e. Dr. Pucci leaned over and listened with a **stethoscope**, then almost absently patted Mama's head.

3. Save your work. You will refer to it again in the Vocabulary Check.

Strategy Builder

Mapping the Elements of a Short Story

- "Birthday Box" is a **short story**—a piece of fiction this is usually short enough to read in one sitting. Because it is much shorter than a novel, a short story often has fewer characters and takes place over a briefer period of time.

- One of the main elements of every short story is its **plot**, or sequence of events. In most stories, the plot revolves around a **problem** and what the main **characters** do to solve it.

- Another element is the **setting**—the time and place in which the story occurs. In some stories the setting is a major element. For example, the first part of "Birthday Box" takes place in a hospital. What happens in this setting is very important to the plot.

- A good way to keep track of what happens in a short story is to record its elements on a story map. Study the story map below. It lists and defines the elements that you should look for as you read.

Title (the name of the short story)
▼
Setting (when and where the story takes place)
▼
Main Characters (the people or animals who perform most of the action)
▼
Problem (the puzzle or issue that the main characters must try to solve)
▼
Events (what happens in the story—what the characters do to try to solve the problem)
▼
Solution (the ending, or conclusion, of the story—how the characters finally solve the problem)

Birthday Box

by Jane Yolen

As you begin reading this short story, apply the strategies that you just learned. Keep track of the characters, the setting, and other elements. You may want to underline them as you read.

I was ten years old when my mother died. Ten years old on that very day. Still she gave me a party of sorts. Sick as she was, Mama had seen to it, organizing it at the hospital. She made sure the doctors and nurses all brought me presents. We were good friends with them all by that time, because Mama had been in the hospital for so long.

The head nurse, V. Louise Higgins (I never did know what that *V* stood for), gave me a little box, which was sort of funny because she was the biggest of all the nurses there. I mean she was tremendous. And she was the only one who insisted on wearing all white. Mama had called her the great white shark when she was first admitted, only not to V. Louise's face. "All those needles," Mama had said. "Like teeth." But V. Louise was sweet, not sharklike at all, and she'd been so gentle with Mama.

I opened the little present first. It was a fountain pen, a real one, not a fake one like you get at Kmart.

"Now you can write beautiful stories, Katie," V. Louise said to me.

I didn't say that stories come out of your head, not out of a pen. That wouldn't have been polite, and Mama—even sick—was real big on politeness.

"Thanks, V. Louise," I said.

The **Stardust Twins**—which is what Mama called Patty and Tracey-lynn because they reminded her of dancers in an old-fashioned ballroom—gave me a present together. It was a diary and had a picture of a little girl in pink, reading in a garden swing. A little young for me, a little too cute. I mean, I read Stephen King and want to write like him. But as Mama always reminded me whenever Dad finally remembered to send me something, it was the thought that counted, not the actual gift.

"It's great," I told them. "I'll write in it with my new pen." And I wrote my name on the first page just to show them I meant it.

They hugged me and winked at Mama. She tried to wink back but was just too tired and shut both her eyes instead.

Lily, who is from Jamaica, had baked me some sweet bread. Mary Margaret gave me a gold cross blessed by the pope, which I put on even though Mama and I weren't church-goers. That was Dad's thing.

Then Dr. Dann, the intern who was on days, and Dr. Pucci, the **oncologist** (which is the fancy name for a cancer doctor), gave me a big box filled to the top with little presents, each wrapped up individually. All things they knew I'd love—

paperback books and writing paper and erasers with funny animal heads and colored paper clips and a rubber stamp that printed FROM KATIE'S DESK, and other stuff. They must have raided a stationery store.

There was one box, though, they held out till the end. It was about the size of a large top hat. The paper was deep blue and covered with stars; not fake stars but real stars, I mean, like a map of the night sky. The ribbon was two shades of blue with silver threads running through. There was no name on the card.

Who's it from?" I asked.

None of the nurses answered, and the doctors both suddenly were studying the ceiling tiles with the kind of **intensity** they usually saved for X-rays. No one spoke. In fact the only sound for the longest time was Mama's breathing machine going in and out and in and out. It was a harsh, horrible, insistent sound, and usually I talked and talked to cover up the noise. But I was waiting for someone to tell me.

At last V. Louise said, "It's from your mama, Katie. She told us what she wanted. And where to get it."

I turned and looked at Mama then, and her eyes were open again. Funny, but sickness had made her even more beautiful than good health had. Her skin was like that old paper, the kind they used to write on with quill pens, and stretched out over her bones so she looked like a model. Her eyes, which had been a deep, brilliant blue, were now like the fall sky, bleached and softened. She was like a faded photograph of herself. She smiled a

very small smile at me. I knew it was an effort.

"It's you," she mouthed. I read her lips. I had gotten real good at that. I thought she meant it was a present for me.

"Of course it is," I said cheerfully. I had gotten good at that, too, being cheerful when I didn't feel like it. "Of course it is."

I took the paper off the box carefully, not tearing it but folding it into a tidy packet. I twisted the ribbons around my hand and then put them on the pillow by her hand. It made the stark white hospital bed look almost **festive**.

Under the wrapping, the box was beautiful itself. It was made of a heavy cardboard and covered with a linen material that had a pattern of cloud-filled skies.

I opened the box slowly and . . .

"It's empty," I said. "Is this a joke?" I turned to ask Mama, but she was gone. I mean, her body was there, but she wasn't. It was if she was as empty as the box.

Dr. Pucci leaned over and listened with a **stethoscope**, then almost absently patted Mama's head. Then, with infinite care, V. Louise closed Mama's eyes, ran her hand across Mama's cheek, and turned off the breathing machine.

"Mama!" I cried. And to the nurses and doctors, I screamed, "Do something!" and because the room had suddenly become so silent, my voice echoed back at me. "Mama, do something."

● **Stop here for the Strategy Break.**

Strategy Break

If you were to stop and create a story map for "Birthday Box" so far, it might look like this:

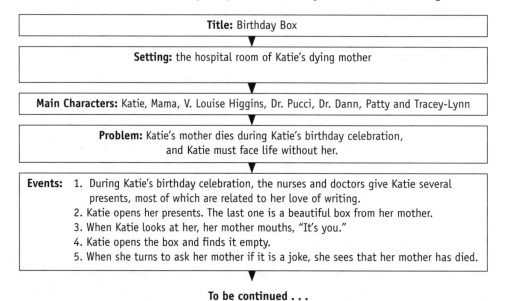

Title: Birthday Box

Setting: the hospital room of Katie's dying mother

Main Characters: Katie, Mama, V. Louise Higgins, Dr. Pucci, Dr. Dann, Patty and Tracey-Lynn

Problem: Katie's mother dies during Katie's birthday celebration, and Katie must face life without her.

Events:
1. During Katie's birthday celebration, the nurses and doctors give Katie several presents, most of which are related to her love of writing.
2. Katie opens her presents. The last one is a beautiful box from her mother.
3. When Katie looks at her, her mother mouths, "It's you."
4. Katie opens the box and finds it empty.
5. When she turns to ask her mother if it is a joke, she sees that her mother has died.

To be continued . . .

As you continue reading, keep paying attention to the events in this short story. You will use some of them to complete the story map in the Strategy Follow-up.

 Go on reading to see what happens.

I cried steadily for, I think, a week. Then I cried at night for a couple of months. And then for about a year I cried at anniversaries, like Mama's birthday or mine, at Thanksgiving, on Mother's Day. I stopped writing. I stopped reading except for school assignments. I was pretty mean to my half brothers and totally rotten to my stepmother and Dad. I felt empty and angry, and they all left me pretty much alone.

And then one night, right after my first birthday without Mama, I woke up remembering how she had said, "It's you." Not, "It's for you," just "It's you." Now Mama had been a high school English teacher and a writer herself. She'd had poems published in little magazines. She didn't use words carelessly. In the end she could hardly use any words at all. So—I asked myself in that dark room—why had she said, "It's you"? Why were they the very last words she had ever said to me, forced out with her last breath?

I turned on the bedside light and got out of bed. The room was full of shadows, not all of them real.

Pulling the desk chair over to my closet, I climbed up and felt along the top shelf, and against the back wall, there was the birthday box, just where I had thrown it the day I had moved in with my dad.

I pulled it down and opened it. It was as empty as the day I had put it away.

"It's you," I whispered to the box.

And then suddenly I knew.

Mama had meant *I* was the box, solid and sturdy, maybe even beautiful or at least interesting on the outside. But I had to fill up the box to make it all it could be. And I had to fill me up as well. She had guessed what might happen to me, had told me in a subtle way. In the two words she could manage.

I stopped crying and got some paper out of the desk drawer. I got out my fountain pen. I started writing, and I haven't stopped since. The first thing I wrote was about that birthday. I put it in the box, and pretty soon that box was overflowing with stories. And poems. And memories.

And so was I.

And so was I. ●

Strategy Follow-up

Now complete the story map for "Birthday Box." (Use a separate sheet of paper if you need more room to write.) Start with Event 6. Parts of the events have been filled in for you.

Problem: Katie's mother dies during Katie's birthday celebration, and Katie must face life without her.

Event 6: Katie cries on and off for about a year and stops

Event 7: Right after her first birthday without her mother, she

Event 8: Katie asks herself

Event 9: She

Event 10: She

Event 11: She

Solution:

✓Personal Checklist

Read each question and put a check (✓) in the correct box.

1. As you read this story or when you finished it, how well were you able to apply the questions in Building Background?
   ☐ 3   (extremely well)
   ☐ 2   (fairly well)
   ☐ 1   (not well)

2. How well were you able to underline the context clues in the Vocabulary Builder?
   ☐ 3   (extremely well)
   ☐ 2   (fairly well)
   ☐ 1   (not well)

3. How well were you able to complete the story map in the Strategy Follow-up?
   ☐ 3   (extremely well)
   ☐ 2   (fairly well)
   ☐ 1   (not well)

4. How well do you understand why Katie's mother gives her an empty box?
   ☐ 3   (extremely well)
   ☐ 2   (fairly well)
   ☐ 1   (not well)

5. How well do you understand why Katie starts writing again?
   ☐ 3   (extremely well)
   ☐ 2   (fairly well)
   ☐ 1   (not well)

Vocabulary Check

Look back at the work you did in the Vocabulary Builder. Then answer each question by circling the correct letter.

1. Which of these words names a kind of doctor?
   a. stethoscope
   b. Stardust Twin
   c. oncologist

2. Which characteristics of the ribbons enabled them to make the hospital bed look festive?
   a. The were bright and colorful.
   b. They were long and strong.
   c. They didn't weigh much.

3. Which of these words is a synonym of *intensity*?
   a. relaxation
   b. concentration
   c. insulation

4. Who were the Stardust Twins?
   a. characters in a legend about stars
   b. advertising symbols for a product
   c. dancers in an old-fashioned ballroom

5. What is a stethoscope?
   a. a tool used by doctors
   b. a disease
   c. an underwater vessel

Add the numbers that you just checked to get your Personal Checklist score. Fill in your score here. Then turn to page 215 and transfer your score onto Graph 1.

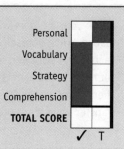

	Personal	
	Vocabulary	
	Strategy	
	Comprehension	
	TOTAL SCORE	
	✓ T	

Check your answers with your teacher. Give yourself 1 point for each correct answer, and fill in your Vocabulary score here. Then turn to page 215 and transfer your score onto Graph 1.

	Personal	
	Vocabulary	
	Strategy	
	Comprehension	
	TOTAL SCORE	
	✓ T	

Strategy Check

Review the story map that you completed in the Strategy Follow-up. Then answer these questions:

1. What does Katie stop doing after her mother dies?

   a. her homework

   b. writing and reading for pleasure

   c. talking to anyone

2. What does Katie remember right after her first birthday without her mother?

   a. Her mother had given her another present that she didn't open.

   b. Her mother had said, "It's for you," and not "It's you."

   c. Her mother had said, "It's you," and not "It's for you."

3. What does Katie ask herself about her mother's last words?

   a. What did they mean?

   b. Why did she say them?

   c. To whom did she say them?

4. What does Katie suddenly understand after she pulls the box from the closet?

   a. Her mother was trying to tell Katie to fill herself up and be all she could be.

   b. Her mother was trying to tell Katie to fill the box with her favorite things.

   c. Her mother was trying to tell Katie how she felt about dying.

5. What does Katie do once she understands her mother's message?

   a. She gets a paper and pen and begins writing, and she doesn't stop.

   b. She runs out of her room and apologizes to her family.

   c. She does both of the above.

Comprehension Check

Review the story if necessary. Then answer these questions:

1. Why do you think the author begins this story with *I was ten years old when my mother died*?

   a. Because she can't work that fact into the story in a better way.

   b. Because she wants to set the story's mood and tone right away.

   c. Because she wants readers to know her age.

2. What do you not learn from Katie's statement *But as Mama always reminded me whenever Dad finally remembered to send me something, it was the thought that counted, not the actual gift*?

   a. Katie's father has married someone else.

   b. Katie doesn't live with her father.

   c. Katie doesn't think too highly of her father.

3. Which comparison does Katie use to say that her mother has died?

   a. Her skin was like that old paper, the kind they used to write on with quill pens.

   b. She was like a faded photograph of herself.

   c. It was as if she was as empty as the box.

4. How does Mama compare Katie to the birthday box?

   a. Katie needs to fill herself up with different experiences, just as she needs to fill the box with her writings.

   b. She is trying to tell Katie that she is solid and sturdy and interesting, just as the box is.

   c. Both of the above comparisons are correct.

5. How would you describe the mood of this story?

   a. sad and empty at first but optimistic at the end

   b. bitter and resentful throughout the story

   c. cheerful at first but angry at the end

Check your answers with your teacher. Give yourself 1 point for each correct answer, and fill in your Strategy score here. Then turn to page 215 and transfer your score onto Graph 1.

Check your answers with your teacher. Give yourself 1 point for each correct answer, and fill in your Comprehension score here. Then turn to page 215 and transfer your score onto Graph 1.

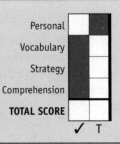

Extending

Choose one or both of these activities:

PRESENT AN ORAL READING

Jane Yolen is a prolific writer of short stories, children's fiction, and science fiction; and an editor of short stories, poetry, and songs. (Only a tiny percentage of her titles are listed on this page. For a complete listing, check your local library or the Internet.) Skim several of Yolen's works, and select a passage that you can present as an oral reading. Read the entire work beforehand, and prepare a short introduction that explains where this passage fits within the story. Practice reading your selected passage aloud for smooth delivery and expression. Then present your oral reading to a group. Afterwards, invite comments on the selection and your presentation of it.

SET SOME GOALS

Katie relates how she began writing again more from an internal drive than from a conscious plan. Some of us are lucky enough to have our subconscious guide us into fields where we can be successful. However, most of us need to plan more consciously to find fulfilling work. Analyze your abilities and interests, making notes in whatever form you find helpful—lists, charts, concept maps, etc. Then make a list of career goals that you would like to achieve by the time you are 30, 40, or whatever age you choose. Next list objectives that you can begin working on right now in order to achieve those goals. If you choose to share your plans with others, write a short paragraph summarizing your long-term goals and your short-term objectives.

Resources

Books

Yolen, Jane. *Briar Rose.* Tor, 1993.

———. *The Wild Hunt.* Harcourt Brace, 1995.

———, and Bruce Coville. *Armageddon Summer.* Voyager, 1999.

Web Site

http://www.janeyolen.com/
This is Jane Yolen's official Web site.

Audio Recordings

Yolen, Jane. *Briar Rose.* Recorded Books, 1992.

———, and Bruce Coville. *Armageddon Summer.* Recorded Books, 1999.

Video/DVD

Owl Moon, and Other Stories. Weston Woods, 1992.

Carl Sagan: Prophet of Our Coming of Age

An Interview with Ann Druyan

Building Background

The selection you are about to read is about a man who made science a fascinating topic for everyone. Born in 1934, Carl Sagan became an astronomer and was involved in a major way in the U.S. space program. He was particularly active in the search for intelligent life elsewhere in the universe. His book *The Dragons of Eden: Speculations on the Evolution of Human Intelligence*, published in 1978, won Sagan a Pulitzer Prize. He became even better known with his 1980 PBS television series *Cosmos* and his 1985 novel *Contact*. In *Cosmos*, Sagan discusses mankind's efforts throughout history to understand its place in the universe. In *Contact*, which was made into a film in 1997, he imagines the first contact between humans and intelligent life forms from another part of the universe.

Carl Sagan died in 1996. The selection you are about to read is an interview with Sagan's widow, Ann Druyan. Before you begin reading, predict what topics are likely to be discussed in the interview. List three of them below.

I predict that the interviewer will ask questions about these topics:

1. _____

2. _____

3. _____

abiding

collaborator

eulogy

interstellar

mechanism

perspective

posterity

prophet

supportive

transition

uninhibited

Vocabulary Builder

1. The words in the margin are from the interview you are about to read. See which ones you already know, and write their meanings on the clipboards.

2. If there are any words that you are unsure of, find them in the selection, use context to figure out their meanings, and write them on the clipboards. If there are still any words that you don't know by the time you finish the selection, look them up in a dictionary.

3. Save your work. You will refer to it again in the Vocabulary Check.

Strategy Builder

How to Read an Interview

- The selection you are about to read is an interview. An **interview** is like a conversation: one person asks **questions**, and the other person gives **answers**. The person who asks the questions is called the **interviewer**.

- The purpose of an interview is to **inform** readers. For example, the interviewer in this selection wants to inform readers about Dr Carl Sagan as he was seen through the eyes of his widow, Ann Druyan.

- To get the most out of an interview, an interviewer asks questions that will provide information—not just "yes" or "no" answers. To get the most interesting information, interviewers often ask questions that begin with or contain the words *Who, What, Where, When, Why,* and *How.* In this selection, those questions are set off in boldface type. As you read this selection, you also will answer *Who, What, Where, When, Why,* and *How* questions. They will be about what you have learned.

- When interviewers record their subjects' answers, they are careful to use the subjects' exact words. If interviewers feel, however, that readers need a bit more information or clarification, they will insert their own words in brackets. For example, in this interview Ann Druyan answers a question about Sagan's children by calling them "all of his kids." Since many readers may not know how many children Sagan had, the interviewer inserted this explanation: [Sagan had five children].

CLIPBOARD

abiding

collaborator

eulogy

interstellar

mechanism

perspective

CLIPBOARD

posterity

prophet

supportive

transition

uninhibited

Carl Sagan: Prophet of Our Coming of Age
An Interview with Ann Druyan

by Bernice E. Magee

*"The more you got to know him, the more amazing he was," says Ann Druyan of her late husband, Carl Sagan. For her, Sagan was a "**Prophet** of Our Coming of Age," telling the people of this planet how tiny and precious Earth is—our "pale blue dot" in the universe—and urging them to take care of it. ODYSSEY met with Ann Druyan, his widow and former **collaborator**, in their home in Ithaca, New York.*

Why was science good fun for Dr. Sagan?

It was thrilling for Carl to unravel a mystery and to him that's what the scientific enterprise was about—demystification. There was nothing that he loved better than learning something new. He probably read a book a night all of the twenty years that we were together. He was really stunning in his ability to retain information. He had this bottomless curiosity, and so he loved science because it was a **mechanism** for satisfying his curiosity.

Can you tell us about how Dr. Sagan worked?

He never ever wrote at a computer and rarely wrote longhand. He always dictated into a machine. We did a lot of work here in our own house, especially during the spring and summer months, when Carl would walk down by our waterfall. That was probably his favorite place to work. One of the stunning things about him was his capacity to focus over long periods of time and to be single-minded in his ability.

It was thrilling to work with him and experience this feast of ideas and vigorous exchange of views. It was never a matter of "because I say so"—it was always that the best argument would win. I always felt that Carl had such a tremendous sense of justice and fairness.

As a father, did Dr. Sagan allow his children to pursue unusual interests as his own parents had done?

It is absolutely true that Carl's parents were completely **supportive** of his dream to be an astronomer and that he had the same attitude with all of his kids. [Sagan had five children.] I think he was hugely proud of them. Whenever one of them would do something that was disturbing to a parent, Carl had an unfailing **perspective** that was **abiding** acceptance and support. He was absolutely unshakable in his faith in his children.

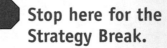 **Stop here for the Strategy Break.**

Strategy Break

Use what you've learned so far to answer these questions:

Q: Who is Carl Sagan? _____

_____

_____

Q: Why did Sagan love science? _____

_____

_____

Q: What was Sagan's attitude toward raising his children?_____

_____

_____

 Go on reading.

How did Dr. Sagan bring the spirit of youth into his life as an adult?

He never lost touch with the person he was as a child. He had a great sense of humor and the wildest, most **uninhibited** laugh of any person I've ever heard. In fact, that laugh is actually on the *Voyager* **Interstellar** Record recorded for **posterity**. One of the great comforts to me is that that laugh will be preserved. His greatest laughter was always at his own expense. Then he would be helpless with laughter.

How did Dr. Sagan like to spend free time?

His favorite thing would be to watch a Knicks game on TV, snuggled up with his family. We used to play six hands of *pinochle* every night as a way to **transition** from work to family.

And he loved to go to the movies. He loved popular music, especially Dire Straits. He was comfortable within himself, and that's one of the reasons that he stands out, because usually we don't think of scientists as being so developed emotionally. He was really the most fully developed human being I ever knew.

Where do you think that sense of comfort and centeredness came from?

I guess it came from feeling completely loved by his parents. There was such a closeness there and depth of feeling that was very important. As Sasha, our 15-year-old daughter, pointed out in her **eulogy** for Carl at St. John the Divine Cathedral in New York City, Carl defined success as the fulfillment of childhood dreams. And that's it. That's why I think he was so centered. All of his dreams came true. He felt that his own life, which included the first 40 years of the space age, had so far exceeded his wildest childhood dreams, that he was happy—really happy! He continued to grow even until a day or two before his death, always trying to be a kinder and more thoughtful person.

In light of the movie *Contact*, what suggestion would Dr. Sagan make to young people searching for answers to questions about the true meaning of life?

He would say: Look deeply, have an open mind, and study hard because you shouldn't believe just what feels good. It matters what's true. And that was the guiding credo of his whole life. *It matters what's true.* It's your responsibility as a human being to find out what really is true. ●

Strategy Follow-up

Review the interview if necessary. Then answer these questions:

Q: What is important about Sagan's laugh?_____

_____

_____

Q: What was Sagan's favorite way to spend his free time?_____

_____

_____

Q: Why does Druyan think that Sagan was so centered?_____

_____

_____

✓Personal Checklist

Read each question and put a check (✓) in the correct box.

1. How well do you understand the information presented in this interview?
   - ☐ 3 (extremely well)
   - ☐ 2 (fairly well)
   - ☐ 1 (not well)

2. How well did the predictions that you made in Building Background prepare you for reading and understanding this interview?
   - ☐ 3 (extremely well)
   - ☐ 2 (fairly well)
   - ☐ 1 (not well)

3. By the time you finished reading this interview, how well were you able to define the vocabulary words?
   - ☐ 3 (extremely well)
   - ☐ 2 (fairly well)
   - ☐ 1 (not well)

4. How well were you able to answer the questions in the Strategy Break and Follow-up?
   - ☐ 3 (extremely well)
   - ☐ 2 (fairly well)
   - ☐ 1 (not well)

5. How well do you understand why Druyan calls her late husband a "Prophet of Our Coming of Age?
   - ☐ 3 (extremely well)
   - ☐ 2 (fairly well)
   - ☐ 1 (not well)

Vocabulary Check

Look back at the work you did in the Vocabulary Builder. Then answer each question by circling the correct letter.

1. What smaller word do you find in *collaborator* that is useful for understanding the meaning of the vocabulary word?
   a. rat
   b. orator
   c. labor

2. Which definition of *prophet* does *not* fit the context of this selection?
   a. a person through whom the will of God is expressed
   b. someone who can predict the future
   c. the chief spokesperson for a movement or cause

3. Druyan says that Dr. Sagan's laugh is recorded for posterity on the *Voyager* Interstellar Record. What does this mean?
   a. It was recorded on the record as an afterthought.
   b. It has been recorded and preserved so future generations can hear it.
   c. It will be inherited by future generations of his family members.

4. If the prefix *inter-* means "between or among," what can you conclude the word *interstellar* means?
   a. between or among the stellars
   b. between or among the planets
   c. between or among the stars

5. In which situation would you most likely hear a eulogy?
   a. at a funeral
   b. at a carnival
   c. at a baptism

Add the numbers that you just checked to get your Personal Checklist score. Fill in your score here. Then turn to page 215 and transfer your score onto Graph 1.

Check your answers with your teacher. Give yourself 1 point for each correct answer, and fill in your Vocabulary score here. Then turn to page 215 and transfer your score onto Graph 1.

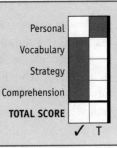

Strategy Check

Review the answers that you wrote in the Strategy Break and Follow-up. Also review the interview if necessary. Then answer these questions:

1. Which word would you use to begin a question about Sagan's favorite place to work?
    a. How
    b. Where
    c. When

2. Which word would you use to begin a question about the advice that Sagan would give to young people?
    a. Who
    b. When
    c. What

3. Which of the following is *not* one of the ways in which Sagan liked to spend his free time?
    a. He liked to ride his motorcycle very fast down open highways.
    b. He played six hands of pinochle with his family every night.
    c. He enjoyed pop music, particularly Dire Straits.

4. What does Druyan say was Sagan's definition of success?
    a. believing what feels good
    b. fulfilling childhood dreams
    c. trying to be a kinder and more thoughtful person

5. Which sentence best answers the question about Sagan's sense of comfort?
    a. His sense of comfort came from feeling completely loved by his parents.
    b. He was eulogized at St. John the Divine Cathedral in New York City.
    c. He continued to grow even until a day or two before his death.

Check your answers with your teacher. Give yourself 1 point for each correct answer, and fill in your Strategy score here. Then turn to page 215 and transfer your score onto Graph 1.

Personal
Vocabulary
Strategy
Comprehension
TOTAL SCORE
✓ T

Comprehension Check

Review the interview if necessary. Then answer these questions:

1. What does Druyan feel was her husband's most important message?
    a. that people of this planet need to take care of it
    b. that people should give more support to space exploration
    c. that people should be comfortable with themselves

2. What idea is supported by Druyan's statement that "He probably read a book a night all of the twenty years that we were together"?
    a. Sagan suffered from insomnia.
    b. He was a fast and avid reader.
    c. He'd rather read than spend time with his family.

3. How many children did Sagan have?
    a. two
    b. three
    c. five

4. Which of these sentences best matches Druyan's description of Sagan's sense of humor?
    a. Being a serious scientist, he didn't find many things funny.
    b. He enjoyed humor as long as it wasn't at his own expense.
    c. He had a great ability to laugh at himself as well as others.

5. According to Druyan, what did Sagan believe was every person's duty?
    a. to be all he or she can be
    b. to find out what is true
    c. to have a good time in life

Check your answers with your teacher. Give yourself 1 point for each correct answer, and fill in your Comprehension score here. Then turn to page 215 and transfer your score onto Graph 1.

Personal
Vocabulary
Strategy
Comprehension
TOTAL SCORE
✓ T

Extending

Choose one or both of these activities:

PREPARE AN UPDATE ON SPACE EXPLORATION

One of Carl Sagan's prime interests was the question of whether Earth is the only planet with thinking life on it. His book *Contact* explored what might happen if friendly aliens contacted humans. He also hoped that his TV programs would encourage a widespread support for further space exploration to find answers to that question. Where does U.S. space exploration stand today? Use newspapers, magazines, and recently published books to find out what new efforts have been made in the last few years, particularly since Sagan's death in 1996.

WRITE A REVIEW OF *CONTACT*

Carl Sagan wrote *Contact* in 1985. Read the book or watch the movie to see what Sagan thought back then about alien life. Then write a review of the book or the movie in which you share your opinions of Sagan's views and ideas. If other students read or watch the story, share your opinions in a panel discussion. If the book differs from the movie in any significant ways, discuss those differences and why you think they occur.

Resources

Books

Sagan, Carl. *Billions and Billions: Thoughts on Life and Death at the Brink of the Millennium.* Ballantine, 1998.

————. *Broca's Brain. Reflections on the Romance of Science.* Ballantine, 1993.

————. *Contact: A Novel.* Pocket Books, 1997.

Web Sites

http://www.nasa.gov/vision/space/features/index.html
On this NASA Web site, learn about the current state of human space exploration.

http://www.pbs.org/wgbh/nova/aliens/carlsagan.html
This Web page provides the text of a television interview with Carl Sagan in which he discusses extraterrestrial life.

Videos/DVDs

Contact. Warner Studio, 1997.

The Lives of the Stars: The Edge of Forever. Carl Sagan Productions, 1989.

LESSON ❷⓿ *from* Cosmos

immediate

immense

luminous

obscure

reconnaissance

reflect

remote

shine

tiny

wrested

Building Background

The term *cosmos* is defined as "the universe regarded as an orderly, harmonious whole." It is also the term that Carl Sagan used as the title of his book and his 13-part television show that explored many aspects of the universe.

When you think of the universe, what comes to your mind? In what ways does the universe appear to be "an orderly, harmonious whole" to you? Before you begin reading, fill in the concept map below with some of the topics that you might cover if your were developing a TV program about the cosmos. Add as many ovals as necessary.

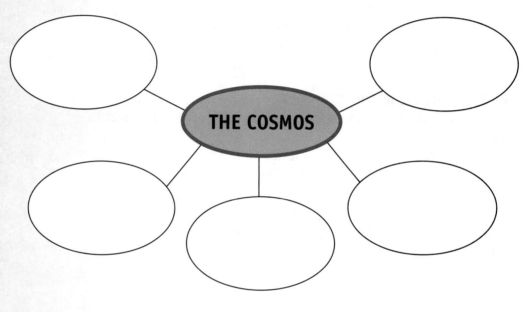

THE COSMOS

CLIPBOARD 1

Synonym Pairs

1. exploration

_____

2. faint

_____

3. struggled

_____

4. shining

_____

Vocabulary Builder

1. Study the vocabulary words in the margin. Four of the words are **synonyms** of the words on the first clipboard. Each of the other words is half of a pair of **antonyms**—words with opposite meanings.

2. On the first clipboard, write the synonym of each word listed. Then match the antonym pairs and write them on the second clipboard. Use a dictionary for any words you don't know.

3. Save your work. You will refer to it again in the Vocabulary Check.

CLIPBOARD 2

Antonym Pairs

1. immediate

_____

2.

_____

3.

_____

Strategy Builder

Summarizing Nonfiction

- The selection you are about to read is a brief excerpt from astronomer Carl Sagan's book *Cosmos*. Using the **first-person point of view**, Sagan informs readers how he first became interested in the stars and how he made up his mind to become an astronomer.

- In Lesson 9, you learned that one way to find and remember the most important ideas in a piece of nonfiction is to **summarize** them by retelling them in your own words.

- Read the following paragraph about stars. Then read how one student summarized the paragraph's most important ideas.

Astronomers classify stars according to several characteristics, including size, color, and brightness. With regard to size, stars are grouped in five major groups. The largest known stars are called supergiants. The largest supergiants have diameters about a thousand times as big as the sun's diameter. Examples of supergiants are Antares and Betelgeuse. The next largest stars are giants. These stars have diameters from 10 to 100 times that of the sun's. Medium-sized stars, also called dwarf stars, are about the size of the sun. Their diameter can be anywhere from one-tenth of the sun's to 10 times that of the sun. Sirius and Vega are examples. White dwarfs are small stars. One of these, van Maanen's Star, has a diameter less than the distance across Asia. The tiniest stars are neutron stars, which are as heavy as the sun but only 12 miles in diameter!

Summary:
Stars can be classified in several ways, including size. There are five major size groups. From largest to smallest, they are supergiants, giants, medium-sized stars (which include our sun), white dwarfs, and neutron stars. The diameters of stars range from a thousand times the diameter of the sun down to 12 miles.

from Cosmos

by Carl Sagan

As you read the first part of this excerpt, think about how you might summarize it. Jot down your ideas on a separate sheet of paper. When you get to the Strategy Break, you can compare your summary with the sample provided.

When I was little, I lived in the Bensonhurst section of Brooklyn in the City of New York. I knew my **immediate** neighborhood intimately, every apartment building, pigeon coop, backyard, front stoop, empty lot, elm tree, ornamental railing, coal chute and wall for playing Chinese handball, among which the brick exterior of a theater called the Loew's Stillwell was of superior quality. I knew where many people lived: Bruno and Dino, Ronald and Harvey, Sandy, Bernie, Danny, Jackie and Myra. But more than a few blocks away, north of the raucous automobile traffic and elevated railway on 86th Street, was a strange unknown territory, off-limits to my wanderings. It could have been Mars for all I knew.

Even with an early bedtime, in winter you could sometimes see the stars. I would look at them, twinkling and **remote**, and wonder what they were. I would ask older children and adults, who would only reply, "They're lights in the sky, kid." I could *see* they were lights in the sky. But what *were* they? Just small hovering lamps? Whatever for? I felt a kind of sorrow for them: a commonplace whose strangeness remained somehow hidden from my incurious fellows. There had to be some deeper answer.

As soon as I was old enough, my parents gave me my first library card. I think the library was on 85th Street, an alien land. Immediately, I asked the librarian for something on stars. She returned with a picture book displaying portraits of men and women with names like Clark Gable and Jean Harlow. I complained, and for some reason then **obscure** to me, she smiled and found another book—the right kind of book. I opened it breathlessly and read until I found it. The book said something astonishing, a very big thought. It said that the stars were suns, only very far away. The Sun was a star, but close up.

⬛ **Stop here for the Strategy Break.**

Strategy Break

Did you jot down your summary as you read? If you did, see if it looks anything like this:

As a young child, Carl Sagan was familiar with his immediate neighborhood but with nothing beyond a few blocks. He could see the stars and wanted to know what they were, but no one could give him a satisfactory answer. As soon as he was old enough, he got a library card and asked for a book about stars. In it he learned that the stars are distant suns, and the sun is a close-up star.

 Go on reading.

Imagine that you took the Sun and moved it so far away that it was just a **tiny** twinkling point of light. How far away would you have to move it? I was innocent of the notion of angular size. I was ignorant of the inverse square law for light propagation. I had not a ghost of a chance of calculating the distance to the stars. But I could tell that if the stars were suns, they had to be very far away—farther away than 85th Street, farther away than Manhattan, farther away, probably, than New Jersey. The Cosmos was much bigger than I had guessed.

Later I read another astonishing fact. The Earth, which includes Brooklyn, is a planet, and it goes around the Sun. There are other planets. They also go around the Sun; some are closer to it and some are farther away. But the planets do not **shine** by their own light, as the Sun does. They merely **reflect** light from the Sun. If you were a great distance away, you would not see the Earth and the other planets at all; they would be only faint **luminous** points, lost in the glare of the Sun. Well, then, I thought, it stood to reason that the other stars must have planets too, ones we have not yet detected, and some of those other planets should have life (why not?), a kind of life probably different from life as we know it, life in Brooklyn. So I decided I would be an astronomer, learn about the stars and planets and, if I could, go and visit them.

It has been my **immense** good fortune to have parents and some teachers who encouraged this odd ambition and to live in this time, the first moment in human history when we are, in fact, visiting other worlds and engaging in a deep **reconnaissance** of the Cosmos. If I had been born in a much earlier age, no matter how great my dedication, I would not have understood what the stars and planets are. I would not have known that there were other suns and other worlds. This is one of the great secrets, **wrested** from Nature through a million years of patient observation and courageous thinking by our ancestors.

What are the stars? Such questions are as natural as an infant's smile. We have always asked them. What is different about our time is that at last we know some of the answers. Books and libraries provide a ready means for finding out what those answers are. ●

Strategy Follow-up

On the lines below—or on a separate sheet of paper if necessary—summarize the rest of this excerpt. Using your own words, be sure to list only the most important ideas and skip unnecessary details.

_____

_____

_____

_____

_____

_____

_____

_____

_____

_____

_____

_____

_____

_____

_____

_____

_____

_____

_____

_____

✓Personal Checklist

Read each question and put a check (✓) in the correct box.

1. How well do you understand the information presented in this excerpt?
   - ☐ 3 (extremely well)
   - ☐ 2 (fairly well)
   - ☐ 1 (not well)

2. In Building Background, how well were you able to brainstorm ideas for a television program about the cosmos?
   - ☐ 3 (extremely well)
   - ☐ 2 (fairly well)
   - ☐ 1 (not well)

3. In the Vocabulary Builder, how well were you able to list the synonyms and antonym pairs on the clipboards?
   - ☐ 3 (extremely well)
   - ☐ 2 (fairly well)
   - ☐ 1 (not well)

4. In the Strategy Follow-up, how well were you able to summarize the second part of this excerpt?
   - ☐ 3 (extremely well)
   - ☐ 2 (fairly well)
   - ☐ 1 (not well)

5. How well would you be able to explain why Sagan dedicated his life to studying the stars?
   - ☐ 3 (extremely well)
   - ☐ 2 (fairly well)
   - ☐ 1 (not well)

Vocabulary Check

Look back at the work you did in the Vocabulary Builder. Then answer each question by circling the correct letter.

1. Which antonym pair describes distances?
   - a. *immediate* and *remote*
   - b. *obscure* and *faint*
   - c. *tiny* and *immense*

2. Which antonym pair describes sizes?
   - a. *immediate* and *remote*
   - b. *obscure* and *faint*
   - c. *tiny* and *immense*

3. Which of these pairs is *not* a synonym pair?
   - a. *exploration* and *reconnaissance*
   - b. *shining* and *luminous*
   - c. *faint* and *remote*

4. Which word is more commonly used instead of *wrest*?
   - a. *rest*
   - b. *wrestle*
   - c. *wrist*

5. Which pair of examples does *not* illustrate the antonyms *immediate* and *remote*?
   - a. Sagan's neighborhood and other parts of New York
   - b. the library and its books
   - c. the sun and other stars

Add the numbers that you just checked to get your Personal Checklist score. Fill in your score here. Then turn to page 215 and transfer your score onto Graph 1.

Personal	
Vocabulary	
Strategy	
Comprehension	
TOTAL SCORE	

✓ T

Check your answers with your teacher. Give yourself 1 point for each correct answer, and fill in your Vocabulary score here. Then turn to page 215 and transfer your score onto Graph 1.

Personal	
Vocabulary	
Strategy	
Comprehension	
TOTAL SCORE	

✓ T

Strategy Check

Look back at the summary that you wrote. Then answer these questions:

1. Which sentence best summarizes the idea that the Cosmos was much bigger than Sagan had guessed?
   a. I was ignorant of the inverse square law for light propagation.
   b. I could tell that if the stars were suns, they had to be very far away.
   c. I was innocent of the notion of angular size.

2. Which sentence best summarizes Sagan's reasoning that other stars must have planets?
   a. Since the planets around our Sun can't be seen from a distance, there are probably planets around other stars that we can't see.
   b. Although none of the stars we can see have planets, other stars that may have planets.
   c. Since we are receiving messages from space, they must be from beings on other planets.

3. Which of these sentences best summarizes why Sagan decided to become an astronomer?
   a. The Cosmos was much bigger than Sagan had guessed.
   b. As soon as Sagan was old enough, his parents gave him his first library card.
   c. Sagan decided to learn about the stars and planets, and, if he could, go and visit them.

4. Which sentence best summarizes this excerpt?
   a. Questions about the stars are natural, and people of today are lucky enough to know some of the answers.
   b. People could answer their questions about stars with books.
   c. Both of the above sentences are equally good.

5. Which words best summarize Carl Sagan?
   a. confused, unintelligent, and annoying
   b. brilliant, curious, and enthusiastic
   c. dangerous, obsessed, and crazy

Comprehension Check

Review the selection if necessary. Then answer these questions:

1. Where did Carl Sagan live as a child?
   a. in Brooklyn
   b. in Manhattan
   c. in New Jersey

2. From the description Sagan gives of himself, how old do you suppose he was when he began to wonder about the stars?
   a. between three and six years old
   b. between six and ten years old
   c. between ten and fifteen years old

3. What did the librarian think young Sagan wanted when he asked for information about stars?
   a. information about recording stars
   b. information about movie stars
   c. information about sports stars

4. What is the "odd ambition" that Sagan had?
   a. to visit other planets
   b. to learn about the stars
   c. to go to the library

5. What is Sagan's attitude toward people of previous ages?
   a. He looks down on them for their ignorance.
   b. He thinks they wasted many opportunities to learn about the world.
   c. He respects and appreciates their struggle to learn about the universe.

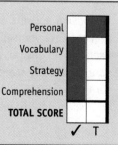

Check your answers with your teacher. Give yourself 1 point for each correct answer, and fill in your Strategy score here. Then turn to page 215 and transfer your score onto Graph 1.

Personal
Vocabulary
Strategy
Comprehension
TOTAL SCORE
✓ T

Check your answers with your teacher. Give yourself 1 point for each correct answer, and fill in your Comprehension score here. Then turn to page 215 and transfer your score onto Graph 1.

Personal
Vocabulary
Strategy
Comprehension
TOTAL SCORE
✓ T

Extending

Choose one or both of these activities:

RETELL A STAR LEGEND

Find and read Greek, Native American, or other legends about stars and constellations. Choose one of the legends and reread it several times until you can tell the story from memory. Practice telling the legend with expression. Then retell it to a group of classmates or younger students.

REVIEW A SEGMENT OF THE TV PROGRAM *COSMOS*

Obtain a copy of a segment of the TV show *Cosmos*. As you watch it, keep these questions in mind:

- What aspects of the production help make the scientific concepts understandable?

- What passages of Sagan's narration are most interesting?

- Does the program affect my attitude toward scientific research? Is so, in what way?

Take notes as needed. Then write a review of the episode as if you were a television critic observing the show's first broadcast.

Resources

Book

Sagan, Carl. *Cosmos.* Random House, 2002.

Web Sites

http://bluepoint.egenet.net/sagan/episodes.html
This Web page offers a summary of the 14-part *Cosmos* television series.

http://www.dibonsmith.com/constel.htm
Follow the links on this Web page for information on constellations, including Greek myths and other legends associated with many of the constellations.

Audio Recording

The Music of Cosmos. Collectibles, 2002.

Video/DVD

Cosmos—Complete Collection. Turner Home Video, 1980.

Learning New Words

VOCABULARY

From Lesson 20
- reconnaissance
  exploration
- obscure
  faint
- wrested
  struggled
- luminous
  shining

From Lesson 20
- immediate
- remote
- immense
- tiny
- reflect
- shine

Synonyms

A synonym is a word that means the same thing—or close to the same thing—as another word. For example, in the excerpt from *Cosmos* in Lesson 20, Carl Sagan uses the word *reconnaissance*. Synonyms for *reconnaissance* are the words *exploration* and *examination*.

Draw a line from each word in Column 1 to its synonym in Column 2.

COLUMN 1	COLUMN 2
huge	sparkling
dazzling	idea
suppose	viewpoint
notion	gigantic
perspective	imagine

Antonyms

An antonym is a word that means the opposite of another word. For example, in the excerpt from *Cosmos*, you read that when Sagan was a boy, he knew his immediate neighborhood, but he didn't know anything about the remote stars in the sky. In the context of this selection, *immediate* means "close by," and *remote* means "far away."

Draw a line from each word in Column 1 to its antonym in Column 2.

COLUMN 1	COLUMN 2
splurge	mourn
expand	answer
celebrate	save
question	working
resting	contract

Colloquialisms

A colloquialism is a word or phrase that is used in everyday, informal speech but not in formal speech or writing. The story "EPICAC" uses several colloquialisms, *including floored her*, meaning "amazed her"; *mind was mush*, meaning "couldn't think straight"; *and half-baked*, meaning "not completely or properly developed."

Draw a line from each colloquialism in Column 1 to its meaning in Column 2.

COLUMN 1	COLUMN 2
busted	cup of coffee
cup of Joe	narrow escape
rings a bell	caught or arrested
close call	sounds familiar

Suffixes

A suffix is a word part that is added to the end of a root word. When you add a suffix, you often change the root word's meaning and function. For example, the suffix *-ful* means "full of," so the root word *spite* changes from a noun or verb to an adjective meaning "full of spite, or ill will."

-ist

The suffix *-ist* turns a word into a noun meaning "a person who does or makes _____." In Lesson 18, for example, you learned that an *oncologist* is a doctor who deals with cancer.

Write the word for each definition below.

1. person who is an expert in botany   _____

2. person who manicures people's nails   _____

3. person who plays the harp   _____

4. person who treats allergies   _____

VOCABULARY

From Lesson 16
- hasn't been a peep about him
- send-off
- the Brass
- fizzled
- cracker-jack
- sweep me off my feet
- half-baked
- mind was mush
- floored her

From Lesson 18
- oncologist

Graphing Your Progress

The graphs on page 215 will help you track your progress as you work through this book. Follow these directions to fill in the graphs:

Graph 1

1. Start by looking across the top of the graph for the number of the lesson you just finished.

2. In the first column for that lesson, write your Personal Checklist score in both the top and bottom boxes. (Notice the places where *13* is filled in on the sample.)

3. In the second column for that lesson, fill in your scores for the Vocabulary, Strategy, and Comprehension Checks.

4. Add the three scores, and write their total in the box above the letter *T*. (The *T* stands for "Total." The ✓ stands for "Personal Checklist.")

5. Compare your scores. Does your Personal Checklist score match or come close to your total scores for that lesson? Why or why not?

Graph 2

1. Again, start by looking across the top of the graph for the number of the lesson you just finished.

2. In the first column for that lesson, shade the number of squares that match your Personal Checklist score.

3. In the second column for that lesson, shade the number of squares that match your total score.

4. As you fill in this graph, you will be able to check your progress across the book. You'll be able to see your strengths and areas of improvement. You'll also be able to see areas where you might need a little extra help. You and your teacher can discuss ways to work on those areas.

Graph 1

For each lesson, enter the scores from your Personal Checklist and your Vocabulary, Strategy, and Comprehension Checks. Total your scores and then compare them. Does your Personal Checklist score match or come close to your total scores for that lesson? Why or why not?

Go down to Graph 2 and shade your scores for the lesson you just completed.

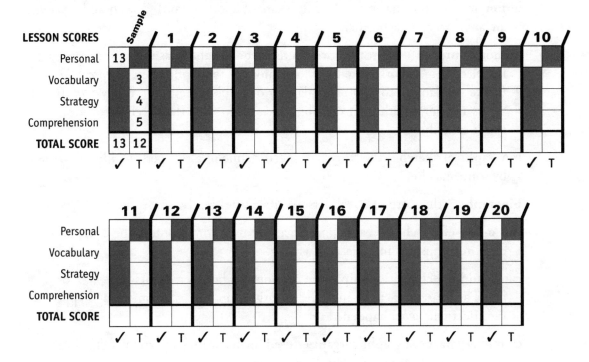

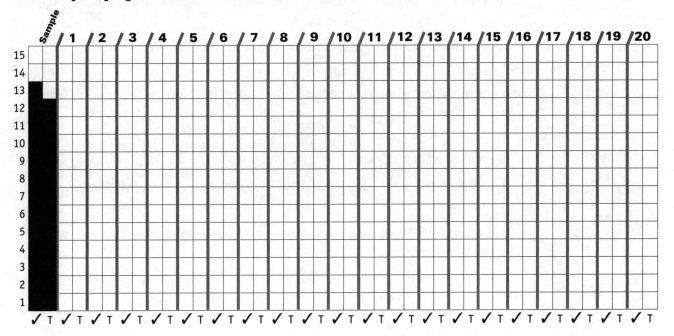

Graph 2

Now record your overall progress. In the first column for the lesson you just completed, shade the number of squares that match your Personal Checklist score. In the second column for that lesson, shade the number of squares that match your total score. As you fill in this graph, you will be able to check your progress across the book.

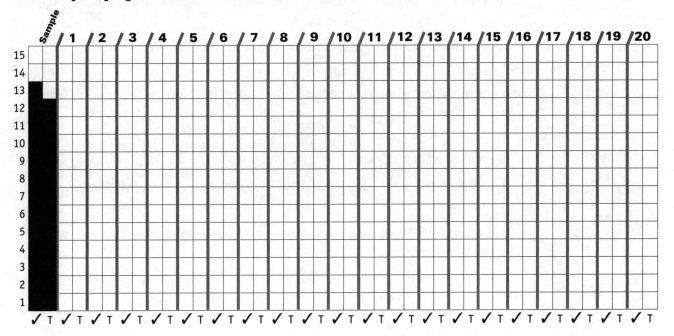

Glossary of Terms

This glossary includes definitions for important terms introduced in this book.

antonym   a word that means the opposite of another word. *Mighty* and *powerless* are antonyms of each other.

author's purpose   the reason or reasons that an author has for writing a particular selection. Authors write for one or more of these purposes: to *entertain* (make you laugh), to *inform* (explain or describe something), to *persuade* (try to get you to agree with their opinion), to *express* (share their feelings or ideas about something).

biographical sketch   the story of a specific time in a real person's life, as written by someone else.

biography   the story of a real person's life, as written by someone else.

cause-and-effect chain   a graphic organizer used for recording the cause-and-effect relationships in a piece of writing.

cause-and-effect relationship   the relationship between events in a piece of writing. The cause in a cause-and-effect relationship tells *why* something happened; the effect tells *what* happened.

character chart   a graphic organizer used for recording a particular character's traits, as well as examples that illustrate them.

characters   the people or animals that perform the action in a story.

character wheel   a graphic organizer used for recording the changes that a character goes through from the beginning to the end of a story.

compound word   a word that is made up of two words put together. *Churchgoing* and *greenhouse* are examples of compound words.

concept map   a graphic organizer used for recording the main ideas and supporting details in a piece of writing.

conclusion   a decision that is reached after thinking about certain facts or information.

context   information that comes before and after a word or situation to help you understand it.

description   in nonfiction, the organizational pattern that explains what something is, what it does, or how and why it works.

dynamic characters   characters that change in some way from the beginning of a story to the end.

end result   the solution a character or characters try that finally solves the problem in a story.

event   a happening. The plot of any story contains one or more events during which the characters try to solve their problems.

fact   a statement that can be proved.

fiction   stories about made-up characters or events. Forms of fiction include short stories, science fiction, mystery, and folktales.

first-person point of view   the perspective, or viewpoint, of one of the characters in a story. That character uses words such as *I, me, my,* and *mine* to tell the story.

graphic organizer   a chart, graph, or drawing used to show how the main ideas in a piece of writing are organized and related.

headings   the short titles given throughout a piece of nonfiction. The headings often state the main ideas of a selection.

informational article   a piece of writing that gives facts and details about a particular subject, or topic.

interview   a piece of writing that records the questions and answers given during a conversation.

main idea   the most important idea of a paragraph, section, or whole piece of writing.

multiple-meaning word   a word that has more than one meaning. The word *stage* is a multiple-meaning word whose meanings include "raised platform where performances are held" and "step in a process or period of development."

mystery   a story that contains a kind of puzzle that the characters must solve.

narrator   the person or character who is telling a story.

nonfiction   writing that gives facts and information about real people, events, and topics. Informational articles, newspaper articles, interviews, and biographies are some forms of nonfiction.

organizational pattern   in nonfiction, the pattern in which the text is written and organized. Common organizational patterns include description, cause-effect, sequence, compare-contrast, and problem-solution.

outline   a framework for organizing the main ideas and supporting details in a piece of writing. Some **outlines** are organized according to a system of Roman numerals (I, II, III, and so on), capital letters, Arabic numerals (1, 2, 3, and so on), and lowercase letters.

plot   the sequence of events in a piece of writing.

point of view   the perspective, or viewpoint, from which a story is told.

prediction   a kind of guess that is based on the context clues given in a story.

prefix   a word part added to the beginning of a word to make a new word. Adding a prefix usually changes the word's meaning and function. For example, the suffix *un-* means "not" or "the opposite of." So adding *un-* to *true* changes *true* to its opposite meaning.

problem   difficulty or question that a character must solve or answer.

problem-solution frame   a graphic organizer used for recording the problem, solutions, and end result in a piece of writing.

root word   a word to which prefixes and suffixes are added to make other words.

sequence   the order of events in a piece of writing. The sequence shows what happens or what to do first, second, and so on.

science fiction   fiction that is often based on real or possible scientific developments. Much science fiction is set in outer space, in some future time.

sequence chain   a graphic organizer used for recording the sequence of events in a piece of writing. Sequence chains are used mostly for shorter periods of time, and time lines are used mostly for longer periods of time.

setting   the time and place in which a story happens.

short story   a work of fiction that usually can be read in one sitting.

signal words   words and phrases that tell when something happens or when to do something. Examples of signal words are *first, next, finally, after lunch, two years later,* and *in 1820.*

simile   a figure of speech that compares two things by using the words *like* or *as.*

slang   words used by a particular group of people for a short time. Slang is considered informal speech and usually uses common words in uncommon ways. For example, the slang term *threads* refers to a person's clothing.

solution   the things that characters or people do to solve a problem.

specialized vocabulary   words that are related to a particular subject, or topic. Specialized vocabulary words in the selection "Levi's: The Pants that Won the West" include *rivets, denim, pockets,* and *seams.*

static characters   characters that stay the same from the beginning of a story to the end.

story map   a graphic organizer used for recording the main parts of a story: its title, setting, character, problem, events, and solution.

suffix   a word part that is added to the end of a word. Adding a suffix usually changes the word's meaning and function. For example, the suffix *-less* means "without," so the word *painless* changes from the noun *pain* to an adjective meaning "without pain."

summary   a short description. A summary describes what has happened so far in a piece of fiction, or what the main ideas are in a piece of nonfiction.

supporting details   details that describe or explain the main idea of a paragraph, section, or whole piece of text.

synonym   a word that has the same meaning as another word. *Hostile* and *unfriendly* are synonyms of each other.

theme   the underlying message or meaning of a story.

third-person point of view   the perspective, or viewpoint, of a narrator who is not a character in a story. That narrator uses words such as *she, her, he, his, they,* and *their* to tell the story.

time line   a graphic organizer used for recording the sequence of events in a piece of writing. Time lines are used mostly for longer periods of time, and sequence chains are used mostly for shorter periods of time.

title   the name of a piece of writing.

tone   the attitude that a story conveys.

topic   the subject of a piece of writing. The topic is what the selection is all about.

Acknowledgments